LISTENING *to*
Latina/o Youth

mediated
youth

Sharon R. Mazzarella
General Editor

Vol. 13

The Mediated Youth series is part of the Peter Lang Media
and Communication list.
Every volume is peer reviewed and meets
the highest quality standards for content and production.

PETER LANG
New York • Washington, D.C./Baltimore • Bern
Frankfurt • Berlin • Brussels • Vienna • Oxford

Kristin C. Moran

LISTENING *to*
Latina/o Youth

Television Consumption Within Families

PETER LANG
New York • Washington, D.C./Baltimore • Bern
Frankfurt • Berlin • Brussels • Vienna • Oxford

Library of Congress Cataloging-in-Publication Data

Moran, Kristin Clare Engstrand.
Listening to Latina/o youth: television consumption within families /
Kristin C. Moran.
p. cm. — (Mediated youth; v. 13)
Includes bibliographical references and index.
1. Hispanic American television viewers. 2. Hispanic American teenagers.
3. Television and youth—United States. I. Title.
HE8700.66.U6M67   302.23'4508350973—dc22   2011003748
ISBN 978-1-4331-0728-3 (hardcover)
ISBN 978-1-4331-0727-6 (paperback)
ISSN 1555-1814

Bibliographic information published by **Die Deutsche Nationalbibliothek**.
Die Deutsche Nationalbibliothek lists this publication in the "Deutsche
Nationalbibliografie"; detailed bibliographic data is available
on the Internet at http://dnb.d-nb.de/.

© 2011 Peter Lang Publishing, Inc., New York
29 Broadway, 18th floor, New York, NY 10006
www.peterlang.com

FOR

MADISON & RYAN

Contents

Acknowledgements

This book is the culmination of many years of thinking about the ways in which the mainstream media industry have responded to the growing numbers of Latina/os living in the United States. I too was swept up in the trendy music of Ricky Martin and Jennifer Lopez as Selena, which led me to think more broadly about representation. Throughout the journey of data collection and writing many people were instrumental in the completion of the book.

I would like to send my heartfelt thanks to all the families who welcomed me into their homes and found the time to speak with me about their perceptions of the changing media environment. I learned so much from them and hope I represent their voices in ways that showcase their thoughtfulness. Wrapped up in an academic setting, it is easy to forget how important it is to listen to audiences. The young people and their parents interviewed here have a lot of important things to say.

I would like to thank my colleagues at the University of San Diego, who offered their support in myriad ways. Discussions with faculty and students helped me organize my thoughts while navigating through the piles of literature and hours of interviews. Our department research group held me to deadlines and kept me focused.

I am grateful to my colleagues in BINACOM (Binational Association of Schools of Communication) who have engaged in ongoing discussions about what it means to live in this border region. Talking with faculty in Mexico helped to provide perspective on the interpretations of the interviewees, especially those who were closely tied to Mexico. The goal of the organization is to demystify the stereotypes associated with the border region, and I hope that this book assists in that process.

I would like to thank my mother, Iris Engstrand, who sparked my interest by taking me with her to Mexico and Spain and keeping us connected through cultural events and exchanges. And to Cindy van Stralen, who served as a careful editor of many early drafts of the manuscript.

I am most grateful to my family, who patiently excused my absence while I was busy completing the manuscript even though they would rather have had me home. In discussing my claims with my husband, Dan, after a long day of writing, he would keep me in check by questioning my arguments in ways that ultimately made them stronger. His unwavering support keeps me grounded. I want to thank my children, Madison and Ryan, who made sure I included their favorite programs as well as being a constant inspiration reminding me of the importance of working to create a more equitable and just future for all youth.

Introduction

The changing demographics of the United States have prompted much discussion for business owners, educators, public officials and the general public. The recent wave of immigrants from all over the world is an influential component in the social, political and cultural fabric of daily life. Latina/os as a group have been in the spotlight as demographic data reveals significant population growth. As a result, Latina/o children are an important part of youth culture, and understanding the ways in which they use and understand mass media will help provide insight into the dynamic role media play in the everyday life of all youth. By focusing the research on youth in the context of their family dynamic, this investigation exposes media consumption patterns in hopes of unraveling the stereotypes and opening up the discourses regarding Latinidad.

The media industry has built great fortune by relying on stereotypes for pan-ethnic programming, so there has been little incentive to change this approach, but as new media technology challenges the industry to contend with new delivery systems, it must reinvent itself. Traditional media—newspapers and television—must learn to survive within a multiple platform media environment. Even though it appears that new media have replaced many of the traditional forms, it is clear that television viewing still plays a dominant role in the leisure time activities of families, especially in the home. In fact, the average American's viewing time is close to four hours per day. Television has remained relevant in the current multimedia environment by reassessing its strategies; prime-time television has found success with competitive reality shows, dramatic series and the ever popular situation comedy, while cable networks are succeeding with niche programming aimed at narrow audience segments. Examples of narrowcasting include Spanish-language networks and Latino-themed programs that aim to reach the emerging Latina/o[1] population.

Since the release of the 2000 Census and subsequent information confirming the expansion of the Latina/o population, industry executives have been interested in selling this audience to advertisers as a way to capitalize on what is seen as an emerging market. The collection of data for the 2010 Census, which should further place Latina/os at the forefront of the debates on the changing character of the United States, will provide information to inform agencies within the federal government, education systems, and the media industry hoping to contain, manage and sell the audience. The U.S. Census Bureau has launched a variety of campaigns encouraging Latina/os to respond to Census inquiries ensuring that the population estimates are as accurate as possible. In addition to traditional advertising aimed at Spanish-speaking populations urging the completion of the survey, the Bureau has teamed up with National Parents and Teachers Association and the Children's Defense Fund to use *Dora the Explorer* to encourage families to return their Census form. During the 2000 Census, it is estimated that over one million children were not counted and many of them were under five. Dora is an iconic figure for preschool age children and their parents, and as a spokesperson, is likely to catch their attention. The "Children Count Too" campaign featuring Dora consists of television and radio public service announcements, web advertising, posters and handouts (Woodard, 2010).

In another campaign aimed at encouraging Spanish-speakers to complete the Census, the ureau teamed up with Telemundo[2] to incorporate a Census storyline into an existing telenovela,[3] *Más sabe el diablo, (The Devil Knows Best),* produced in the United States. According to Brian Stelter (2009), the immense popularity of telenovelas, especially among Spanish-speaking first generation immigrants, "mak[es] them a prime way to encourage Hispanics to be counted next year." The story features Perla Beltrán, who has suffered as a result of her husband's murder and other problems and who will become an employee for the U.S. Census Bureau. The telenovela will follow her as she is approached by a Census recruiter, applies for the job and performs the Census. There is hope that the storyline will eliminate fears, especially among undocumented immigrants, and encourage them to report their presence. While accurate accounting of the Hispanic population is optimal for a variety of reasons, Telemundo support is not surprising; Telemundo hopes to highlight Latina/o presence because the more viewers it reaches the more it can charge for advertising on its channels. Spanish-language media stand to gain financially as the numbers of Hispanics in the United States grow. Don Browne, president of Telemundo, told the *New York Times* that "If you think it's a good business now, wait until after the Census" (Stelter, 2009) indicating the continued belief in the success of Spanish-language and Latino-themed media. Alternatively, one might fear the continuation of a pan-Latino identity imposed by institutional forces that look to exploit the numbers in the name of the market.

In 2009, Latina/os made up close to 15% of the U.S. population, and projections point to Latina/os comprising 29% of the population by the year 2050. In California and Texas, over 35% of the population is Latina/o. Many Latina/o adults are bilingual, with 68% of adult children of immigrants speaking both English and Spanish (PewHispanic.org). Young Latina/os, especially those born in the United States, are eager for media products that reflect their interests—in English, Spanish or both. As a result it is important to look at Latina/os as part of the broader American landscape to uncover patterns of behavior that shape the social process.

The relationship audiences have with media can be viewed from a variety of perspectives. Within communication studies, media use among Latina/os has been linked with identity formation (Subervi & Rios, 2005; Mastro, 2003a; Moran & Chung, 2008), hybridity (Rinderle, 2005; Molina Guzmán, 2006; Molina Guzmán & Valdivia, 2004; Straubhaar, 2007) and cultural maintenance (Rios & Gaines, 1998; Mayer, 2003; Mato, 2005), stereotyping and its consequences (Cortés, 2000; Mastro & Behm-Morawitz, 2005; Casas Peréz, 2005), addressing the cultural and social implications of representation (Dávila, 2001a; Valdivia, 2008a; Aparicio, 2003;

Guidotti-Hernández, 2007), and from an economic perspective, the growth of new media outlets seeking an audience (Callow & McDonald, 2005; Liesse, 2007; Consoli, 2008; Romano, 2003). This book connects these perspectives to expose the context in which Latino families find themselves when interacting with media products within the home. The Spanish-language television industry has enjoyed attention from advertisers who see it as economically successful in the current television market, where English-language networks have seen audiences slip away (Wentz, 2008).

The purpose of this investigation is to respond and add to the work of communication scholars who are engaging in the examination of media texts created for Latina/o audiences as well as those who are studying the reception process of these audiences. In this sample, the participants, who were interviewed as family units, provide an opportunity to uncover the diversity of the Latina/o experience and to highlight the dynamics of media use within a natural setting—the family and the home. The research presented demonstrates that the respondents in the families I spoke with choose their content based on a variety of factors commonly seen in other studies focusing on the Latina/o audience (Barrera & Biebly, 2001; Mayer, 2003b; Dávila, 2002; DeSipio, 2003). Family members are drawn to programming that is relevant to them at a particular moment in time. To better understand how and why family members come to the television set, it is important to put together many pieces of the puzzle—social and cultural identity, content availability, and the economics of the industry. This book provides a context in which the reader can hear the family members through dialogues that were produced during in-home interviews with families who have emigrated from and/or have ancestry in Mexico. While the book's title uses the term Latina/o, I am careful to underscore that the explanations reflect the experiences of Mexicans and Mexican Americans living in San Diego County, mostly in central and southern urban areas. These families speak for themselves, and while it is unwise to generalize based upon their experiences, they do provide a rich understanding of the complexity of media consumption that may point to broader commonalities across audience segments. A total of ten families were interviewed during February and March 2008. In March 2010, a second round of interviews were conducted and were focused more keenly on Latina/o children. Each family consisted of participants where at least one parent identified as Latina/o. Family units ranged from three to five members and were interviewed together in their homes. When possible all members of the family who lived in the home were present. Each of the children had at least one parent who identified as Latina/o.

At times I feel under-qualified to investigate issues of Latinidad because I am an outsider. I am a native of San Diego, the daughter of a Swedish American father and a mother with mixed heritage including French, German, and Algonquin from the U.S. Atlantic coast. I am close to friends who are deeply connected to Mexico, and as a child, I spent summers travelling with my mother, a historian, to Mexico and Spain, where she investigated eighteenth-century scientific exploration. My early experiences molded my understanding of the culture while my body codes me as ethnically outside of Latinidad. As a member of the dominant class, I do not pretend to understand what daily life feels like for many members of families who spoke with me. My language skills do not exclude me from peer groups, social situations, education, or the general mass media. In fact, bilingualism has always been an advantage for me. As a child living in Mexico and Spain, I was part of the investigating other and not an immigrant trying to negotiate a new social system and acculturate. My mother, too, experienced the privilege that came with her status; it was her blonde hair and young age, as well as her foreign university credentials, that rendered her access. The looks from museum guards and stubborn archivists were softened with a nod, *"sí la rubia puede"* (yes, the blonde can), and she (we) entered. These early experiences later shaped my interpretations of mainstream media stereotypes I encountered as I navigated media through my elementary and teenage years. I remember *The Cosby Show* and *The Fresh Prince of Bel-Air*, but I do not remember many Latina/os on television except for "Ponch" on *CHiPs*[4] and the secondary characters who were maids, cantina girls or gardeners. These images did not resonate with my own experiences with friends both in Mexico and in the U.S. As a young adult I remember listening to debates around California Ballot Propostition 187,[5] which came on the heels of many years of anti-immigrant rhetoric. I remember a family acquaintance disgruntled because of "those people" (the migrant workers he employed on his farm) who sent their kids to school, where he imagined they were not required to speak English. Because of the tone, I remember being shocked at his overt racism, but realized that I was hearing an opinion that would not be shared with those coded as Latina/o. These experiences have shaped my interest in studying the ways in which Latina/os use media to investigate how meaning is constructed and contested within U.S. society. It is important to recognize Latina/os as part of the mainstream U.S. audience rather than as a separate niche to be understood as Other.

My children are part of the most diverse generation the United States has witnessed, and it is my hope that they will grow up to embrace difference and not see it as something to be overcome. We must teach them that differences exist but that difference does not mean worse or better. One afternoon while I was listening to a recorded interview, my daughter asked what I was doing. I told her I had just finished listening to a father describe his annoyance with all little Latina girls with bobbed haircuts being called Dora. My daughter asked why; after all she had been a fan of Dora. I explained that it upset him that Dora was the only reference people could think of to describe young girls with dark eyes and dark hair, and I asked her to think of her two friends, Julia (Mexican American) and Liana (mixed heritage—Spanish, French —looks "Latina") and asked if they looked alike. She said "no." I asked her if they like the same things. She said "no" and described that Julia loves "girl stuff" while Liana is a fan of *Star Wars*. I told my daughter that she understands the differences between her friends because she knows them, but others may see them as the same because they both look Latina with dark hair and eyes. I explained that the frustration for the father who I interviewed was when others assumed that being a Latina girl is defined as being like or even looking like Dora because she is their most salient cultural reference. The lived experience of a pan-Latina/o identity can be frustrating because there exists complexity and diversity within the group that is not explored in media portrayals. This simplified explanation goes to the heart of the book. By listening to families describe their media use as well as their perceptions about Spanish-language television and the representations of Latina/os in mainstream media, it became clear that the industry response to this group should be scrutinized. Latina/o children have a wide variety of interests and see themselves as central to the American experience. As media respond to this demographic, it is important to recognize that similar to any other group, it is impossible to capture their complexity within a limited range of media.

The book is organized into six chapters. Chapter 1, "Latina/os in the Audience," introduces readers to the current demography of the Latina/o population and how that is connected to the growing interest in the media industry to justify the creations of products that will attract this newly sought after group. Further, there is an explanation of the role that Nielsen Media Research plays in collecting and distributing information pertaining to the best ways to reach Latina/os. Chapter 2, "The Latina/o Youth Market," discusses the growth of the Spanish-language television industry as well as describing new bilingual and Latino-themed networks. In addition, children's programming that features characters who speak English and Spanish is analyzed to provide the reader with a context from which to understand the interview data. Networks such as MTVtr3s and mun2 are introduced to explain their concentration on U.S. Latina/o teenagers. After analysis it appears that these networks perform a "syncretic identity" (Molina Guzmán, 2006) that glosses over difference and diversity within the teenage experience to present a united Latinidad. Programs such as *LatiNation* and *American Latino TV* attempt to present a "hybrid identity" (Molina Guzmán, 2006; Martínez, 2004, 2007) by acknowledging the diversity as well as bicultural status of its target audience.

Chapters 3, 4, and 5 report the primary findings from the interviews. Chapter 3, "Latina/o Media Consumption," discusses general viewing habits of family members focusing on young people's media choices, which highlight a hybrid reality for many participants (Molina Guzmán, 2006; Mayer, 2003b). The children in the families see themselves as typically American in their media use. Their favorite activities are consistent with most accounts of American children's viewing habits; the only distinction is their exposure to Spanish-language television, which leads to a bicultural outlook. Chapter 4, "Connecting to 'Home,'" analyzes the attraction Mexican American families have for their home media. Many families report watching telenovelas as a way to connect to an imagined home, even for those participants who have not been to Mexico in many years. In addition, the novelas act as educational supplements for the children in the home who learn about being Mexican from the programs (Mayer, 2003a; Rios, 2003; Casas Peréz, 2005). Further, while the younger participants did not report watching much news, the older children and parents responded that their preference was for news from Mexico because it was more international and kept them connected leading to a more cosmopolitan perspective. Chapter 5, "Concerning Representation: Latina/os in English-Language media," critiques the images of Latina/os in mainstream media (Valdivia, 2007; Harewood & Valdivia, 2005; Markert, 2007; Johnson, 2000; Lichter & Amundson, 1997). Participants engage in negotiated readings (Hall, 1980; Radway, 1984; Lull, 1995; Rojas, 2004) of the texts that are informed by their hybrid positioning within mainstream culture (Straubhaar, 2007; Kraidy, 2005; Rinderle, 2005; Mayer, 2003a; Dávlia, 2001a). While there was optimism as family members recalled the success of some Latina/o actors, there was a consensus that there could be more programming that integrates Latina/o characters naturally into the storylines. Finally, Chapter 6, "(Re)Imagining a Latina/o Audience," concludes by addressing the relationship audience members have with television both in English and in Spanish. The complexities of language and identity are addressed to provide insight into the ways in which Latina/o youth navigate the media landscape. The stereotypes associated with the Latina/o audience are challenged, and readers will gain a better appreciation for the rich diversity of the group. I propose that the industry resist forcing Latina/os into a market niche. What I heard time and time again from the family members is that they do not want to be isolated from the mainstream, but rather they would prefer to be included. Listening to Latina/o youth will better serve the industry if it responds to the diversity by creating programs that include their experiences and will expand the possibility for media programming that can be enriching for all.

Chapter One

Latina/os in the Audience

My interest in investigating the ways in which Latina/os, or more specifically Mexican American families in southern California, negotiate their television viewing began when I witnessed the increasing advertising and programming created for what some have labeled a new or emerging audience. As new programs and networks enter the television marketplace to reach a particular type of audience member, I question whether this niche programming is desired, essential, effective or at worst functioning to segregate one community from another. Over the course of writing the book, it became clear that the effort to design bicultural and bilingual programming has intensified with networks, such as MTVtr3s, mun2, SiTV, and V-me, competing for this market. For a communication scholar, the questions go beyond whether U.S.-born Latina/os and new immigrants enjoy these programs and become questions about the role of this programming in the socialization of Latina/os into the broader American landscape. How do the programs impact the growth and development of young people living within this bicultural reality? Have the new programming efforts offered something beneficial to the youth market or does the desire to sell Latina/o youth as an audience outweigh any sincere efforts to create enriching television?

The opportunity to investigate family viewing habits allows for a rich view of the audience by interviewing subjects in a natural setting, their home, to discuss a normal part of their daily routines. As the book unfolds the family members explain perceptions about the mass media focusing on positive and negative aspects. While many have opinions about the efforts of the U.S. Spanish-language networks, few mentioned seeking out Latino-themed programs. The parents of young children did acknowledge an in-crease in Latina/o characters in preschool shows, but this was not the primary reason they encouraged their children to watch; par-ents look for educational programming regardless of the ethnicity of the characters. Overall, most family members agreed that they would like to see more diversity across the mainstream mass me-dia and do not want to be thought of as a separate but equal audi-ence.

Television viewing remains a popular leisure time activity, even in the current media environment that offers consumers so many platforms from which to choose that it appears as if family members are isolated from enjoying entertainment together. No longer do we envision the family gathered around the one televi-sion set choosing among the "big three" networks. Now each mem-ber is likely to have his or her own computer, cell phone, and multiple televisions to watch programming from hundreds of channels and recorded shows from days earlier. It would seem to be a rare program that brings the whole family together, but it happens, and in fact, according to most reports, it happens more often than we think. Television viewing still plays a dominant role in the leisure time activities of families, especially in the home (Kotler, Wright, & Huston, 2001; Rideout & Hamel, 2006; Roberts, Foehr, & Rideout, 2005; Jordon, 2004).

The Changing Demography

Often the changing demography of the United States is used to justify the study of Latina/os as a separate group, but it is clear that the reason to investigate how Latina/o audiences make sense of media is not because they have become an important part of the American landscape, but because they have always been part of the American landscape. It is incumbent upon communication scholars to take the process of meaning making seriously and, as content providers produce more programming attempting to delin-eate audience segments from each other, we should assess what happens as young people and their parents engage with media.

The release of the 2000 Census that showed that the Hispanic population was the fastest growing minority segment in the U.S. sparked an interest in the media industry that launched efforts to tap that market. The rush to be on the Latina/o bandwagon does not seem to be slowing down. The expectation is that the 2010 Census will solidify interest in the group ensuring that media catering to Latina/os is here to stay.

The experience of Mexican Americans is an integral part of the complex narrative that shapes the story of the United States. In the Southwest, explorers from Spain and Mexico arrived prior to establishment of the original thirteen colonies. As a result, the history of the southwestern United States is intertwined with the history of Spain and Mexico, leaving a lineage of Americans who trace heritage to these countries. In 1848, as a result of the Treaty of Guadalupe Hidalgo, Mexico ceded 525,000 square miles of territory, nearly 50% of its land, into what now makes up the Southwest United States. Mexicans who were settled in the region had the right to become U.S. citizens and to retain title of their property; however, many were not successful in petitioning for the title and struggled in court battles leaving them without the promised land (Engstrand, 1998; Hayes-Bautista, Chameline, Jones, Cornejo, Cañadas, Martinez, & Meza, 2007). Between 1901 and 1965, omigration from Mexico was not restricted and Mexicans were recruited to work in agriculture between 1942 and 1965. After 1965, immigration policy toward Mexico changed, making it much more difficult to enter the United States legally (Hernández, Siles, & Rochin, 2000). Currently, the process to legally emigrate from Mexico is lengthy and complex and many immigrants come to the U.S. without legal documents.

Unlike other regions that border Mexico, San Diego County is more economically, socially, and culturally diverse. While there are disparities between communities with high concentrations of Mexican immigrants and Latina/os and those without, these differences are often masked by the vast urban environment that shapes the region. Not only is San Diego County a large metropolitan area, the region extends east to Imperial County, and if Tijuana and Mexicali are included, there are 12 million residents in this transnational space (Valero, Villaseñor, & Roman, 2008; Naughton & Love, 2006; González Hernández, 2008). There is a circle of connection in the border region: many people in the Imperial Valley cross through Calexico/Mexicali, and near San Diego, Tijuana/San Ysidro, the busiest border in the world, sees an estimated 300,000 border crossers daily. For many who live comfortably in both countries, the border is a physical, troublesome barrier while their understanding of home is borderless. It is unknown how many cross through other means to arrive in California, but it is clear that San Diego County is a gateway for immigrants from all over the world.

According to U.S. Census Bureau reports, the Hispanic[6] population reached 45.5 million people, or 15.1% of the U.S. population, in 2007. California has the largest Hispanic population with 13.2 million in 2007. Latina/os are also the fastest growing minority group with a 14% increase in the last four years and projected to reach close to 60 million people by 2020. As of 2008, there were just over 12 million Hispanic television households. After 2020, according to the U.S. Census Bureau, the Hispanic population is projected to add more people to the U.S. population every year than all other race/ethnic groups combined (Rodríguez, 1999a). In California, half of the state's children live in families where at least one parent is an immigrant and of those 67% are Latina/o (Newhouse, 2007). In San Diego County, 38% of children under 18 identify as Latina/o, and in some communities as much as 74% of the children are Latina/o; 85% of that group are of Mexican descent (Naughton & Love, 2006).

In December 2009, the Pew Hispanic Center released a report highlighting the characteristics of Latina/o youth. The data show that this wave of immigration, driven by people from Latin America, is the largest in U.S. history; nearly half of the 40 million immigrants that have come since 1965 are from Latin America. The reality of Latina/o youth, however, indicates that they are not immigrants. While the story of the growth of the Latina/o population has been tied to stories of immigration, the data show that among youth, most are native-born Americans. In 1995, nearly 50% of Latina/os between the ages of 16 and 25 were immigrants; that number dropped to 34% in 2009 (Pew Hispanic, 2009). In contrast to perceptions of Latina/os not speaking English well, among foreign-born, 48% and, among second generation, 98% speak English "very well or pretty well" (Pew Hispanic, 2009). Of second generation, 79% are also proficient in Spanish, and 70% of bilingual speakers engage in some form of Spanglish. Spanglish use peeks among the second generation.

The reality of Latina/o youth is not devoid of complications, and second generation and beyond face a myriad of challenges. The obesity rate among Latina/o youth is higher than other ethnicities in all age groups (Key Facts, 2006). The availability of healthful food and cultural attitudes contribute to these discrepancies, and the long-term well-being of Latina/os is a serious consequence (Alban, 2009). Young Latina/os are becoming teen parents at a rate higher than other ethnic groups in the United States. According to the 2009 Pew Hispanic Report, while the overall numbers of teen birthrates have declined since 1990, 26% of Latinas are becoming mothers before the age of 19. In 1990, the teen birthrate was at 44%, indicating an important drop. It is important to remember that the children born in the 1990s to teen mothers are now teenagers, many of whom are struggling to succeed. Many second generation and beyond Latina/os, especially those of Mexican heritage, are familiar with gangs, indicating that they know someone who is a current or former gang member (Pew Hispanic, 2009). The dropout rate for Latina/o youth is three times as high as white teenagers, and second generation Latina/o youth dropout of high school at a rate of 9%, with three quarters of those who dropout citing financial pressure to support their families. The drop out rate is highest among immigrants (32.9%), lowest among the second generation (8.5%) and begins to creep back up at the third generation or higher (11.5%). Most Latina/o youth believe that a college degree is important for "getting ahead in life" (Pew Hispanic, 2009, p. 10), and of high school graduates 46% enroll in college. According to Fry (2002), however, they are less likely than white college students to graduate with a degree.

Latina/o youth are aware of the subtle and not so subtle differences among members of the pan-Latino coalition. According to the

Pew Report (2009) "young Hispanics say there are more cultural differences (64%) than commonalities (33%) within the Hispanic community in the U.S." (p. 8). The differences bear out as young people describe themselves much more often in terms of their family's country of origin rather than using the term "Latina/o" or "Hispanic." This challenges the efforts on the part of marketers and media industry executives who are drawn to creating Latino-themed media when in fact there is much diversity among the group. What is common is a diluted sense of difference from the mainstream culture. How do these differences get made into something that defines a generation of young people? What are the consequences of rejecting diversity in the name of apolitical benign multiculturalism? Is it easier for the dominant culture to accept "Latina/os" into the broader U.S. culture if they are sold as a package rather than a complex group of people who are Mexican, Cuban, Puerto Rican, Venezuelan, Honduran, among others?

The Hispanic Market

The reality of the changing demography did not go unnoticed by business executives, who saw Latina/os not merely as a group of new Americans, but rather as an untapped market ready to spend. The potential buying power of the group has led to the creation of many media outlets hoping to sell the supposedly new demographic to advertisers. In the United States, there are roughly 35 million Hispanics with a potential buying power of $951 million per year (Humphreys, 2008)—a market too large for most advertisers to ignore. The Spanish-speaking market is the fastest growing in the country, both in population and purchasing power. These facts make advertising in Spanish a perceived necessity. By 2025 it is estimated there will be 60 million Hispanics nationwide, and the Hispanic population will surpass the Anglo population in California and San Diego County. Dean Calbreath, writing for the *San Diego Union Tribune*, stated: "Walter Meneses, who runs Meneses Research & Associates in San Diego, said that in San Diego County, many third- or fourth-generation Hispanics flip between English and Spanish stations on their televisions. But, according to his research, as many as 85% prefer to communicate in Spanish" (Calbreath, 2002). The creation of Spanish-language media has been shaped by the dual forces of desire on the part of Latina/os to access programming that is relevant to their experiences and the desire of corporations who think the best way to reach them is through the Spanish language. In addition, Spanish-speakers recall advertisements more often when the ads are presented in their native language, which is the benefit of advertising in Spanish-language media outlets.

In San Diego, 89% of Hispanics speak Spanish and, according to some reports, Spanish-language television advertisements are 4.5 times more likely to influence purchasing decisions than English-language ads. According to Magazine Publishers of America (www.magazine.org/market profiles), Hispanic audiences have a 61% better ad recall and have a 57% better comprehension rate when the ads are in Spanish. The recognition that Latina/os prefer to watch programming in Spanish will continue to persuade corporations to produce advertisements in Spanish, which in turn will continue to support the Spanish-language media industries in the United States In fact, according to Wentz (2008), Spanish-language TV ad spending grew 1.5%, accounting for approximately $4.4 billion spent in 2007, and advertising firms continue to seek ways to "speak" to this audience (Liesse, 2007; Callow & McDonald, 2005; Luna & Peracchio, 2005; Romano, 2003). In San Diego, Spanish-language advertising was once isolated in communities with a high percentage of Mexican immigrants and Mexican Americans. Now it is common to see these advertisements throughout San Diego County.

In an effort to assess the Hispanic market, Meneses Research & Associates, a San Diego based firm, provided an overview of the market in 2010 through a workshop and was interviewed on the local NPR affiliate. According to the statistics, the buying power of the Latino population in the United States is approaching one trillion dollars. As of 2010, close to one third of the population is Latino/a, and one of every two new babies born in San Diego County is in Latino families. Given the proximity to the border, Walter

Meneses explained that 47% of the Latinos living in San Diego
have family ties in Baja California (Brown, Davis, & Stoffel, 2010).
Advertising to Latinos is complex because of the differences in
language, acculturation levels, and immigrant status. Meneses
identified Latinos as "loyal consumers" who are likely to stay with
trusted brands. For example, if they are used to a product that
they purchased in Mexico, it is likely they will continue to purchase that brand when they move to the United States. They are
also a demographic that is highly dependent on word of mouth information from friends and family. It is important to recognize
that the consumer needs of the market are no different than other
groups, but to be an effective marketer, the way in which you
communicate with the group is unique. According to Meneses, 49%
of first generation prefer to communicate in the Spanish language,
which drives much of the translation approach to advertising in
the United States. He cautions, however, that direct translation is
unlikely to be successful because these advertisements are not culturally attuned and miss the value orientation of new immigrants
who have moved from Latin America.

Meneses details the differences between "Hispanic" and "Anglo" markets by listing opposing value orientations. These dichot-
omies   include   formality   vs.   informality;   cooperation   vs.
competition; dependence vs. independence; and obedience vs. follow own rules. He argues that marketers who are uneducated
about these differences can potentially alienate their intended
market. It must be noted, however, that this succinct explanation
is based on stereotypes that are not necessarily reflective of the
diversity of either group nor are they the easy answer to the best
way to reach Latina/os. While there are certainly advantages to
learning more about the cultural norms of a group before creating
strategies to appeal to their spending habits, it must be recognized
that the most widely adopted standard is not the only way.

In addition to using the Spanish language and Spanish media
outlets, another approach has been to capitalize on "Latino identity" by creating advertising that incorporates elements of what has
been determined as Latina/o in order to sell products (Brown,
2004; Martinez, 2004, 2007; Mayer, 2003b; Callow & McDonald,

2005; Luna & Peracchio, 2005). The goal of the advertisers is not necessarily to promote Latinidad, but rather to use the cultural markers as a type of shorthand to hail particular members of the audience. Michael Callow and C. Gibran McDonald (2005) explain that advertisers are more likely to tailor the language of the advertisement in ways that mimic the outlet in which it is placed, but point to a trend of Spanglish where a Spanish word is inserted into an English sentence. As predicted, this practice is seen more and more. David Luna and Laura Peracchio (2005) conclude that the inserting of Spanish words into English sentences does enhance attention from a bicultural audience. This strategy has been used in a variety of forms and can be found on promotional websites for Latino-themed networks such as MTVtr3s. Further, "Hispanic marketing firms thus work to promote a hybrid authentic standard of Latina/o ethnicity consisting of the cultural and language knowledge of recent immigrants and the affluence of the middle class" (Macias, 2004, p. 303).

Marketers have tried to capture and stabilize what it means to be Latina/o, but the vibrant and varied lives of Latina/os cannot be easily situated (Dávila, 2001a, 2002; Molina Guzmán, 2006; Rojas, 2004; Rivadenerya, 2006). Some brands are moving away from the niche marketing perspective, recognizing that young people who hail from different cultural and ethnic backgrounds have more in common with each other than with older members of their same ethnicity. Young people across demographic groups are being branded as "youth," which in today's global market is driven more by an attitude—trendy, urban, hip—than by ethnic differences. A young Latino may see himself as more similar to a young African American schoolmate than to his father, who may have been born in another country and is Spanish-language dominant. We can see the United States as a test for global marketing trends because the target market is already diverse so that, if these approaches work here, it is likely that they will be used across borders. Transnational corporations see the advantage of appealing to a global teenager rather than being concerned about the subtle differences between teenagers. According to an *Advertising Age* article, Neil Golden, chief marketer of McDonald's USA, believes that consumers are embracing diversity, and that needs to be represented in advertising efforts. Proving that ethnic diversity in advertising is good for business, 40% of McDonald's customers are ethnic minorities.

Within a global framework international marketing campaigns are becoming more common using an ambiguous strategy that appeals to youth. Within the global approach to branding there is the need to sell multiculturalism in uncontested ways. In a textual analysis of *America's Next Top Model*, Hasinoff (2008) examines the way in which the discourses of race are articulated through a neo-liberal framework that highlights ambiguity as marketable and therefore desirable. The race becomes another element of their identifiable physical features that can be sold and promoted to clients. The more flexibility in their racial codes, the better they can serve a variety of needs. Valdivia (2004) makes the point that most successful Latina actors have been those that can play across the ethnic spectrum.

The Role of Nielsen

The A.C. Nielsen Company is the most recognized audience research firm in the world and holds a monopoly over the data collection process that reveals audience media habits. Mass media industries, including television, radio and more recently the Internet, rely on Nielsen to gather data about who is using a particular medium at a particular time. In addition, Nielsen provides demographic information about the audience including age, ethnicity, and socioeconomic class. The mass media industries use this data to set advertising rates as they sell airtime to advertisers who hope to reach a particular segment of the audience. When Nielsen began collecting information about the Hispanic audience, it legitimized the presence of the Spanish-language media market, and now Nielsen has incorporated Spanish-language networks into its general market sample.

Bill Grimes, who became president of Univisión in 1986, was eager for Nielsen to revamp its data collection system in order to gather more accurate information about the Hispanic audience. In 1992, Univisión and Telemundo paid $20 million to develop new ways of assessing the Hispanic audience. The old methodology used by Nielsen, for example, showed that 8% of the population in Los Angeles watched Spanish-language programming and the new system showed that the viewership was actually 13%. After this methodology was implemented, nationwide figures showed 40% more households tuning into Spanish-language programming than were reported under the old system (Moran, 2004). The methodology was called the National Hispanic Television Index.

According to Nielsen Media Research, the number of Hispanic television households reaches close to 13 million in 2010 and 51% of homes have four or more members. Further, 57% of Hispanic homes have children while only 36% of the total U.S. households have children (Ethnic Trends, 2009). Ad spending on Spanish-language networks topped $3 billion in 2006. In fact, total ad expenditures were down 0.3% overall in the first quarter of 2007, but increased 3.7% in Spanish-language media outlets (Ayala, 2007). Reports for the 12-month period prior to June 2009 showed a decrease of 6.3%, but at $5.5 billion it is still a $2.5 billion increase from 2006. Further, the smallest drop in ad revenue was in the television market with only a loss of 2% (Wentz, 2009). The market share of the Spanish-language media industry is significant.

Nielsen announced in August 2007 that it was including Spanish-language networks in the general National People Meter to put "Spanish-language television on a level playing field with English-language television" (Holmes, 2007). As a result, Nielsen retired the National Hispanic People Meter, which had measured television use in Hispanic households since 1992. This may be a response to the criticism that the Hispanic sample that Nielsen relied on did not accurately reflect U.S.-born Latina/os' television habits (Houpt, 2006). The removal of the Index demonstrates that "Latinos are now so important to the overall TV ratings picture that it would be misleading to relegate them to a separate system" (James, 2007).

The information that Nielsen provides the industry is that the best way to reach Hispanics is by advertising with Spanish-language media, and many corporations have done just that. According to Nielsen, between 2007 and 2008 there was an 8% increase in ad spending for Spanish-language commercials spurred by the knowledge that the Spanish-language networks, Univisión and Telemundo, had 11% more viewers overall last season and a 6% increase in the 18–49 demographic (Kaplan, 2009). This indicates that more than new immigrants are watching Spanish-language television. Again the industry conventional wisdom is to utilize language as the way to reach this market. Market research shows that bilingual consumers have stronger recall, score higher on a likability scale, and are more emotionally connected to ads in Spanish when comparing the same product spot in English.

The creation of more advertising in Spanish was bolstered by this information, which is driving the development of more Spanish-language outlets. Research that is independent from a marketing framework and independent from Nielsen paints a very different picture of media use for bilingual, U.S.-born Latina/os, which is further discussed in Chapter 2. In fact, many researchers have found that third-generation plus Latina/os in the United States prefer to watch television in English and many watch television in both languages (DeSipio, 2003; Mayer, 2003b; Straubhaar, 2007) In addition, many would indeed like to see more diversity, particularly more Latina/os in English-language fare (Moran, 2010).

Nielsen's monopoly over the market has not just been a concern for those interested in getting accurate readings of the habits of Latina/o consumers. Across the board, networks have been dissatisfied with the data collection and distribution process (Dávila, 2008). In fact, as reported by Carter and Elliot (August 14, 2009) in the *New York Times*, NBC Universal (which owns Telemundo) has been a driving force behind an initiative to create a consortium that would devise a new audience measurement system. For years it was cost prohibitive to compete with the ratings giant, but new technologies such as digital video recorders (DVRs) have enabled a possible competitor (Elliot, 2009).

The interest in the market should not overshadow the fact that cultural visibility does not always equate with civil liberties (Dávila, 2000) and "the commercial use of Spanish is not about the recognition of Latina/os but about constituting them as contented consumers" (Dávila, 2000, p. 84). Further, as we consider Latina/os as a group, it is important to interrogate the essentialist notion of the label. As the family members reveal in later chapters, the audience is diverse, and it is often the media texts themselves that contain Latinidad to a few stereotypes such as immigrant, Spanish-speaking, urban. The media industry has always tried to sell one way of being—teenager, mother, boy—because it works to create an ideology of defining normal. What is the "normal Latina/o"? What we can conclude is that ideological constructs of Latinidad do not reflect the diversity of the Latina/o experience within the U.S., but that should not be surprising and should not lead to a fatalistic attitude that accepts this normality as the end of the story. The media can tell a different tale. The process of rearticulation can challenge commonsense beliefs that stabilize the status quo. The market-driven mass media version of Latindad does not have to be the narrative of Latina/o youth in this country.

Mass Media and the American Family

The role of the mass media in the social fabric of the American family has become so intertwined that many take its presence for granted and are unable to imagine a life without technology. While the time young people spend interacting with some sort of screen is increasing, their parents too are enjoying streaming television online, Facebook, and other media that are now part of family life. It is as common to see fathers and sons playing video games together as it is to see them playing catch.

According to the Kaiser Foundation that studied media use among young people and the household media environment, media have become a central component of family life, and it is no surprise that as of 2005, children use media for nearly 6½ hours per day with most of the time devoted to television (Roberts et al., 2005; Jordon, 2004). All children spend a considerable amount of time using the mass media. Further, it has been shown consistent-

ly that black and Latina/o children spend more time with media
than white children (Blosser, 1988; Bickham, Vadewater, Huston,
Lee, Caplovitz, & Wright, 2003) and minority children are more
likely to have television and other media in their bedrooms leading
to more media exposure (Taveras, Hohman, Price, Gortmaker &
Sonneville, 2009). It is also true that children in families with lower household incomes and less education are more likely to use
media for longer periods of time (Roberts et al., 2005; Taveras et
al., 2009).

In addition to the overall time spent with the mass media,
most children are multi-tasking with their media use. It is common to see a child on the computer with the television on in the
background while keeping in touch with friends on a cell phone.
Nevertheless, television still remains a dominant source of entertainment for American families and an activity that multiple generations can enjoy together. In fact, according to Dafna Lemish
(2007), it has become so much a part of everyday life that its existence is taken for granted. For many it is a daily ritual that occu-
pies time in deliberate ways, but often it is part of the background
noise of life. It is incumbent on scholars to continue to investigate
the role of television in the socialization process even as other
technologies vie for our attention. While many bemoan the ritualistic use of television as a leisure time activity, for some familial
viewing can be an important part of shared experiences. The ritual
of watching sporting events or dramas may be just as satisfying as
other more nostalgic activities such as game playing or storytell-
ing. Strasburger, Wilson, and Jordan (2009) explain that the home
has become a multimedia environment whereby parents socialize
their children by modeling media behaviors. Ecological systems
theory has been used to situate children's media use within the
home environment to explain how media fit into larger social systems that impact a child's development. The media are part of the
"exosystem" defined as "those social settings that influence a
child's development but in which the child does not necessarily
have a direct role" (Strasburger et al., 2009, pp. 510–511). An of-
ten-cited example of this is the parents' workplace whereby events
occur that are not related to the child, but that impact the parents'

attitude or behavior in a way that impacts the child. In the case of the media, decisions are made, narratives formed, characters chosen, all of which are independent from the child, but do have an impact when the child is exposed. From the perspective of the Latino child, the impact of media content is dependent on the ecological systems that inform attitudes toward patterns of media use.

Studies of Latino families[7] in the United States have identified characteristics that are differentiated from the dominant middle-class culture. "Familialism" has been identified as a key characteristic in the culture of the Latino family (Vázquez García, García Coll, Erkut, Alaracón, & Troop, 2000; Cauce & Domenech-Rodríguez, 2002; Marín & Marín, 1991), which can been seen through family members' strong identification, loyalty, and attachment to each other. Vázquez García et al. (2000) explain how the term "normal enmeshment" has been used to describe Latino families' pattern of "overinvolvement, dependence, and discouragement of self-differentiation among family members" (p. 239). Further, the authors describe how *respeto* (respect) has been used to identify patterns of generational and gender role boundaries. Latino families, more so than the dominant culture, place a strong emphasis on respect for elders and interact in ways that demonstrate strict norms of behavior based on age. Children are taught to conform to traditional sex roles and to respect the elderly and other authority figures (Vázquez García et al., 2000). In terms of parenting and family structures, *marianismo* has been a term used to emphasize the role of the mother and her self-sacrifice for her children, while *machismo* makes reference to the role of the father as provider and reinforcing elements of a strict patriarchal structure (Cauce & Deomenech-Rodríguez, 2002). Latino families in the United States face numerous challenges, many of which are exacerbated in immigrant families. In California, Latina/o teenagers have high dropout rates with an estimated 25% of high school students not completing their education. Many Latino families are living below the poverty line. For families with a foreign-born head of household, the poverty rate exceeds 19% while for U.S.-born families it is just above 14% (Just the Facts, 2009). Children raised in Latino families have a myriad of experiences that connect with other children in the United States. In today's multi-generational and bicultural environment, children growing up in Latino families are learning to negotiate traditional values with those promoted within the dominant culture.

As children access mainstream mass media, they may encounter a lifestyle that is at odds with their cultural traditions. When they perceive this difference between their traditions and mainstream culture, children may experience dissonance when trying to reconcile conflicting ways of being (Perreira, Chapman, & Stein, 2006). Reducing dissonance by engaging with media that speaks to them may provide an opportunity to feel at ease. Therefore, programming with a bicultural approach may indeed validate Latina/o teenagers' feelings by highlighting or even making fun of the process of living between two cultures. For example, a program on MTVtr3s is called *Music My Guey* playing on the Spanish word *Guey* (slang for "dude" or used more negatively for "jerk"), but it sounds like "way" so the title of the program in English sounds like Music My Way, with a wink to the in-group.

In one of the first comprehensive studies to assess media use habits among Mexican Americans, Greenberg, Burgoon, Burgoon, and Korzenny (1983) found that children in Mexican American homes watch more television than Caucasian children and this finding has remained consistent over time. Further, in assessing access to Spanish-language television, children in Spanish-speaking homes were exposed to Spanish-language television as a family viewing activity. Since the early 1980s the television landscape has changed significantly with the availability of Spanish-language and Latino-themed programs; what remains, however, is that many of the viewing patterns have stayed fairly consistent. The conclusions of the 1983 Greenberg et al. study on Mexican American youth posit that "...the cultural duality does persist for these youngsters, a wish to maintain some specific language tie with their ethnic roots. The majority mass media may wish to consider means of accommodating this preference, rather than merely deferring to more specialized media" (p. 199). In other words, the authors indicate that it would be better to incorporate some of this "cultural duality" into mainstream English-language programming rather than relying on Spanish-language or niche programs to address Mexican American viewing preferences. Close to thirty years after this initial investigation, there is a significant increase in the bicultural approach to programming targeting Latina/o youth, but it is not part of the mainstream TV landscape and therefore it is viewed as niche programming appealing to a specific audience. Questions remain regarding the impact of this programming on the socialization of the audience.

For children, the relationship with media, and specifically television, remains complex and like all children, Latina/o children come to the television set with their own unique set of experiences that impact how they interpret media content. As de Block and Buckingham (2007) caution, a child's ethnicity is not the only factor determining media use and preferences, and other factors such as age, gender, and class all interact in children's media choices. The broad term Latina/o incorporates many different life experiences. Children may have moved with their families to the United States when they were young and in this case children tend to adopt the mainstream pop culture fairly rapidly. Latina/o children who are second generation and beyond are fully integrated into mainstream U.S. pop culture. New immigrants who come as older children like their parents are typically more connected to their home media. What makes the role of television more complex in these families is that there is an opportunity to remain fully connected to media from home—especially from Mexico—through U.S. outlets such as Univisión and Telemundo. If the parents choose to watch television in Spanish, then it is more likely that their children are exposed to this programming. If you ask children, however, when they have the opportunity to choose, they are more likely to choose mainstream popular programs; they watch what is cool. Most young children do not articulate the language of multiculturalism, and few are critical of the representations they see; however, they will explain how they like seeing other children similar to them. For example, children in Latino families are likely to watch Disney's *Handy Manny* because it is popular and promoted with an official line of Handy Manny toys, but it is harder to determine whether the fact that he is Latino brings them to the TV set with more frequency than a program without Latina/o characters. Nevertheless, such programming provides more diverse characters on television to which children are exposed.

For children living within immigrant families, media can play a dual role of connecting the family to their home culture and providing information about the new culture. The Spanish-language media, especially news, have long seen its role as informing immigrants about their new environment. For immigrant parents who have limited English, media in Spanish become their primary source of entertainment and information. Their children, who often become proficient in English faster because of school attendance, will navigate through both the English- and Spanish-language media landscape (DeSipio, 2003). For immigrant children, the characters on television provide models of behavior of "American life," especially in the beginning when they are more isolated from local children (Lemish, 2007; Elias & Lemish, 2008). Sometimes parents feel the media in the new country contradict their traditional value system and limit exposure, but many parents recognize the benefit of national television in helping children "settle in" (de Block & Buckingham, 2007, p. 105). While "very little is known empirically about the various roles that media actually play in the lives of immigrant children who undoubtedly face unique personal challenges, as well as, inter-generational tensions" (Lemish, 2007, p. 132) the families described later in the book provide insight into this complex relationship.

Children Understanding Television and Other Media

Much research has been conducted on the role of television on the socialization process of children. Research into the effects of television exposure has centered on two primary avenues: negative effects—increased aggression, early sexual activity, body dissatisfaction, stereotyping of others—and the positive impact—cognitive skills, pro-social lessons, and cultural awareness. Research into how children process media at different ages is based on cognitive development research highlighting how the cognitive skills of children at different ages impacts how they interpret media content. While the role of television in the lives of American families has been documented (see, for example, Kotler et al., 2001), attention to media use within Latina/o and/or Spanish-speaking homes has been limited (Subervi-Vélez, 1999; Subervi-Vélez & Colsant, 1993). Nevertheless, the relationship between children's cognitive abilities and their ability to understand and process different types of mass media (Lemish, 2007; Strasburger, Wilson, & Jordon, 2009) has undergone extensive research over the past fifty years (Pecora, Murray, & Wartella, 2007).

It is clear that certain imagery and sound attract a child, even as an infant, to the mass media. Programs that include bright colors, cheerful high-pitched sounds, and fuzzy characters all seem to resonate with even the youngest of audience members. As more media products are available for the very young, parents are persuaded by advertisers, peers, and their children to bring these products into their homes. As children age, their attention to content is driven more by the story and development of characters and they begin to differentiate between fantasy and reality. My son at age 4 responded to questions posed by characters because he saw them talking to him in a very direct manner. A conversation with my daughter, however, revealed that at age 7 she understood that the tween[8] targeted sitcoms are not real in the sense that they are actors playing pretend, but she had difficulty differentiating between the possible and probable (Strasburger et al., 2009) because she believed that the issues and situations the characters face are realistic and accurately represent a probable reality. Children identify with characters not just as friends, but as important role models. Through the process of identification, children may form parasocial relationships with characters that prove to be significant as audiences learn and take advice from mediated friends. These characters demonstrate a myriad of behaviors that may be incorporated into a child's personality, impact behavior, and change attitudes—at least for a time.

Teenagers' cognition levels are approaching the sophistication of an adult, but there are key developmental trends that occur during adolescence that impact the ways in which teens use and interpret media content. Media executives interested in attracting a teen audience often exploit these characteristics in order to gain notoriety. Media outlets draw teenagers by showcasing risk-taking behaviors and/or by providing content that is offensive to adults. One key milestone of adolescents is the process of identity formation that is molded through, among a variety of other things, mediated experiences such as listening to music, watching teen-centric television, or using social networking sites to chat with friends. Teens experiment with identity, and those teens who are socialized in a bicultural environment have many versions of "self" from which to experiment. As a child reaches his or her teenage years, real life experiences, including gender, ethnicity and family values, all become part of how they process media content. For children growing up in a Latino family, their attention to media content may be shaped by being Latina/o or that may have little to do with their choices. Because the sophisticated marketing strategies, product tie-ins, and traditional commercials persuade children in powerful ways, it appears that for most children, regardless of heritage, the popularity of mainstream media personalities or trends can predict what they are watching.

As the demographics of young people in the United States change so do the industry attempts to make media that will be popular. It is perhaps no coincidence that one of Disney's most popular programs, *The Wizards of Waverly Place,* features a family with an Italian-American father and Mexican mother whose children struggle with bridging Mexican traditions and dominant American customs. For example, in one episode, Alex, the 15-year-old daughter, struggles to learn Spanish even though her mother is bilingual. We can posit that Disney is attempting to provide more diverse programming for altruistic purposes, or we can expect that as a successful business, the company understands the reality of many of their tween audience members and wants to appeal to their experiences.

As children mature they become savvy about their media choices. Older children are actively engaged in deciding what to watch. As families bring more media devices into the home, it is likely that children will have more autonomy over their viewing patterns because they may have their own device rather than sharing a communal television that was once housed in the living room. As their tastes become sophisticated, they too become better able to process the information they receive. As children age, they are increasingly adept at distinguishing between fantasy and reality. They are able to understand more complex narrative structures while incorporating their own experiences into judging a character's motivations and actions (Strasburger et al., 2009; Calvert, 1999). Older teenagers have more elaborate schemas from which to evaluate media content and become more sophisticated at critiquing content based on their own worldview.

Two traditions of research have formed our understanding of the role of media in a child's socialization. From a social science perspective, theories such as social cognitive theory and cultivation theory have been systematically investigated and explain a process by which children and adolescents who are exposed to media content are more likely to think and behave in certain ways. Social cognitive theory posits that through identifying role models in the mass media children will be more or less likely to imitate behavior that is rewarded or at least not punished (Bandura, 1986; Calvert, 1999; Strasburger et al., 2009). In terms of learning about diversity, the assumption is that by producing programming featuring culturally diverse characters engaging in prosocial behaviors, audiences may become more tolerant of other races provided that tolerance is modeled in other aspects of the child's environment. Therefore, by increasing the number of diverse characters, more salient role models become available for all children (Calvert, Strong, Jacobs & Gonger, 2007; Cortés, 2000; Li-Vollmer, 2002; Mastro & Behm-Morawitz, 2005; Mastro, Behm-Morawitz, & Kopacz, 2008). Within the empirical tradition, cultivation is often used in conjunction with social cognitive theory to describe how the frequency of media use impacts children's understanding of the real world. Cultivation theorists have shown a correlation between the amount of exposure to media content and related perceptions and attitudes about their environment. Cultivation hypothesizes that small changes in attitudes can, over time, prove to be significant and the modes of understanding the world are shaped by what children see in the mass media (Gerbner, 1998).

Empirical modes of inquiry provide a foundation from which to access a deeper understanding of the relationship children and their families have with television. The critical/cultural perspective holistically identifies the ways in which media work in relation to other societal factors to mold children's understanding of themselves and others. Scholars argue that the mainstream media function in ways that reinforce dominant cultural codes, and most media, even children's programming that tries to be enriching, function in ways that perpetuate long held stereotypes which then impact how we think about ourselves and others. Latina/o media scholars, working from the critical tradition, point out that attempts at multicultural children's programs are constrained by market forces that limit their liberating potential (Harewood & Valdivia, 2005). The commercialization of the marketplace, however, makes it difficult to determine whether children are choosing media because they authentically enjoy it or because it is being sold to them in a way that preempts their choices. Media for children have become so much a part of a larger commercial structure that selling children as an audience for more products, including those associated with their favorite television characters, influence how we understand the media available. The creation of more television programs featuring Latina/o characters may be an attempt to provide more diverse programming, or it may be a way to reach children as consumers, or perhaps a little of both.

It is clear from these perspectives that the media children are exposed to have an impact on their socialization. It also makes sense to assume that the varied experiences of children will impact this process. Latina/o children bring to the television set their unique cultural positioning, which will impact how they negotiate the meaning from the text. Relatively little is known about how Latina/o children, especially those living in a Spanish-speaking environment, process the mass media. In 1999, Federico Subervi-

Vélez described the need to create communication scholarship relevant to Latina/os. He explains three avenues of inquiry that are relevant to understanding the relationship between Latina/o children and the mass media. First, he calls for educational/informational programming that promotes cultural sensitivity that is related to and relevant for Latina/os but "must not portray Latinos and their culture as foreign and exotic" (p. 135). Second he believes more attention needs to be paid to the unique reality in which bilingual Latina/o children find themselves—a world that engages with television in English and Spanish. Finally, he asks that more attention be given to the role of Spanish-language networks in serving the educational and informational needs of children as outlined by the Children's Television Act (Subervi-Vélez, 1999; Subervi-Vélez & Colsant, 1993; Moran, 2007). Angharad Valdivia (2008c) also calls for more investigation into Latina/o youth audiences to better understand their relationship with media and popular culture, which "promises to become a growing area of research" (p. 111). There are opportunities to change the way Latina/o youth are conceptualized, and listening to them is the first step.

Chapter Two

The Latina/o Youth Market

Most texts about American mass media ignore or relegate Spanish-language media to a footnote in their descriptions of the industry. The purpose of this chapter is to expose how powerful Spanish-language media are not only in terms of advertising revenue, but in their ability to compel English-language media to take notice of the Latino audience pushing the creation of bicultural programming. Spanish-language media have been an integral part of the audiovisual landscape in the United States since the 1930s when Mexican entrepreneurs first entered into the American radio industry. Since that time, the Mexican broadcast industry has pursued access to Spanish-speaking audiences in the United States, and as the population of American Latina/os continues to grow, the Spanish-language media outlets have continued to expand. Because of the close proximity to neighboring Tijuana, San Diegans have been able to access radio and television in Spanish even before the development of a dedicated Spanish-language industry in the United States. Two radio stations—XEMO-AM and XEAZ-AM—date to the 1940s. The growth of the Latina/o population in recent decades has led to the development of Spanish-language mass media throughout the United States and notably in San Diego County.

The Development of
Spanish-Language Television

In order to understand more clearly the evolution of Spanish-language media in San Diego, it is necessary to examine historically their development throughout the nation. As early as the 1950s, the response to the presence and growth of Latina/os in the population spurred action by television entrepreneurs who saw not just a Spanish-speaking minority, but an untapped market available to sell to advertisers. Essentially, the purpose of creating Spanish-language television was born out of the desire to reach Spanish-speakers in a way that would entice them to buy and become loyal to products advertised on these stations.

Like most television industries, the Spanish-language industry was created from the foundation of Spanish-language radio, which had been dominated by the Azcárraga family of Mexico. Emilio Azcárraga Vidaurreta, known as "el Leon," and his son Emilio Azcárraga Milmo, called "el Tigre," along with grandson Emilio Azcárraga Jean have held majority ownership of Televisa since its formation in 1972, which developed out of Azcárraga's Telesistema Mexicano. The elder Emilio died on September 23, 1972, and his son took over operations that year and built the international and national empire Televisa. In 1997, grandson Azcárraga Jean inherited the principal ownership of Televisa (Rodríguez, 1999a; Fernández & Paxman, 2000; Sinclair, 1999).

Televisa, the most watched television network in Mexico, has grown into an international multimedia corporation and is the second largest exporter of television programming worldwide. For U.S. television investors, the Spanish-speaking market in the United States was so small and poor during the 1950s that it was not even considered a viable audience to sell to advertisers through television programming. From the Azcárraga family's point of view, however, "the millions of Mexican immigrants and Mexican Americans living in the United States were one of the largest and wealthiest Spanish language markets in the world" (Rodríguez, 1999a, p. 36). Therefore, as a result of Mexico's geographical proximity and Azcárraga Vidaurreta's assumption that Mexicans living in the United States would watch Mexican produced programming, the development of a Spanish-language television industry began in the 1960s.

The Spanish International Communication Corporation (SICC) became the umbrella corporation through which a string of U.S.

Spanish-language stations began in areas that had significant numbers of Spanish speakers. The first cities with Spanish-language television stations owned by SICC were San Antonio (1961), Los Angeles (1962), New York (1968), and Miami (1971). Because of FCC regulations stating that "aliens" or persons acting for them can own no more than 20% of stock in a television station, Azcárraga Vidaurreta officially owned only 20% of SICC. The other investors were U.S. citizens, including Rene Anselmo, who later became president of the corporation. Anselmo had a close relationship with Azcárraga Vidaurreta and essentially acted on his behalf in all aspects of the business (Sinclair, 1999). After the stations were purchased, the need arose for programming to fill the airwaves. Thus, the Spanish International Network (SIN) was formed in order to supply programming exclusively produced by Telesistema Mexicano and to sell airtime to advertisers (Rodriguez, 1999). Azcárraga, through SIN, supplied SICC with telenovelas, news, and other entertainment programming. Although often compared to American soap operas, which are ongoing serials without end (until cancellation by the network), in contrast Latin American telenovelas are drama serials that have a duration of 150–200 episodes. Prime-time telenovelas appeal to a broad general audience and have gained international popularity while telenovelas aired in the afternoon and early evening are for younger audiences (Moran, 2003; Rios, 2003; McAnany & La Pastina, 1994).

By the end of 1972, Televisa resulted from the consolidation of the two most powerful networks, Telesistema Mexicano and its competitor Televisión Independiente de México, and continued to support the Spanish-language market in the United States (Sinclair, 1999). SICC and SIN were operating together under Rene Anselmo but were not financially successful, and even though the Televisa Corporation was supplying programming, SIN did not make a profit for its first seven years of operation (Sinclair, 1999). By 1975, American investors including Frank Fouce, Jr., a majority stockholder in SICC, grew tired of the growing debt, which by this time was nearly $2 million. Fouce's father, Frank Fouce, Sr., of Fouce Amusement Enterprises—a chain of Spanish-language movie theaters—had been associated with the Azcárraga family since the early 1960s in Los Angeles and San Antonio. Fouce Jr. brought a civil lawsuit against Anselmo and SICC, which exposed the relationship between SIN, SICC, and the Azcárragas. As a result, in 1980 the Spanish Radio Broadcasters' Association filed a charge with the FCC that in fact SICC was under foreign control, which triggered an investigation that concluded the corporate structure of SICC and SIN violated section 310b of the Communication Act of 1934 because Anselmo was acting on behalf of "aliens," resulting in de facto foreign ownership of American airwaves. Thirteen of SICC stations and all of SIN's stations had to be sold to U.S. citizens (Sinclair, 1999; Rodriquez, 1999a).

Two major players acquired SICC and SIN interests. The Reliance group acquired enough Spanish-language stations to form the Telemundo network in the mid-1980s, and Hallmark Cards Inc. acting with First Capital Corporation of Chicago out-bid other interested parties to acquire control over SIN and its individual stations. The 1987 Hallmark takeover was considered friendly since the cozy relationship continued between the Azcárraga family, Televisa, and the American network. The new Hallmark network was named Univisión. For the first ten years Univisión had the first option to purchase Televisa-produced programs, giving Televisa a distribution outlet in the U.S. Televisa had free advertising time on the Univisión stations for its products and services (Sinclair, 1999). Because of the advantage of its relationship with Televisa, Univisión quickly rose in popularity and gained notoriety in the U.S. as *the* Spanish-language network.

The direct importation of Mexican news and entertainment on Univisión created frustration among some Latina/o groups in the U.S. who claimed that the programming did not reflect the experiences of Spanish-speaking Americans. They wanted to be more than a dumping ground for Mexican imports. Since the Telemundo network could not buy products from Televisa because of its arrangement with Univisión, Telemundo began producing programming in the U.S., in Spanish, to reach Latina/os who were looking for an alternative to Mexican television. Because Telemundo was headquartered in New York, it tried to appeal to Puerto Ricans,

Cubans and people from Central and South America. When Telemundo moved its operations from New York to Miami, it began producing a U.S. news program in 1987, *Noticiero Telemundo,* and also a telenovela that integrated stories of Mexican, Puerto Rican and Cuban immigrant families. Univisión was quick to respond and by 1991 had set up its own production studios in Miami and began airing shows such as *Sábado Gigante,* a live variety show, and *Cristina,* a talk show, both of which became popular with Spanish-speaking audiences.

In 1992, Spanish-language television entered a new era marked by significant changes in the industry. Nielsen Media Research began tracking "Hispanic Audience" media use and provided a more accurate account of the audience share devoted to Spanish-language television. Hallmark Cards Inc. sold its interest in Univisión to A. Jerrold Perenchio, a Hollywood television producer, who acquired 50% of the Univisión Network Partnership and 76% of Univisión Television Group, which operates individual stations. Careful to remain in compliance with FCC regulations, Televisa acquired 25% of the Network Partnership and 12% of the Television Group. Venevisión, the most influential television network in Venezuela, which also produces telenovelas, purchased the remaining portion of the corporation. For both Venevisión and Televisa, access to the U.S. market became increasingly important especially because Nielsen Media Research was taking notice of the Spanish-language market (Sinclair, 1999). The power of Univisión to attract the Spanish-speaking audience has continued to grow, especially in the 8–10 p.m. timeslot, during which the most popular Mexican telenovelas are aired. According to the Nielsen ratings, nearly every week the top ten most-watched programs by Latina/os are on Univisión.

The more accurate estimates of viewers did not help Telemundo, however, which was coming in a distant second to Univisón, which had successfully cornered the market with its exclusive partnership with Televisa. Telemundo filed bankruptcy in 1992, restructured the corporation and, by 1994, became a public company controlled by Apollo Advertisers, a U.S. firm backed by Europe's largest bank, Crédit Lyonnais, and Bastion Capital, a

U.S.-based firm. Even with a new corporate structure, Telemundo continued to struggle without access to Televisa or Venevisión telenovelas, which proved to be the most watched programs among Latina/os. Telemundo turned to TV Azteca, a Mexican network started in 1994, and arranged to purchase their telenovelas. Telemundo, purchased by NBC Universal in 2001, became the second largest provider of Spanish-language television in the United States.

Univisión continues to be the leader in attracting the Spanish-speaking audience and has consolidated its power over the marketplace by merging with the Hispanic Broadcasting Corporation (HBC), the largest Spanish-language radio network. As a result of this 2003 merger, one corporation gained control over more than 70% of the national advertising dollars spent on Hispanic media (Gregor, 2003). The merger also gave the "conservative conglomerate the economic muscle to compete with mainstream media" (Casteñada, 2008b, p. 211). Some Latina/o activists expressed concern about the limited voices representing the Latina/o community and opposed the merger because of the fear that it would have a negative impact on the creation of local news and limit creative entertainment programming (Casteñada, 2008b). Nevertheless, both the FCC and FTC approved the merger resulting in Univisión becoming the fifth largest media organization in North America. Joe Uva, an Italian-American with limited Spanish-language skills, is the current CEO; his non-Latino status has drawn some criticism, but his expertise in the media marketplace has served Univisión well.

In San Diego County, Spanish-language television began as a result of San Diego's geographic location and television broadcast signals' ability to cross international borders. XETV, channel 6, was San Diego's second television station and first to broadcast programs in Spanish. The call letters were designated because of its transmitter in Tijuana, which allowed the station's owner to get around the FCC's television licensing freeze from 1948 to 1952. Partnering with Mexican television entrepreneur Emilio Azcárraga Vidaurreta, the station was licensed by the Mexican government and began broadcasting in 1953. Programs in English and

Spanish could be seen on both sides of the border. XETV affiliated with mainstream U.S. networks, first with ABC until 1973 and currently as San Diego's FOX affiliate choosing to broadcast exclusively in English. Because XETV is licensed in Mexico, officially it does not have to follow FCC regulations, although it does remain in compliance with U.S. policies. In 1960, XEWT, channel 12, began broadcasting programs exclusively in Spanish, and although it was a station owned and operated in Tijuana, it served Spanish-speaking households in the San Diego region. XEWT, a Televisa affiliate, gained popularity with Spanish-speaking San Diego audiences, who had direct access to Mexican television.

San Diegans have long been able to access entertainment programming and national news in Spanish through cable and Tijuana stations, but local Spanish-language media, specifically news, is relatively recent. In 1990 KBNT, channel 17, a Univisión affiliate, went on the air in San Diego and has grown in popularity (Moran, 2004). Just within 2004, audience ratings increased over 200% in the coveted 18–34 year-old market (Turegano, 2004). Owned by Entravision Communications, its local news broadcast and entertainment programming have been successful in reaching the Spanish-speaking audience throughout the city and county. During July 2009, KBNT outperformed all other evening newscasts in the 18–49 year-old demographic (Univisión San Diego Outperforms, 2009) and demonstrated an increase in ratings across their schedule (Univisión San Diego Turns Up the Heat, 2009). San Diego audiences can access all of Univisión's national programming via KBNT, which includes morning talk shows, children's programs, afternoon talk shows, national news, and telenovelas during the prime-time evening hours. For those families accessing cable, Galavisión, Univisión's cable network, offers national news, movies, and other entertainment programming (Moran, 2004).

XHAS, channel 33, a Tijuana station affiliated with Telemundo, began broadcasting local programming to San Diego audiences in 2002, while competitors KBNT and XHAS are both owned by Entravision Communications Corporation. To circumvent FCC regulations that prohibit one corporation owning more than 35% of a given television market, XHAS is licensed through the Mexican government, while KBNT receives its license from the United States. The shared corporate structure makes the relationship between the Univisión affiliate and the Telemundo affiliate a bit peculiar since both stations are housed in the same facility on Ruffin Road in San Diego. XHAS broadcasts its local news, *Noticiero 33,* from San Diego, but it is relayed through a transmitter in Tijuana. The mission of the newscast is to appeal to audiences on both sides of the border. The general manager, Carlos Sanchez, explained that "Our goal is to open the borders of local communication with a global vision living up to our slogan *Abriendo Fronteras* (Opening Borders)" (Turegano, 2002). In addition to the local news broadcast, channel 33 provides national Telemundo programming including telenovelas and its national news program *Noticiera Telemundo.* Television programming from Tijuana is available over the air, making Mexican television free and easy to access. Telemundo's cable stations are available in the San Diego market, providing an alternative to Univisión's Televisa dominated programming. Telemundo continues to have access to programming from Mexico through TV Azteca, but is still second to Univisión in terms of national television ratings.

Spanish-Language Television for Young People

Because the expansion of Spanish-language media outlets in the U.S. is directly tied to the assumption that Spanish-speakers prefer to watch programming in Spanish, even when they understand and speak English fluently, cable networks targeting young Latina/os in Spanish have increased. Univisión, a broadcast network, must air 3 hours of children's programs a week to be in compliance with the Children's Television Act[9] (CTA). At one point Univisión used a telenovela to fulfill requirements placed on broadcasters to comply with the CTA. The telenovela *Complices al rescate (Friends to the Rescue)* that featured 11-year-old twins who swap identities was labeled a core program that served the "educational and informational" needs of children by Univisión and used by many of its affiliates to fulfill the "3 hour rule" mandated by the

Act. While the program was mildly popular among young Spanish-speaking children, the E/I component was questioned. The FCC launched an investigation centered on a complaint filed against WQHS-TV, an Univisón affiliate in Cleveland, Ohio, for failing to serve the Spanish-speaking children in the audience. In his affidavit filed with the FCC as part of the complaint, Subervi-Vélez (2005) concludes "the telenovelas that WQHS claims fulfill its educational and informational obligations do not meet the FCC's requirements. At best, these programs present incidental moral lessons that are sporadic and brief. The predominant content of those telenovelas is a very complex mix of adult themes and situations with only sporadic segments that contain intertwined moral lessons on appropriate or inappropriate behaviors for children." The telenovela was entertaining, but not appropriately educational. At the conclusion of the investigation, the FCC determined the Univisión affiliate was not in compliance with the mandates of the Act, a decision which impacted the broadcast of that program on all member stations. The network agreed to pay a $24 million fine, the largest in FCC history (Labaton, 2007). Univisión could continue broadcasting the telenovela, but needed to include more overtly educational shows for children under 12. Since then, Univisión has aired programs that are explicitly educational. According to the 398 Report filed for the fourth quarter of 2009, the network broadcasts primarily Spanish-dubbed versions of English-language educational programs and is in compliance with the CTA.

Few of the new networks directly target Spanish-speaking children. ¡Sorpresa!, launched March 15, 2003, is the first children's network in the U.S. to broadcast in Spanish and reaches children with programs that "adequately reflect their lifestyle, blending culturally appealing educational and entertainment programming" (www.firestoneinc.com/news_200202.asp). Most of the animated programming on the channel is imported from countries outside the U.S. such as Spain, Japan and Canada. ¡Sorpresa!, which is in approximately 1 million U.S. cable homes, was purchased in August 2009 by Olympusat, a cable distributor that will include the channel among its 11 networks' Hispanic Package

(Olympusat buys Sorpresa, 2009). Other Spanish-language channels include dubbed versions of English-language networks such as Disney en Español and DiscoveryKids en Español.

The first public television network in Spanish was launched in the U.S. in March 2007. V-me, pronounced veh-meh, from the Spanish *ve me* meaning "see me," aims to entertain and educate families in Spanish by featuring programs "specially adapted for American Latinos" (www.v-me.tv). The V-me network broadcasts thirty-six hours of children's programming per week in Spanish. What causes concern about the preschool programming on the network is that many of the programs are imported from Canada or the UK and then translated into Spanish without any cultural adaptation or localization. These programs include *Lunar Jim* produced by Alliance Atlantis in conjunction with the British Broadcasting Corporation (BBC) and Canadian Broadcasting Corporation (CBC). On V-me it airs as *Jim de la luna. Franny's Feet (Los pies magicos de Franny)* and *Connie the Cow (Connie la vaquita)* are both CBC productions translated into Spanish. In addition, *LazyTown,* an imported program from Iceland, is part of the preschool line-up without any cultural adaptation apart from dubbing. *Las tres mellizas bebes (The Baby Triplets)* is imported from Spain. None of these programs for children, however, hold any particular relevance for the Latina/o child in the United States. In fact, most of the programs do not even feature Latina/o characters in the cast. A recent addition to the V-me lineup includes a Spanish version of eebbee, a puppet popular with English-speakers, now coupled with a Latina sidekick. The one exception that will hold relevance for immigrants from Latin America is *Plaza Sésamo*, a co-production between Sesame Workshop and Mexico's Televisa broadcast throughout Latin America. In 2009, V-me was available in 80% of U.S. Hispanic households and is carried on basic digital cable in the top 35 Hispanic markets (LazyTown, V-me, 2009).

Writing in 2000, Arlene Dávila criticized the Spanish-language networks for their lack of attention to the experiences of U.S.-born Latina/os. Dávila (2000) explains, "Simply put, language means money and this equation is likely to continue to affect the correlation of Latinos with Spanish, impairing attempts to broaden the media's definition of Latinos, or at least what they sell as 'Latinos' to marketers and corporate clients" (p. 89). In other words, the conventional wisdom among marketers that Latina/os want more programming in Spanish leads to the creation of more outlets in Spanish whether or not there is an actual desire. As we listen to the sample families discuss their media use in the following chapters, the questions are: who watches Spanish-language programming in the U.S. and why?

Latino-themed Programming

Although the availability of Spanish-language television grows for all audience segments, some networks have a bilingual and bicultural approach to programming as a way to reach U.S.-born Latina/os, including children. Sí TV, for example, advertises "Speak English. Live Latin" (Wentz, 2004). Mun2, a cable network owned by Telemundo, a subsidiary of NBC Universal, broadcasts programming in both Spanish and English (Hoffman, 2006). The program *LatiNation*, aimed at young adults, broadcasts news features and commentary about Latina/os in the United States. Programming for young children, however, has historically received much attention from television executives who are interested in diversifying casts and appealing to broad audiences. *LatiNation* and *American Latino TV* are now produced by LATV networks, but the original concepts were created by Robert Rose, who saw an opportunity to provide unique programming to an underserved audience.

Robert Rose began his career at Univisión, where he worked to sell advertising spots to companies trying to reach the Hispanic market. The information he was given by his employer revealed that the best way to reach U.S. Hispanics was by using media outlets in Spanish such as Univisión. This did not resonate, however, with his personal experience with U.S.-born Latina/os. Therefore, he conceptualized a smarter approach and created a vehicle that would attract bicultural and bilingual Latina/os. *American Latino*

TV was launched in 2002 to tell the stories of inspiring Latina/os. According to its website:

> *American Latino TV* is a nationally syndicated, half-hour program that celebrates American Latino Pride. The weekly, award winning half-hour show sets the standard for culturally relevant television for young, U.S.-born Latinos in the United States. In a typical episode of *American Latino TV,* you'll see interviews with Latin celebrities, musical artists, features on cultura, fashion, barrios and, most importantly, everyday American Latinos doing extraordinary and inspirational things!
> We tell stories that need to be heard, that must be heard! (http://www.americanLatino.tv/index.php).

LatiNation, created by Rose two years later, appeals to a younger audience with a more casual approach. Its website boasts:

> *LatiNation* is a nationally syndicated, half-hour program that is broadcast to over 90 markets across the United States, Puerto Rico and the Virgin Islands. Join hosts Desi and Jose as *LatiNation* takes an entertaining look at the impact of Latino culture in the U.S. and all things fun and cool. (http://latination.tv/index.php).

In an interview with Rose (personal communication, 19 March 2009) he discussed his perceptions of the role these television programs have in the broader television landscape and his ability to sell this programming to independent stations across the United States. The impetus for the creation of these shows was to serve what he perceived to be an underserved market—U.S.-born Latina/os who were fluent English speakers, unlikely to view Spanish-language television, and felt underrepresented in the English-language general market television. Since this audience was more likely to view mainstream youth programming than anything in Spanish, Rose created programming that would appeal to the coveted 18–35 youth market by using a bicultural strategy to feature the U.S. Latina/o experience.

Robert Rose is critical of Nielsen for promoting the idea that all Hispanics watch Spanish-language television because this perception of the market made it difficult to sell a Latino-themed show in English. According to independent audience research aiming to dispute Nielsen's claims, "...73% of Hispanic immigrants favor

Spanish, only 25% of their children do. That number falls to 15% by the second generation" (Sass, 2007). Rose is also critical of Spanish-language television imported from Mexico that dominates the U.S. market for perpetuating the stereotype that Latina/os are "cheesy, sexy, and sexist" and "different" from mainstream U.S. culture. In addition, because first generation immigrants are so well served by the Spanish-language networks, they remain outside the dominant U.S. culture, which may function to segregate groups instead of bring them together.

As an independent producer, however, Rose went to selected markets with a high percentage of Latina/os and pitched the idea of programs that would highlight the accomplishments and experiences of U.S.-born Latina/os. He confesses that he may have had an advantage since he is Caucasian and was able to connect with the station managers by selling the economics of the idea. He critiques Hispanic marketing for relying on the personal experiences of staff rather than marketing research to sell the audience. Because he is an outsider, he had to rely on research and not his personal preferences. For second generation and beyond, what ties Latina/os together is the common experience of being the children of Latina/o immigrants, not necessarily the Spanish-language, although they may use it too.

In 2002, Latino-themed English-language programming was new, and the approach in the production was to break down stereotypes that had long been associated with Latina/o representation. The first two stereotypes Rose wanted to challenge were that all Latina/os speak Spanish and all Latina/os are immigrants. Latina/os have been part of the fabric of this country for hundreds of years. Therefore, Hispanic does not equal immigrant. Rose's programs have been platforms to represent a broad range of Latina/os including: young Latina/o skateboarders, NBA players and Afro-Latina/os. The best way to open the representation, according to Rose, is through "subtle but purposeful representation and to include three dimensional characters and stories" (personal communication, 19 March 2009). Rose sees his niche market as U.S.-born English-speaking Latina/os and he believes that to move beyond that and include more ethnic diversity would water down the programming. Because of the long held industry thinking that the best way to reach Latina/os is with Spanish, Rose admits it was difficult to get advertisers to buy time on these networks and during these programs and it has been difficult for them to find an audience.

In the current marketplace more and more programs are following suit with programming that incorporates a bilingual and bicultural focus, some succeeding more than others. Three networks that target young U.S.-born Latina/os are MTVtr3s, mun2, and Sí TV. Robert Rose is quick to critique MTVtr3s and mun2 for creating programming that is "unauthentic" to the audience. Because of their corporate structures—MTV is owned by Viacom and mun2 is owned by Telemundo/NBC Universal—they are restricted from creating innovative programming. Because *LatiNation* and *American Latino TV* are independently produced they have the advantage of freedom. It appears that programming on MTVtr3s mimics other MTV networks with shows that follow the same formula. For example, *My Super Sweet Sixteen,* a reality show on MTV that follows a spoiled teenager who plans an over-the-top sixteenth birthday party, becomes *Quiero Mis Quinces* on MTVtr3s, a reality program that follows a fifteen-year-old Latina planning her *quinceañera.*[10] In addition, the network has imported a teen-centered telenovela from Venezuela, *ISA TKM,* and features other programs such as *Music My Guey* and *Pimpeando,* similar to *Pimp My Ride.* The strategy of MTVtr3s has been to use the format of successful shows on MTV while including what is perceived to be "Latin flavor" peppered with Spanish phrases. According to the network, MTVtr3s is available in 7 million U.S. Hispanic households and a total of 38 million television households nationwide. According to Viacom's description, "MTVtr3s is capturing the attention of one of the most influential demographics in the United States. Latina/o culture is brought to life on MTVtr3s through customized MTV music franchises, news documentaries and lifestyle series...which genuinely reflect the culture, trends and icons of young bicultural U.S. Latinos."

Mun2 has responded to the marketplace by rolling out six new prime-time telenovelas between fall 2009 and the end of 2010

(Gibbons, 2009). According to Telemundo's president, Don Browne, mun2 is the "fastest growing Hispanic cable network." Browne also remarked that Telemundo is ready to respond to requests for product placements in their new telenovelas. One of the most anticipated is a remake of the TV Globo hit *O Clone* (first broadcast in Brazil in 2001–2002), which will be remade with the title *O Clon* broadcast in Spanish with English subtitles. Other programming includes *"The mun2 Look,* a multiplatform fashion initiative shot in New York" (Gibbons, 2009).

Sí TV, founded in 1997, established itself as an independent production company creating English-language Latino-themed programming. In 2004, Sí TV launched the first cable network under the same name dedicated to capturing 18 to 34-year-old Latina/os who prefer their television content in English. While Sí TV has been in the market longer, it does not have the household penetration of MTVtr3s nor mun2. As of 2009, Sí TV was found in 18 million homes. Original programming includes *Model Latina*, an adaptation of *America's Next Top Model,* and *Freddie*, a sitcom starring Freddie Prinze, Jr., as well as *American Latino TV* and *LatiNation*. According to its company profile its mission is "to deliver authentic and original programming in English while portraying Latinos in non-stereotypical roles."

HBO Latino has also changed its business strategy to be more relevant to U.S. Latina/os, but according to scholar Katynka Martínez (2007) that may not be good enough: "HBO Latino programming continues to consist primarily of Spanish dubs of the English-language programming that airs on the main HBO channel" (p. 203). More recently, HBO Latino has imported a successful dramatic series from Argentina, *Epitifios* (which can be seen with English subtitles on HBO2), as well as films and other products from Latin America. According to its daily schedule, it still features primarily U.S. movies in Spanish.

English-language networks have also included Latino-themed programming, notably ABC's *The George Lopez Show*. While it is not necessarily intended for youth audiences, it does provide an example of family programming in the broadest sense. George Lopez, playing the main character, embodies being Mexican Amer-

ican, highlighting cultural elements that illustrate his Mexicanness. George's wife, Angie, played by Constance Marie, provides a cultural contrast; Angie's family is from Cuba and the
program at times depicts differences between the groups demonstrating some diversity within Latinidad. The program has been
criticized by some for perpetuating stereotypes of Latina/os while
others have praised its cultural aspects that work to examine stereotypes. Researcher John Markert (2007) concludes that the portrayal of Latina/os in the program is generally positive and "is
likely to promote pride among fellow Latinos at the same time that
it challenges some of the stereotypes about poor, rural, illegal immigrant Hispanics that are so pervasive within the wider society"
(p. 162).

Programming for Younger Children

Nickelodeon, the top-rated cable network for children, is committed to producing programming that is "child-centered" and as a
result has found success in the competitive market (Baent-Weiser,
2007). Further, according to Seiter and Mayer (2004) "Nickelodeon's record on racial and ethnic diversity is notewor-
thy....Nickelodeon has invested in two shows with Latino
characters when other networks shy away from offering any" (p.
125). The authors note that "with the representation of Latinos,
Nickelodeon has deliberately sought qualified producers and con-
scientiously pursued Latino families as a potentially lucrative
market; here Nickelodeon has positioned itself favorably and is
well ahead of the networks" (Seiter & Mayer, 2004, p. 132). Based
on its initial success, Nickelodeon has created additional programs
with Latino themes, and other networks have followed a similar
pattern. The most widely known example of this type of programming is *Dora the Explorer,* and in an effort to reach older Latina/o
children, Nickelodeon premiered *El Tigre: The Adventures of Manny Rivera,* a stylized animated program, in March 2007 as part of
its "Teen Nick" programming block.

Dora the Explorer features a 7-year-old bilingual character who takes audiences on adventures using primarily English but including Spanish words that are repeated at least three times. The program has characters that speak exclusively Spanish, while others, such as Dora's best friend Boots, speak English. Dora is special because she is bilingual and can communicate in both English and Spanish with all the characters. Brown Johnson, Nick executive creative director, explained: "Spanish becomes through Dora this sort of magical thing. The ability to speak another language [becomes] really cool and powerful" (Clemens, 2006).

The spin-off *Go, Diego, Go* uses a similar approach. Diego is Dora's cousin and is an 8-year-old bilingual adventurer. His 11-year-old sister, Alicia, is also bilingual. Diego does not have a specific nationality but is definitely Latino and lives in a world that is based on the geography of Latin America. The program aims to expand Spanish vocabulary through songs and the animals' actions (Fernández, 2005). *Dora* and *Diego* account for seven of the top ten most-watched programs for preschool age Hispanics (Clemens, 2006), and among all ethnic groups, *Dora the Explorer* is the number one rated preschool program. Although the character of Dora as well as the stylized setting has been criticized for masking the diversity of the Latina/o experience (Harewood & Valdivia, 2005), she is a Latina character who resonates with American children.

The Disney Channel has followed the bilingual trend and began airing *Handy Manny* in September 2006. Animated character Manny García and his tools occasionally speak Spanish and live in a town with other Latina/o characters. Although the creation of bilingual programs is market driven by the population growth of Latina/o children in the United States, the consequence of this diversification is significant for children of all ethnic backgrounds. *The Wizards of Waverly Place* is a Disney Channel favorite and features a family that brings together an Italian American (wizard) who gives up his powers in order to marry a Mexican mortal and have a family. The Russo family includes three children; the star of the program is the middle child, Alex Russo, played by Selena Gomez, a Texan whose father is from Mexico. The program integrates Mexican culture with episodes that show young Alex unable to learn Spanish from her mother and another episode about the character's *quinceañera* that brings in elements of the Mexican traditions. Unlike other Latino-themed programs, *Wizards* does not necessarily highlight Latino culture in every episode. Instead the culture is more thematic and integrated subtly into the characters' interactions. *The Wizards of Waverly Place the Movie* premiered on the Disney channel as 2009's most-watched telecast on cable averaging 11.4 million viewers, with 4.5 million between the ages of 6 and 11 (Stelter, 2009). As commercial networks, both Disney and Nickelodeon have found economic success with programs that include Latino themes and have Latina/o characters.

Public television in the United States has long been the place to which parents turn for educational programming. When *Sesame Street* debuted in 1969, it cemented PBS's place in the children's television industry. Because of the non-commercial nature of the network, children's programs were given more room to take chances on the educational potential of the medium. "PBS has always been a leader in developing groundbreaking programs that reflect cultural diversity, particularly for younger audiences" (Lisotta, 2004, p. 36). *Sesame Street* highlights bilingual characters such as María and the muppet Rosita and each episode offers a "Spanish word of the day." From its inception, *Sesame Street* has been committed to creating a program that celebrates diversity in an attempt to role model interethnic friendships to encourage preschool audiences to play with children of different races (Truglio et al., 2001).

The Misadventures of Maya & Miguel produced by Scholastic Entertainment, a U.S. based company specializing in educational products for children, is also aired on PBS and features a Mexican-American family and targets 6- to 11-year-olds. Maya and Miguel are 10-year-old twins who interact with a group of multicultural friends. Even though the main characters are bilingual, the program is not intended to teach English or Spanish, but to promote cultural diversity and help children feel more comfortable about being bilingual. Maya and Miguel are U.S.-born and speak English without accents; the cousin, Tito, moved from Mexico with his family and serves as the show's model of an English-learner (Lisotta, 2004). In addition, the program aims to "smash stereotypes by portraying Hispanic families in a positive light" (Sigler, 2004, p. 68). The educational goals of *Maya & Miguel* are twofold:

> 1. To encourage children to value, respect and better understand a variety of cultures, perspectives, tradition, languages and experiences.
> 2. To support children in building their understanding of the English language, with a special emphasis on vocabulary (www.pbskids.org).

In the December 2004 issue of *Hispanic,* Deborah Forte, president of Scholastic Entertainment, exclaimed: "We think we have the chance to allow Latino children to see themselves, to take pride in who they are and maybe even more importantly, for non-Latinos to see and visit with this fabulous family that is so funny and smart and loving and colorful—that's really a great opportunity for us" (Sigler, 2004, p. 68).

Maya & Miguel may hold particular relevance for Latina/o children growing up in the United States. Latina/o children will be more likely to identify with the characters because of their brown hair and eyes. In addition, the characters speak in complete sentences in Spanish to their grandmother, who emigrated from Mexico. The representation of Latino culture is more relatable because of the program's focus on the importance of family and the cultural issues children face at school.

Is More Better or Is It Just More?

It is clear that as a result of the interest in Hispanics as a market, the media landscape has changed to include more programming that features Latina/o characters and the Spanish-language. Do these programs serve audiences in ways that may be empowering or do they reinforce long-standing relationships of power? For some, the addition of the new programs to the marketplace is seen as justice for the historic absence of Latina/os from the English-language media. Is the addition of more programs

beneficial or do they function as part of a larger additive multiculturalism that masks the power deferential and politics that are
inherently intertwined within the Latina/o experience in the United States? In discussions of the representation of African Americans on television, Herman Gray (1995) and Sut Jhally and Justin
Lewis (1992) provide a lens from which to problematize Latina/o
representation. In analyzing audience response to *The Cosby
Show,* Jhally and Lewis found how even the positive portrayal of
blacks can be interpreted in ways that reinforce the status quo rather than providing substantial contribution to debates about civil
rights. In addition, Esteban del Río (2006) warns that even new
programs that highlight Latina/os need to be questioned so that
the celebratory voice that comes from industry professionals can
be interrogated within the politics of the representation.

Many of the Latino-themed networks that are part of larger
media conglomerates tend to follow the formats that have found
success in other markets. Format adaptation has become a proven
way of localizing programming in an international context
(Straubhaar, 2007). For example, reality program formats such as
Big Brother have been exported to a variety of countries, versions
of *Pop Idol* can be seen around the world and adaptations of popular telenovelas have been produced in a variety of countries. What
is unique about the United States is that the localization process is
happening within the nation. MTVtr3s, a U.S. adaptation of a U.S.
network, must reinvent itself to serve a unique audience defining
Latina/o as the Other. As a result, Viacom describes the channel:

> A PLACE FOR OUR LATINO AUDIENCE TO CALL THEIR OWN. MTV
> Tr3s is capturing the attention of one of the most influential de-
> mographics in the United States. Latino culture is brought to life on
> MTV Tr3s through customized MTV music franchises, news documen-
> taries and lifestyle series including *MiTRL, Sucker Free Latino, Quiero
> Mis Quinces* and *Pimpeando,* which genuinely reflect the culture, trends
> and icons of young bicultural U.S. Latinos. The brand features bilingual
> VJs, plus artists that range from popular Latin American singers like
> Juanes and Paulina Rubio, to English-dominant artists including Mariah
> Carey.

The implication of the description is that Latina/o teens are not at home when they watch MTV's main channel. As much as the network tries to bring Latina/o audiences together, it excludes non-Latina/os from its target. MTVtr3s attempts to reach U.S. Latina/o teenagers with the performance of a "syncretic identity" (Molina Guzmán, 2006) that seamlessly brings together mainstream popular culture with what is identified as Latina/o— Spanish phrases and tropical and/or salsa inspired music. Nowhere is this more obvious than on their promotional websites that promise "authentic" experiences all contained within the MTV experience. For example, in a post to promote the MTV awards the website boasts: "Increíble! If you thought Los Premios MTV 2009 were already heating up, think again porque the first wave of performers have just been announced and trust us—este es un show you will not want to miss!" The use of Spanish peppered in hails a certain Latina/o viewer who is positioned as a member of the Latina/o audience because he or she is different from a viewer who only speaks English.

Programming for young children should be taken seriously within the discourses of representation and programs such as *Dora the Explorer,* which are created to appeal to mass general audiences, further perpetuate long-standing assumptions about the Other (Harewood & Valdivia, 2005; Calvert, Strong, Jacobs & Gonger, 2007). The multicultural framework from which diversity is celebrated on Nickelodeon and Disney, and to some extent PBS, erases difference by making every character common. For example, in their critique of the representation of Dora, Harewood and Valdivia (2005) conclude that "Dora is the embodiment of syncretic tropicalizing discourses. Her brownness, situated in an unspecific tropical space, is emblematic of the commodification of this new constructed audience that we now know as Latinos" (p. 99). The notion of Dora herself still positions a Latina as Other and by emphasizing her as different perpetuates the "us versus them" mentality that is infused in so much of the Latino-themed programming.

While programs such as *LatiNation* and *American Latino TV* attempt to present a "hybrid identity" (Molina Guzmán, 2006;

Martínez, 2004, 2007) by acknowledging the bicultural status of their target audience, the question of authenticity comes to the forefront. The creator of the programs, Robert Rose, saw an opportunity in the market and filled it with programs that speak to U.S.-born Latina/os. The programs themselves have had varying success in markets across the United States. In San Diego, the programs are broadcast on MyTV13 on Sunday afternoons. In July 2009, *American Latino TV* at 4 p.m. averaged 5,000 television households and *LatiNation* at 4:30 p.m. averaged 7,000 television households. The strategy has been to respond to stereotypes by opening up discourses about young Latina/os. According to Rose, the programs have resisted essentialist notions of "who these people are." There is more diversity of the Latina/o experience on both these programs; the problem may be that not many viewers are exposed to them.

It is not surprising that the media industry has sliced the Latina/o youth market in ways that appeal to advertisers. The commercial demands that focus unmistakably on the bottom line need to follow proven methods of doing business. There is little room for risk taking and proven formulas of previous programming have served the industry well. The question remains: does it serve the audience?

Studying the Audience

As the media industry develops to include more opportunities for Latina/o audiences to find information that is reflective of their experiences, it is necessary to examine the process through which audiences select and interpret media messages. Audiences actively negotiate meanings that are influenced by multiple factors that work together to create meaning. The relationship between media and audiences is more than a cause and effect relationship, rather the media as a whole "work ideologically to promote and prefer certain meanings of the world, to circulate some meanings rather than others, and to serve some social interests better than others" (Fiske, 1987, p. 20). The challenge of reception studies then is to illuminate the relationship audiences have with texts and provide insight into the lived experiences of Latino families.

The heart of critical audience study is Stuart Hall's encoding/decoding model (Hall, 1980), informing scholars to look at both the process of the production of the text as well as the potential readings of audiences. Hall moves textual theorists into an analysis of the moment of reception to understand how the social positioning of audiences determine the meaning. For media scholars interested in the relationship between audiences and texts it is crucial not to underestimate the process through which audiences create meaning that may or may not be determined by construction of the text. Hall proposes three potential readings now commonly referred to as dominant, negotiated, and oppositional. Audience members typically understand the dominant or preferred meaning but are able to engage in a process of *negotiation* through their situated logic of understanding to produce alternatives to the dominant discourse. In other words, a young Latino teen who enjoys watching *The George Lopez Show* negotiates his understanding of the stereotypes of Mexican Americans, while his mother rejects the program through an oppositional reading. While Hall's proposal can be seen as liberating in that the power of the meaning is situated squarely in the audience, he cautions that the systems of production are never outside ideology. David Morely (2006) further unravels value of the encoding/decoding model within audience research suggesting that scholars must not be overly optimistic nor dismissive of the ability of the audience to resist and/or reinterpret meaning.

Because audience studies were optimistic about the power of audiences to use media in sometimes unpredictable and liberating ways, Celeste Condit (1989) cautioned scholars about "the limits of polysemy." The ability of audiences to deconstruct texts through multiple systems of meaning can provide evidence that not all audiences are systematically persuaded in similar ways. Condit (1989) argues that what many claim is polysemy is better articulated as polyvalence, highlighting that audiences do not necessarily produce multiple meanings; in fact they understand the text in similar ways, but attach nuanced valuations to those messages in ways that demonstrate variance (Condit, 1989). As Latina/o media scholars (del Río, 2010; Vargas, 2008; Cepeda, 2008; Rojas, 2004; Mayer, 2003) have taken on audience studies from the critical tradition, new variations on the delicate and systematic process of negotiation within this audience is revealed.

Systems of production as described in this chapter point to the methods through which the media expressly designed for Latina/os have been coded to position the audience. What is seen in the creation of texts for Latina/o audiences is the repetition of certain signs that are used to signify Latino cultural practices. For example, the use of bright colors, the sound of tropical music, and casting actors with dark hair and tanned skin are all part of the process of creating texts that are assumed to attract Latina/os. While these conventions have become common across U.S. popular culture, insight into how the Latina/o audiences interact with these and other texts has been more limited. In the case of the Latina/o audience, the texts available in the United States are encoded within a culture that has defined Latinidad from an essentialized perspective giving way to interpretation that is imbedded with a particular ideology coded within a system of either stereotypical representation or one of benign multiculturalism that situates Latinidad for consumption rather than liberation. Examples of this celebratory multiculturalism can be seen most clearly in children's programming that highlights Latino culture and the Spanish language as conventions to promote cultural diversity. In this way "multiculturalism, in the neoliberal sense, limits its own challenge to the hegemony of white supremacy by avoiding direct confrontation with structural inequality and racial injustice" (del Río, 2010, p. 146). The incorporation of Latina/o characters and themes into the English-language, and sometimes Spanglish, programming is read by audiences in complex ways.

From a social scientific perspective the Latina/o audience has been seen as a group that challenges assumptions about media use as it finds multiple ways of engaging with mainstream and more specialized and/or Spanish-language media indicating a dual process of embracing U.S. culture while remaining tied to a Latina/o heritage (Rios & Gaines, 1998; DeSipio, 2003). Further study has uncovered the role mainstream media play in reinforcing stereo-typical perceptions among Latina/o (Rivadeneyra, 2006) or Cauca-sian (Mastro, Behm-Morawitz, Kopacz, 2008; Lee, Bichard, Irey, Walt, & Carlson, 2009) audiences. Rocio Rivadeneyra (2006) con-cludes that Latina/o viewers recognize the stereotypical represen-tations, but she warns that not all audience members are influenced in the same way. Lee, Bichard, Irey, Walt and Carlson (2009) used cultivation theory to investigate the potential differ-ences among heavy and light television viewers to determine if those with heavier usage had more stereotypical attitudes toward ethnic groups. Curiously, the researchers found that there were few significant differences between heavy and light viewers re-garding their perceptions of Latina/os, leading the team to con-clude that "the lack of findings indicate a need for further inquiry" (Lee et al., 2009, p. 106). It may also be that the stereotypes asso-ciated with other ethnic groups do not fit the complicated category of Latino/Hispanic, which may also be further complicated by the fact that there are still few representations of Latina/os in main-stream English-language programming.

Much of the empirical research comparing Latina/o media con-sumption with other groups in the U.S. has limited explanatory power because the construction of "Hispanic" as an ethnic variable fails to account for the diversity within the group and therefore typically renders it meaningless. More often than not, the experi-ence of Latina/os within a comparative study is relegated to a sen-tence describing how the group is the same as or different from Caucasian or African American audiences. For example, Calvert, Rideout, Woolard, Barr, and Strouse (2005) studied the computer use of young children and determined "regardless of income, edu-cation, and family structure, African American and Latino families were less likely to have Internet access, and Latino families were less likely than Caucasian families to report that they owned a computer" (p. 602). What is missing from this research is a thor-ough investigation of the dynamics of Latino families. In fact, the authors admit that the data for Latino families came from a "rela-tively small sample size for certain subgroups such as Latino chil-dren" (p. 604). Further, the Hispanic category has not been a good predictor of media use among Latina/o children (see, for example, Bickham, Vandewater, Huston, Lee, Caplovitz, & Wright, 2003; Anand & Krosnick, 2005). Bickham et al. (2003) assessed variables to uncover the similarities and differences within media use among European American, African American and Hispanic American children based on previous research that show differences among these groups of children. Overall, the conclusions related to specific predictors of media use—family life, economic status, education—were similar across the three groups, differences were seen in the time spent with television and electronic games especially between European and African American children and, "for the most part, Hispanic American children fell in between the other two groups" (Bickham et al., 2003, p. 128). While the authors intended to describe the variations within each ethnic group, there are many questions to raise about these ethnic categories. Are we to assume that European American children are white, and if so, where does an immigrant child from Spain get placed? In which category is a child who was born to Haitian parents in France and then moved to the United States placed? While ethnic categories are useful to organize data to determine patterns of behavior for groups, Hispanic as a variable is problematic because there are many different ways to identify someone of Hispanic origin. It is important to investigate variations between groups using empirical and/or quantitative approaches, but there must be more attention paid to meaningfully categorizing participants. Susana Rinderle (2005) posits: "Lack of sufficient attention to labels and their identity meanings may account for some of the variations in study results on the communication dynamics between people of Mexican descent and European Americans" (p. 295).

One way to move beyond ethnicity specifically related to the Latina/o experience is to focus instead on home language use. For U.S.-born Latinos who speak English, their perceptions of the influence of television on children do not differ significantly from other groups. Further, when parents were asked about the desire for more Latina/os in television programming, either for adults or children, no significant findings emerged between ethnic groups. When language was differentiated from ethnicity new patterns emerge. Spanish-speaking parents agreed that they would like to see more Latino-themed and Spanish-language programming, while English-speakers did not feel this way (Moran, 2010).

Media use among Latina/o youth has increased and Latina/os as a whole remain heavy users of all types of media. In the Kaiser Family Foundation's report updating the information from 2004 regarding 8- to 18-year-olds' media use, the authors conclude that in 2009 children spent more time with media than ever before (Rideout, Foehr, & Roberts, 2010). Young people in the United States have unprecedented opportunity to access media and the availability of technology reaches across demographic lines. The total time spent with media (including media multitasking) for La-tina/os reached close to 13 hours per day. If you control for multi-tasking, Latina/os between the ages of 8 and 18 are using media for on average 9 hours and 14 minutes per day (Rideout et al., 2010). Television remains the most used medium, with Latina/o youth spending about 5 hours and 21 minutes per day engaging with television on a variety of platforms. In the new media envi-ronment the category for television use was extended to include time-shifted viewing, DVDs, and viewing TV on other platforms such as the Internet (Rideout et al., 2010). Latina/o children and teenagers report higher television than white children who spend 3 hours and 36 minutes per day with the medium. The Kaiser Family Foundation report establishes that young people, especial-ly Latina/os, are completely integrating the media into their daily lives, but what demands further attention is how youth navigate and understand the images they see and how those representa-tions impact their understanding of themselves, others, and the world around them. Scant audience research has been conducted with primarily Latino families, and few have looked at the differ-ences between primarily Spanish-speaking and English-speaking families with young children. Spanish-speaking parents held more favorable perceptions about the influence of television, believing that exposure to programming would have a positive impact on their child (Moran, 2010). This may provide some insight into why Latina/o children are spending more time using mass media. If parents believe that media use will have a positive effect, it is less likely they will restrict its use. For English-language learners, many encourage English-language media use by their children as a way to improve their own skills. Moreover, the U.S. production of Latino-themed programming positions the audience as belonging to a pan-Latinidad warrants investigation into reception practices. Studying the audience is a difficult task; they are illusive, unpredictable and complicated. Nevertheless, the modes of reception can be examined to gain insight into the dynamics of interpretation.

Chapter 3

Latina/o Media Consumption

Latina/o media consumption remains a mystery to those who hope to explain a neat and precise pattern of behavior that could be counted on to access this group of audience members. For example, marketing firms are interested in determining a predictable way of tapping into this audience. But media consumption among Latina/os is not mysterious; in fact it is common in its complexity and unpredictability. For decades, media scholars have looked to uncover the nature of the audience's relationship with media and have found that it is constantly in flux and vigorously negotiated. The tradition of audience studies from both an empirical and critical perspective provides insight into variances between audience use, interpretation, and potential effects related to media consumption. Critical audience study has matured into a field of inquiry that imagines an audience actively engaged in a negotiated process that is always already informed by the cultural norms from which a text is produced. As audience members derive pleasure from media texts, we must ask how these texts impact the ways in which audiences see themselves and others. The relationship audiences have with media can be viewed from a variety of perspectives. A common way to think about the influence of media is by assessing how audiences use the media as a part of their identity formation (Subervi-Vélez & Rios, 2005; Mastro, 2003; Moran & Chung, 2008), including conceptualizing hybrid identities (Rinderle, 2005; Molina Guzmán, 2006; Molina Guzmán & Valdivia, 2004; Straubhaar, 2007). Susana Rinderle (2005) argues that Mexican Americans constitute a diaspora distributing characteristics that include "a yearning for the homeland; alienation from the hostland; a complex structural relationship among homeland, hostland, and diaspora; and a collective identity largely defined by the relationship between homeland and hostland" (p. 301). The connection among Mexican Americans in the United States is strengthened by the availability and use of Spanish-language media produced in the U.S. and the availability of Mexican and other Latin American media imported to Spanish-language networks as well as the ability for audiences to access television directly from Mexico.

The audiovisual landscape in the United States is unique in that domestic media are produced in both English and Spanish with an additional flow of programming coming from Latin America, most notably Mexico. The availability of media in both languages provides an interesting entrance into audience behavior. In global studies of media consumption, often it has been scholars' intention to determine whether audiences prefer domestic (local) or foreign media. Within international communication, early research cautioned against cultural imperialism, fearing that the one-way flow of media products from the global north would lead to a loss of local cultural practices (Thussu, 2006). Of course, the underlying assumption of the cultural imperialism thesis was that audiences preferred foreign (mostly U.S.) programming and as a result of that exposure would adopt the values embedded in such programming, which were assumed to be at odds with the local culture (Elsmar, 2003). Audience research has determined, however, that people in fact preferred local programming when it was available (Straubhaar, 2003, 2007). The geographic location of production and language are part of what makes a program proximate, but other factors, such as class and education, influence audience choice. Joseph Straubhaar (2003) explains the relationship between cultural capital and cultural proximity to determine what influences media preferences. Straubhaar draws on Bourdieu's definition of cultural capital, indicating that education and social class impact cultural capital. The more educated, higher class standing, and a wider cross section of social and professional networks, the more cultural capital, which in turn leads to a more diverse breadth of experiences. This then leads to a broader appetite when it comes to a media diet. Further, the media can also be a source of cultural capital as well as a consequence. In other words, the more access to cultural capital, the more likely audiences were to access transnational programming.

Cultural proximity theory provides a relevant foundation for analyzing audience behavior in the U.S., but with a caveat. As we imagine the Latina/o audience, how do we label foreign and domestic programs? Immigrant audiences are likely to find the foreign programming most culturally relevant, which is to be expected. However, the availability of domestic U.S. productions, both news and entertainment, in Spanish complicates the puzzle. In fact, Ksiazek and Webster (2008) wonder whether the contra-flow of media products "might polarize culturally diverse populations within a given country into different audience groups who rely on entirely different media for their news and entertainment" (p. 488). I pose a similar question related to the differences in domestically produced English- and Spanish-language news. If audiences selectively expose themselves to news in either Spanish or English, are they learning about their community in a way that may be ultimately divisive (Moran, 2006)? It is important to uncover the selective processes of Latina/o youth to better understand the ways in which they navigate through the multifaceted media environment.

Latino Family Participants

The first two chapters provide a foundation to understand the current media environment with attention to the development of Spanish-language and Latino-themed programming. In the following chapters we hear from families who share their perspectives on media consumption to paint a broad picture of the context in which Latino families find themselves when interacting with media products within the home. It has been assumed that the Latino audience will be more likely to watch this type of programming and specific Latino-themed networks because of the cultural relevance. This expanding market share predicates the need to investigate the relationship audiences have with media. While the

Spanish-language television industry has enjoyed attention from advertisers who see it as a successful element in the current television market (Wentz, 2008), families choose to watch or not to watch based on personal content choices (Barrera & Bielby, 2001; Mayer, 2003b; Dávila, 2002; DeSipio, 2003) that are not necessarily driven by the marketing framework.

A total of ten families were interviewed during February and March 2008 in San Diego County, California. Each family consisted of participants where at least one parent identified as Latina/o. Family units ranged from three to five members and were interviewed together in their homes. When possible all members of the family who lived in the home were present. Consistent with the demographic characteristics of Latina/os in San Diego County where most Latina/os are of Mexican descent, all families were from or had familial connections to Mexico. As an incentive to participate, the families were given a $25 gift card to a popular store. Interviews were recorded with a digital video camera. The parents' education levels ranged from high school completion to advanced degrees, and their occupations varied from cook and day-care provider to middle management positions to a museum scientist. The children in the families ranged from 2–23 years old. Nine of the ten families had children under the age of eighteen who lived at home. Nine of the ten families can be defined as "immigrant families" (Newhouse, 2007) with at least one parent who moved from Mexico to the United States.

A second round of interviews was conducted in March 2010 focusing on children and teenagers as the primary interview participants. The interviews were conducted in the home with other family present, but questions involved media consumption among youth. A total of seven interviews were conducted with ten children. Each child was given a $15 gift card to a popular store. The parents of younger children provided observations as well as an explanation of their purposeful use of media for particular goals. The children ranged from 3 to 17 years old.

Of the seventeen families that participated in the interviews, eight speak primarily English in the home, five families speak primarily Spanish, and four families speak both languages with equal frequency. Every member who participated spoke both languages to varying degrees. The diversity of the sample provided the opportunity to gauge a range of viewpoints and while the sample reflected a diversity of opinions, there was consistency among the sample that may point to broader trends in the Latina/o experience.

Families make up their own interpretive community that is part of a larger segment of an imagined Latina/o audience, either imposed by the industry for marketing purposes or because of a genuine shared identity among members within the group. Interpretative communities are defined as a group of persons "who share strategies for classifying and decoding certain texts" (Lindlof, 1991, p. 29) and the family unit remains a strong force of collective identity that informs media use and interpretation. Even when families do not use media at the same time, their readings are still influenced by the family dynamics. Further, parents of young children are very interested in managing their media exposure and are influential in how the children interpret the content. In this case, the purpose of the interviews was to provide insight into the general perceptions and media habits of audiences. No single text was used to determine specific readings to analyze differences among audiences related to that text. Audience members were asked generally about television programs and websites but were not exposed to a single source. The flexible nature of the interview process allowed for nuanced understandings of the relationship family members have with popular culture.

The interviews lasted between 45 and 90 minutes and were conducted in both English and Spanish depending on the preference of the family, allowing for a more natural flow of conversation (Lugo Steidel, Ikhlas, Lopez, Rahman, & Teichman, 2002; Marín & Marín, 1991). Some interview participants engaged in code switching—speaking both languages. The style of the interviews was conversational to also permit a natural flow of dialogue between family members and the interviewer (Perreira, Chapman, & Stein, 2006). One of the advantages of interviewing respondents in family units is the dialogue that happens between family members. The narratives during the interviews seemed to continue discussions that had occurred previously in the family. Often, children would question or challenge their parents, or alternatively children would answer questions in ways that would surprise parents. Even when the primary interview participant was the child, the parents often would interject their opinion related to a specific topic. The author, who is a native English speaker but also speaks Spanish, conducted all the interviews. The language of the interview depended on the respondents who took the lead. All of the families live in a bilingual environment and often spoke English and Spanish interchangeably. The interviews conducted in Spanish were transcribed in Spanish by a fluent Spanish speaker and then translated into English by the author. English interviews were transcribed in English. For a full demographic description of each family see Appendix A.

Spanish- vs. English-language Television

Before delving into the ways in which family members process the images presented in media texts, it is first important to determine the trends of exposure. Many industry professionals assume that audiences prefer media texts in Spanish and respond more positively to advertisements in their native language, even when they have mastered English. While it is true that many first generation immigrants use Spanish-language media, their motivations vary. Further, borderland viewing is complicated by broadcast signals that are not blocked by political boundaries. It is also the case that their experiences with popular cultural texts are determined more by content than language, indicating a fluid movement between English- and Spanish-language media.

Latina/o households use Spanish-language media for a variety of reasons. First, the desire for Spanish-language programming stems from the desire of audiences to stay connected to their Latina/o culture while being a part of the United States. Spanish-language mass media use is part of a dual cultural process for social integration and sustained ethnic differentiation (Rios & Gaines, 1998; Viswanath & Arora, 2000). In other words, ethnic groups use ethnic media as a way to stay connected to what is familiar—their native culture. They are also in the process of acculturation, however, and being able to access news and entertain-entertainment in their own language helps them to understand their new home. Within first generation families, the children quickly become bilingual users but Spanish often dominates the home. Even as members become more comfortable using English, they are still drawn to Spanish-language media for content that is unavailable on English-language domestic channels. Family members who are proficient Spanish speakers and interested in news and entertainment from Mexico engaged with Spanish-language media more often. Older family members encouraged younger members, who may have never visited Mexico, to access Spanish-language media in an attempt to highlight elements of the culture. This serves as a way to maintain cultural awareness as well as ensuring that younger members feel connected to a Latina/o heritage while integrating into the larger Anglo culture. According to Diana Rios (2003), "Latinos may use media for selective acculturation to gain dominant cultural knowledge and learn cultural interaction and survival skills necessary in an Anglo American world" (p. 60). The family members with limited English or those who want to access programming that is shown exclusively in Spanish do turn to Spanish-language television. Children in the families are more drawn to mainstream English-language programming unless they are co-viewing with family members.

The families in this study were selective in their media use, and for bilingual participants, the content of the program dictated choice. Arlene Dávila (2000) explains that Spanish-language networks have often made the Spanish language central to their own marketing and thus tethering the language to Latinidad. The families who participated in the interviews explained their use of television with attention to both language and culture. Use depended on their mastery of English and/or Spanish, their cultural connection to a Latina/o heritage and a desire for particular content absent from English-language fare.

Based on the interview data, it appears that there is a preference for entertainment television in Spanish among family members who have limited English skills. It must be noted, however, that the preference was not for Spanish-language programming produced and/or distributed in the United States, but for programming broadcast in Mexico. Because of San Diego's proximity to the border, many families watch television stations broadcast in Tijuana, including a direct feed from Mexico City, which can be picked up in San Diego County. In addition, satellite and cable provide access to a variety of Spanish-language networks. It must be noted that for Spanish-speaking families living farther from the Mexican border, their primary access to Spanish-language programming is through U.S. based broadcast networks Univisión and Telemundo as well as Spanish-language cable channels. Nielsen Media Research consistently purports that the most commonly watched programs in "Hispanic Households" are Mexican telenovelas broadcast on Univisión.

As I engaged in the interview process, I tried to make the setting as comfortable as possible so parents and children felt as though we were merely having a conversation about their favorite media. The participants would open to these discussions, and once I began asking questions, they would freely explain their perspectives. I assured the families that I was not collecting information that would be used for marketing purposes, and I stayed clear of any discussion related to legal status as immigrants. I was careful not to imply that there were any "right" answers. Further, I allowed the participants to lead the conversation. It became clear that first-generation immigrant parents watch television in Spanish more often than U.S.-born Latina/os, but also watch English-language programming. Many participants describe a clear connection between the ability to speak English and more economic success in the United States and use watching television and movies in English as a way to improve their language skills. Most families who participated in the study live a bilingual existence, and this is reflected in their media consumption as they engage with both English- and Spanish-language media. The patterns of consumption of these families are consistent with those that have emerged in previous research in this area (DeSipio, 2003; Mayer, 2003b; Dávila, 2001a).

The first generation families in this sample reflect commonalities with participants in Straubhaar's (2007) sample where he describes media use by immigrants this way: "some spoke only Spanish and were focused on Spanish-language television. However, several, particularly those with more years of education, had learned some English before coming to the United States and were using television in both languages" (2007, p. 24). While the older family members had learned some English before moving to the United States, for the most part the first generation parents were primarily Spanish-language media users.

The families interviewed confirmed that they engage in programming in both languages and use television to practice their English or Spanish skills, depending on need. Immigrant parents who are primarily Spanish speakers encourage their young children to watch programming in English and were hopeful that their own English-language media consumption would help with language acquisition. One such family is family #5. José, the father, has been in the United States for eighteen years and his wife, Carmen, emigrated eight years ago. They met in an English class. José is more proficient in English and uses English at his work as a cook in a chain restaurant. Carmen speaks primarily Spanish and works as a house cleaner. She continues to take English classes while José stays home with the children in the evenings so she can attend. Neither of the parents watches Univisión or other U.S. Spanish-language channels, but they occasionally watch Televisa directly from Tijuana. These parents are eager to become proficient English speakers because they hope to continue their life in the United States to provide opportunities for their children. José describes his children's television use this way:

Kristin Moran (KM): ¿Se ven la televisión en inglés o en español? *(Do they watch television in English or Spanish?)*
José: En inglés, casi [nunca en]español...ellos casi todo en inglés. Como Barney, Teletubbies, Mickey Mouse... *(In English, hardly ever in Spanish, the kids watch all in English, like Barney, Teletubbies, Mickey Mouse...)*
KM: ¿Y cuando Uds. ven la televisión, es en español o en inglés? *(And when you watch television, is it in Spanish or English?)*

José: Es casi la mayoría en inglés. La mayor parte. Toda la mayor parte. *(Mostly in English. The majority. Mostly.)*
Carmen: Bueno que él dice pero casi no veo la tele. *(Well, what he said, but I rarely watch TV.)*
KM: ¿Pareces que es importante a ellos ver la televisión en inglés para practicar un poco el inglés? *(Do you think it is important for your kids to watch television in English to practice a little English?)*
José: Yo sí, Jaime aprendió mucho con *Barney*...muchas palabras cuando era chiquito. Aprendió muchas palabras y aparte de que él ve y luego usa la palabra con su hermano y hablan en inglés y repite todo lo que dice su hermano. Y habla todo en inglés en la escuela. *(For me yes, Jamie learned a lot watching Barney...many words when he was little. He learned a lot of words and also he will watch and later use a word with his brother and they speak to each other in English because he repeats everything that his brother says. And, now he speaks only in English at school.)*

The experience of family #5 demonstrates the conclusions of Louis DeSipio's (2003) "Latino Viewing Choices" study where he found "Approximately two-thirds of respondents reported that children in the household preferred English-language programming while just 4 percent preferred Spanish-language programming." In addition, Moran (2010) discovered that 65% of Spanish-speaking parents reported that their child never watches television in Spanish and most children described a preference for English-language media. While it is true that family #5 was eager to describe their preference for the English language, the primary language of the home is Spanish. The parents speak to their children and to each other in Spanish. They rely on their 6-year-old son, who is mildly autistic, to translate information. José does speak English at work, but many employees in the restaurant where he works are Spanish speakers. While this family hopes to become proficient English speakers, it is difficult. Jaime, 6, described his favorite shows on KidsWB, a programming block that included *Batman* and other action-adventure cartoons and demonstrated his pop culture insight discussing his favorite things such as *Teenage Mutant Ninja Turtles*. Jaime and his brother, Juan, 2, are well on their way to engaging with mainstream popular culture.

The members of family #6 speak primarily Spanish in their home. The grown children navigate both English and Spanish equally well and use the content of the programs to dictate in which language to consume content. Both parents moved to San Diego in their twenties and have lived in San Diego for more than twenty years. Victoria, the mother, is Spanish dominant and her job as a housekeeper has not demanded that she learn English proficiently. Her husband uses English at his job in a manufacturing plant. Their neighborhood is primarily Mexican and Mexican American, and much of their daily interactions take place in Spanish. Many of the billboards and other signage is in Spanish. Both children became English proficient in school and speak English with their friends. Angela, 21, is currently attending college, and her brother, Pablo, is a senior in high school. Angela spends a lot of time watching television with her mother, Victoria; both are fans of telenovelas and watch the Tijuana station for entertainment. Angela does turn to the English-language networks for news. Pablo, 17, watches mostly sports and does so in English. Both children are bilingual and throughout the interview spoke in both English and Spanish. The father, who has lived in the United States for approximately 25 years, watches news from Mexico, but enjoys watching American sports—baseball, basketball and football—in English. Victoria admitted that she needs to become a better English speaker and now watches Hollywood movies in English, but at the end of the day she enjoys watching telenovelas to relax. The family members allow the content of the program to drive the language choice. If Angela is in the mood for a novela, she will watch TV in Spanish, although she remembered watching the Disney Channel growing up as well as popular sitcoms including *Full House* and *Family Matters*.

Family #7 includes Victoria's sister Lola, who lives in Chula Vista with her husband and son. The family speaks Spanish in the home, while their son, an eighth grader, speaks English at school and with his friends. While Lola is a fan of telenovelas from Mexico, she prefers to watch the Televisa feed from Tijuana rather than the delayed novelas that are imported through Univisión. Alejandro, her husband, watches channel 57, which is the Televisa affiliate from Mexico City and which he prefers to channel 12, Televisa's Tijuana affiliate. He explained that the prime-time line-up is the same in the evening, but the news is local to Mexico City. He watches ESPN in English to keep up with the American teams and watches local San Diego sporting events in English, even though the Padres, the professional baseball team, broadcast the games in Spanish. Their son, 13, does not watch much television, but prefers to watch American sports in English and soccer in Spanish.

The three families are immigrant families where the parents moved to the United States for better opportunities for themselves and their children. They are not eager to strip themselves of their Mexican roots and selectively choose to relax by watching familiar programming. The children engage with Spanish-language media in a communal setting, such as family #6's ritualistic telenovela viewing in the evening. The teenage boys, who did not describe themselves as watching the soap operas, were connected to popular sports programming across cultures.

Because of the children's bilingual ability they are entrenched in both types of programming reflecting a bicultural reality that is their very existence. The neighborhoods where the families live have strong Latino communities. The Barrio Logan community, home to family #6, is more than 80% Hispanic, mostly of Mexican heritage, and Chula Vista, where family #7 lives, is nearly 50% Hispanic compared with the citywide average of 25%. Both families remain closely connected with both Mexican popular culture and family traditions. The fluid movement between U.S. and Mexican culture is demonstrated by the youth in these families. As they navigate both worlds, they are emblematic of a hybrid, bicultural reality that is common within the second generation. Their home environment situates their Mexicanness by preserving the Spanish language and cultural traditions while their peer groups and mainstream pop culture use draws them into the dominant culture.

The experience is a bit different for Jimena, a 17-year-old high school senior, who is a member of family #16. Although she is young and moved with her family to San Diego when she was 14, she is still very connected to Mexican culture and spends most of her weekends with her grandmother in Tijuana. She attends public high school, but admits she does not socialize much with many classmates outside of the school setting. She is studious and plans to attend San Diego State University. She is bilingual but speaks primarily Spanish with her family at home. She described her media use:

> KM: So what do you like to watch on TV?
> Jimena: I like documentaries, like on channel 15 [PBS affiliate]. I also like to watch movies. I like to watch romance movies, I just love them. I also like action sometimes. So that is what I like watching.
> KM: What's your favorite romance movie?
> Jimena: There are a bunch of movies I like... *Thirteen Going on Thirty.* Yeah, the ones that have comedy and romance together, I just love those ones.
> KM: Who is your favorite actress?
> Jimena: Well, I don't know. I don't watch too much TV in English. But the girl that is in that movie *Thirteen Going on Thirty*, I think she is a really good actress.
> KM: Jennifer Garner?
> Jimena: Yeah, Jennifer Garner.
> KM: So when you watch television you mostly watch in Spanish?
> Jimena: Yeah.
> KM: What do you like to watch?
> Jimena: The news and cartoons. I still like cartoons. Like the *Pink Panther,* those old classics, I just love them.
> KM: When you watch television in here, do you know if you're watching the television from Tijuana?
> Jimena: Yeah, I am watching the television from Tijuana....

It was clear that Jimena was stretching to think of media in English that she enjoyed watching, because she thought I was only interested in U.S. media. When I asked her about television in Spanish she seemed to relax as she described her experiences with her Mexican favorites. As first generation, Jimena told me she identifies with American culture and calls herself Mexican American, but her media selections are squarely connected to Mexican popular culture. Even the programs she watches that are produced in the United States, *Bones* and *Smallville*, she watches in Spanish on the channel from Mexico City. Because of Jimena's proximity to Mexico, she can remain tied to her country of birth. Jimena is nostalgic about her pre-immigrant life, but is realistic about the educational opportunities that living in the United States affords.

Her family moved to San Diego to create better opportunities for themselves, but the move has been difficult. Both Jimena and her brother had to learn English and transition from ESL to "regular" classes. In Mexico, she remembers her mother being home and cooking all the meals; in San Diego both parents work full-time. Jimena's patterns are more closely connected to a first generation adult than to the other teenagers I spoke with who more quickly embraced U.S. teen culture. Jimena criticizes U.S. popular culture by pointing out programs she does not enjoy. "Like *Family Guy* and *South Park* I just don't like those things. I see students from my school that love those programs and I don't like that. It just annoys me." She does not explicitly state the reasons for her annoyance, but the two programs she mentions are satirical programs that rely on understanding current events to get the jokes. Without insider cultural knowledge much of the programs could be read as vulgar and offensive rather than as critiques of dominant ideologies.

Perspectives on Spanish-Language Television

Family #8 moved from Mexico to San Diego in 1997 when the father was offered a position by the Mexican Consulate to work in California. Although they are first generation immigrants their move was predicated on a different set of circumstances in that the father was chosen as an expert in the field of education and therefore had a well-paying, secure job in the U.S. Jorge, the father, is well educated and made several thought provoking comments on U.S.-Mexico relations. The family is still culturally connected to Mexico even though they have been living in the United States for more than ten years. While in their home, I felt like I had traveled to Mexico City. Their sojourner status may help explain the father's nostalgic fondness for his home media, while his daughters are not as invested in Mexican media. The following dialogue is between the father, Jorge, and his younger daughter Diana, 22, currently living in Guadalajara attending art school as well as his other daughter Mona, 23, who lives in Orange County, south of Los

Angeles. As the family discussed their opinions of Spanish-language television, the generational differences became apparent between the father and his daughters, who spent their formative years in high school in the U.S. All agree, however, that the Spanish-language media produced in the United States is poor.

KM: Is there anything else you want to share with me?

Jorge: Yes, I'll tell you something about Spanish television. We have cable and with the dish you can get much things from different parts of Mexico, Mexico City. I love having news from Mexico City. Not about Mexico City, but from Mexico City, because I don't share the opinion of Diana. I think that the television in Mexico City is great.

Diana: Mexico City, but that's not the TV that I watch. That's not the TV that I've seen.

Jorge: Oh. And so the contrast between the television, the Mexican television, and the Spanish speaking television here, is a disgrace. It's *absurdo* [absurd]. Same with radio. Radio the commercials, the advertisements. It's like they say, well maybe that's because the people want this.

Diana: It's because nobody's asking for more.

Jorge: They don't move a finger to prove the culture of the people to...

Diana: It's not what sells.

Jorge: Yeah, so I think it's...

Diana: What shows do you watch from Mexico City?

Jorge: What?

Diana: What shows from Mexico City are excellent?

Jorge: *Las noticias son buenas.*[The news is good.] News, cultural type channels, el canal [channel] 22, and movie channels. Animal Planet, Discovery Channel, that's the only things that I see here.

Jorge: Kristin, I'd like to clear the point, when I'm saying that television in Mexico...*Televisa y TV Azteca son basura., pero basura de alta calidad* [Televisa and TV Azteca are trash, but high quality trash] *Los comerciales, las publicidades,* [The commercials, the advertisements] the level here, you know the reading sign "Buy this"? They're primitive, they're stupid, they're dumb, no creativity, no nothing.

KM: Here or there?

Jorge: Here.

Diana: The Mexican-American television right? The Latina, the Hispanic channels?

Mona: Yeah Telemundo, Televisa. He's comparing them.

Jorge: On the other hand, Mexico City, it's Televisa and it's civilized.

Throughout the interview, it was evident that the criticism of Spanish-language television in the United States was related to their perceived class positioning. While they are first generation, they do not see themselves as part of the target audience for this type of programming.

Members of family #10 had similar sentiments as family #8 and agree that Spanish-language programs in the United States are of low quality. Because most family members are critical of programming available in Spanish in the United States, when they do access media in Spanish they prefer to do so directly from Mexico, which is perceived to be of higher quality. Family #10 also came to San Diego because of a job opportunity for the father, who became a research scientist at San Diego's Natural History Museum. In general, the members of family #10 are interested in having access to more international networks not just from Mexico, but also from Latin America and Europe. They remember living in Mexico City and accessing television from all over the world. They describe the American television landscape as ethnocentric and promoting a worldview that in fact excludes most of the world. And while they were critical of television in general they do have their favorite programs, including *Monk* aired on the USA network. The children, Pilar, 15, and Roberto, 18, have lived with their parents in San Diego since 1998. Roberto criticized the U.S. Spanish-language programming.

> KM: Telemundo and Univisión are U.S. networks that broadcast in Spanish. Do you ever watch those?
> Pilar: I personally don't watch those.
> Roberto: Yeah, I don't know much about it but I think that's just because, yeah like we were talking earlier, the stuff they have on....going through channels to sort of find something desperately...I think, four or five Spanish channels. It's always the same game shows, the same, like you know the flashing colors. It doesn't get boring, it is boring. There's no real substance. And the channels that I've seen maybe if I stay the whole day watching it, I might find something interesting but I'm not gonna do that.

For the second generation and beyond, it is rare for the families to access media in Spanish unless it is in a communal setting.

While most of the family members had negative comments about U.S. Spanish-language television, distinctions emerged based on class. As Viviana Rojas (2004) found, the critique of programming on Univisión and Telemundo was common for both lower SES and higher SES respondents, but the focus of the criticism varied. Class becomes a marker to explain why the programming on the U.S. Spanish-language networks is unappealing or as Jorge says "a disgrace." Members of Jorge's family are well educated and describe the programming as appealing to new immigrant audiences who "don't demand more" from television. This perspective can be compared to Rojas' (2004) description where she concludes: "Some respondents even have a condescending and patronizing view of this audience in regard to the possibility of agency and change" (p. 144).

The families described in this study are not alone in their criticism, but again similar to Rojas' (2004) findings, members of families who had a lower social status centered their critiques on the values presented in the programming. Victoria, the mother of family #6 who emigrated from Tijuana, is concerned about what the messages in telenovelas might teach young children. Although she is a fan, she does not agree with the adultery and sexual promiscuity common in the programs. Carmen, the mother of family #5, also worries about the moral content of the programs on Univisión and does not approve of the violence on programs such as *Lucha Libre* or the "almost naked" women. Carmen and Victoria demonstrate "a less material conception of class" (Rojas, 2004, p. 144), confirming that what separates them from the audience for which these programs are intended is their interpretations of the text through a moral framework. In both cases, the women at other points during the interview revealed a strong religious commitment, which may also factor into their interpretation of the content. Communication scholars have also critiqued U.S.-based Spanish-language media with regard to the reliance on Mexican imports (Mayer, 2003a), the lack of children's shows (Moran, 2007; Subervi-Vélez, 1999) and too many telenovelas (Rojas, 2004).

Contradicting cultural proximity theory, the families with the highest cultural capital were most critical of U.S. media and were more connected to their national programming. The highest educated members of the sample, the fathers in families #8 and #10, praised the media in Mexico for its international focus and lamented the provincial nature of U.S. programming.

Parents of Young Children Talk About the Media

As children age, they become more purposeful in their media choices, but for young children, those under the age of 5, parents (or sometimes older siblings) are often in control of the media choices. The parents in this sample explained different strategies for regulating media exposure from few rules to more substantial tactics related to regulating the content their children see. Bilingual parents discussed how the television plays an important part of introducing their child to the non-native language. Criticism of Latino-themed preschool programming came from higher educated, bilingual parents who saw the construction of Latinidad on these programs as forced. Many agreed that their children enjoyed watching these programs, but were not always pleased with the way in which the Spanish language or Latino culture is incorporated. Some parents were critical of programs such as *Handy Manny* because they saw the presentation of the mixing of Spanish and English as unnatural. Parents remarked that the way Manny uses Spanish does not reflect their own use and they find it "annoying."

Handy Manny is an animated show broadcast on the Disney Channel and features a handyman who interacts with his set of bilingual tools. The episode "The Twisty Turn Twist" (Season 3, Episode 8) provides an example of the characters code switching. The episode opens with the tools working together to fix a rocking horse and talking about what they would do if they did not work in Manny's shop. The saw, Dusty, remarks, "gosh, someday I would like to be a real detective, that would be so much fun." The wrench replies, "Someday I want to be a cowgirl!" Dusty asks Felipe, the Phillips screwdriver, and he responds in an accented tone, "*Quiero ser,* I want to be...hmm...if I didn't fix things, I don't know what I want to be." Just then Manny enters the scene and says, "Hey, you finished fixing the rocking horse, *muy bien*, very good."

Viviana, the mother of five-year-old twins, Marco and Mercedes, in family #14, finds Disney's *Handy Manny* problematic. Viviana self-identifies as Mexican American and is bilingual. She grew up in Texas, where her mother's family has lived for generations. Her father moved from Spain and settled in Texas after marrying Viviana's mother. Viviana moved to California after college and married a Mexican American from Los Angeles. Her husband grew up speaking primarily English and now both parents are committed to teaching their children Spanish.

> Viviana: We were watching *Handy Manny* this morning, there is this idea that everyone who is Mexican or of Hispanic origin speaks with an accent and that bothers me. I think that both of them [her twins] do not identify with Handy Manny. But I think it is easier to identify with someone like Dora or Diego because they don't have accents but they do speak Spanish. On the other hand, they see Dora and Diego as brown but they see themselves as peach, this is this whole other thing so they are not like them. So is there stereotyping? On the one hand I appreciate it but I don't think Mexican Americans speak like that. For example, Handy Manny saying I am going to go get a *regalo* that is a present. I do not think that is natural so it is stereotypical.

The mother explained that when naturally code switching you would not say the same thing twice. The presentation of Spanish on programs such as *Dora the Explorer* and *Go Diego Go* was more tolerated because of their strategy to intentionally teach a specific word during an episode which could then be repeated by the child.

An example interaction on *Dora the Explorer* would include the character demonstrating the action and then repeating the Spanish. In "Dora Saves the Prince" Boots says, "The gate won't open," and Dora responds with, "Let's use the magic word *abre* to open the gate. Say *abre*." There is a pause for the child audience to presumably respond. The gate opens. Later in the episode Dora says, "Let's say the magic word *abre* so each crocodile will open its mouth." Dora and Boots repeat *abre* five times, and each crocodile opens its mouth to protect Dora and Boots from the mean witch. Throughout the episode Dora does not say that the word *abre* is the Spanish word for "open." She calls it a magic word and never translates it, but each time it is used something is shown opening. The audience is encouraged to use the word to help Dora, and when it is time to save the prince the audience is prompted to say the magic word and the characters pause waiting for the child viewers to say the word. The door opens and the prince exclaims, "¡Gracias!" and Dora answers, "De nada." None of the Spanish words are translated; they are understood because of the context. According to Carlos Cortés, consultant for *Dora* and *Diego*, the producers are careful not to translate words from English to Spanish because *abre* is not the Spanish word for *open;* it is the word in Spanish that describes that action. In other words, the producers do not want to privilege English by normalizing its use and making Spanish the "other" language by highlighting the difference. Brown Johnson, Nickelodeon executive creative director, explained: "Spanish becomes through Dora this sort of magical thing. The ability to speak another language [becomes] really cool and powerful" (Clemens, 2006). This logic works for family #9, where Michelle, a mother of two girls now 4 and 5, discussed her older daughter learning from Dora.

> Sofia: I liked to watch Dora.
> Michelle: It was so cute, I made a whole page about it in my scrapbook. She loved Dora. That was the first show she ever started to watch. She used to call her "Goonga". She couldn't say Dora; I don't know where she got "Goonga" from. She loved Dora. And actually the words that they've learned about Spanish, has been from that. She learned how to count to 10 in Spanish because of Dora before she could ever learn it in English.
> KM: Did you like Dora more because it was a Latina girl?
> Michelle: No, I don't think it mattered, I liked the fact they were teaching Spanish, because I had wanted to teach them Spanish.

Michelle articulates an interesting dynamic between ethnicity and language. For Michelle, a third generation Mexican American, being Latina is not necessarily connected to Spanish. The language is important; she wants her girls to speak Spanish, but not because she sees that as central to the Latino experience. While Michelle is bilingual, her language ability does not define her Latinidad.

It is unlikely that a program like *Dora the Explorer* will teach much Spanish to families who are living a bilingual existence, since the language presentation is basic vocabulary, but there is a sense from parents that exposure to Spanish words is beneficial in perhaps intangible ways. Viviana of family #14 explained that Mercedes and Marco, 5-year-old twins, enjoy watching the program. Parents who are third generation and beyond were more likely to explain that they exposed their child to these programs with the intention of the child learning a Spanish word. This is similar to the motivations of non-Latino parents who see programs such as Dora as a way to expose their children to something new.

> Mercedes: I can understand when Dora speaks Spanish!
> KM: She is easy to understand and speaks slowly?
> Mercedes: Yeah.
> KM: Does she have a cousin?
> Mercedes: Yeah. Diego!
> KM: And he speaks in Spanish sometimes? So when Dora or Diego speak in Spanish you can understand them?
> Mercedes: Yeah but Marco can't.
> KM: Is your Spanish better than Marco's?
> Mercedes: Yeah, he can only do the numbers in Spanish.
> KM: Marco, does your sister help you speak in Spanish?
> Marco: Yes. I know how to speak Spanish.

This is a household where the Spanish language is seen as beneficial. Until recently, the children had a Spanish-speaking nanny, Margarita, who cared for them during the week. Viviana wants them to continue using Spanish and considered Spanish immersion school as they searched for the perfect kindergarten. Further, she uses Latino-themed programs and programs in Spanish as a way to expose them to their Mexican heritage.

> KM: Are you interested in continuing their Spanish?
> Viviana: Yes I am. So while we are looking at schools, we are looking at programs that have Spanish lessons and I make them watch one of the PBS programs in Spanish or one of their movies in Spanish because they are losing it. They do understand, like when Margarita comes she speaks to them in Spanish and they understand and respond in English. But if they are forced to they will respond to her in Spanish. But even if my father speaks to them in Spanish they don't respond in Spanish. There has

never been a negative connotation associated with Spanish, but for ex-
ample with Marco, he feels very strongly that we should only speak Eng-
lish.
KM: Do you like to speak Spanish Mercedes?
Mercedes: Yes.
KM: Do you think you would want to watch TV or other shows in Span-
ish?
Mercedes: No, because I can't really understand the language.

The children understand that their mother wants them to
speak Spanish, so Mercedes will offer up her Spanish ability to receive praise, but the dominant language of the house is English.
Marco is more resistant and wants to only speak English and relies on his sister to communicate in Spanish. While Viviana wishes
that their household was more bilingual, she admits the reality is
that they are English dominant.

Family #13 present another example of a second generation
parent who wants to keep Spanish alive within the family, but is
faced with the difficulty of living in an English environment. Sergio, 8, attends a Spanish immersion school and his mother is happy with his Spanish progress.

KM: So as far as your intention for television with them, do you ever
have them watch TV in Spanish?
Marisa: No because Sergio does not need it. He's speaking Spanish all
day and since he is the older one, he has driven a lot of the choices. I
have not done my part to know what is available in Spanish and we don't
have any of the channels that would put Disney in Spanish. There are a
lot of programs I don't care about and even if they are available in English or Spanish I don't want them.

Marisa, the mother, is very careful about media exposure. She
monitors what her children, 5 and 8, watch and records approved
programs on their DVR so they can fast forward through the commercials. She prefers that they watch PBS, and their favorite program is *Cyber Chase*. While she is cautious about commercial and
even public television, the TV area had plenty of movies on DVD
that the children enjoy. Five-year-old Pedro showed me his *G-Force*
DVD and said it was his favorite. While there are limits placed on
what the children access, they are still immersed in much of main-

stream popular culture. Marisa acknowledges that watching media in the non-native language is work and she wants to give Sergio a break from learning since "he's speaking Spanish all day." What is comfortable for her family is English; Marisa herself is bilingual and grew up speaking Spanish with her parents. Her favorite programs are English-language shows such as *Grey's Anatomy*.

On the other hand, family #11 is a blended family where two of the children have recently moved from Mexico and are learning English; however, many of the same issues emerge when considering the purposeful ways parents encourage their children's media exposure. The older children in the family, Armando, 9, and Lupe, 6, provide an example of first generation children living in a bilingual household. Their father, Armando, married Linda, who is a second generation Mexican American from Chicago now living in San Diego. After the marriage, his two children from a former marriage, who had been living in Puerto Escondido, Oaxaca, Mexico, moved to San Diego. Armando and Linda have one son, Jack, who is nearly 3 years old. I asked Linda about whether the children are exposed to English or Spanish-language programming.

KM: They mostly watch TV in English?

Linda: Yes because I have asked them to, when they got here a year ago, I requested that if they want to watch cartoons that they watch them in English because it would help with their English skills. So when they rent movies or they watch movies or cartoons I did not make them, but I requested and strongly suggested that they watch them in English. So if I am not home or not there to supervise and once in a while I will come home and they will be watching in Spanish, I won't stop them but if I am here we are going to start a movie in English.

KM: So have you noticed their English has improved?

Linda: Yes it helps, they primarily speak to me in English but if they can't express themselves they switch over to Spanish. But they only speak to Armando in Spanish because his English is not very good.

KM: And he watches TV mostly in Spanish...

Linda: I watch the news in both because it is so different so I don't want to miss anything either way and he will go either way.

Linda: The siblings speak all Spanish to each other. But when they talk to Jack or me it is all English. It is really interesting around here. I guess I don't pay attention to it anymore.

Linda is faced with the dilemma of wanting her older children to learn English and younger son to learn Spanish and feels that exposure to television in the non-native language is beneficial.

> Linda: We are in a very strange situation because Jack does not want to speak Spanish anymore, so I want him to be bilingual and watch stuff in Spanish but I don't necessarily want them to watch stuff in Spanish because I want them to be working on their English.

While the older children are learning English and speaking it at school, it appears that when left to their own devices they choose to engage with media in Spanish. Linda does not want to force the issue too much because she recognizes that it is challenging for them to learn English and admits when she catches them watching cartoons in Spanish she usually lets it go.

Parents of young children are heavily invested in the experiences of their children, and those with whom I spoke want to carefully manage their child's media diet. The parents were careful to avoid discussing media use as entertainment or as a babysitter since much of the current parenting culture laments that perspective, while at the same time the industry is creating more media products for the very young. When the parents discuss the types of shows the children watch they were seen as having a purpose that elevates the use beyond just watching T.V. Parents articulated the educational benefits of the programming to which their children were exposed. Of course, this management did not always translate into practice as the children themselves often told a different story. Certainly as children age, their parents have less control over the choices.

Children's Choices:
Youth Explain Their Media Use

The family members in the sample reinforce conclusions from previous research (DeSipio, 2003), revealing that television viewing is driven by content choice and that indeed Latina/os engage with both languages. For audience members, being bilingual is seen as an advantage that opens up the availability of different content. Again, consistent with Straubhaar's sample where it was found that "overall, younger people, both adolescents and those of college age, were more likely to watch either just English-language programming or both English and Spanish programming" (2007, p. 248), young people in this sample choose English-language programming over Spanish-language content. Their preferences are for programs that are popular with their age group. The younger children watch cartoons and the tween and teenagers reported low levels of television viewing (although that was sometimes contradicted by their parents) and high levels of Internet use for games and social networking.

Latina/o youth are influenced by their own experiences as members of their family as well as other systems of influence, including peers and marketing efforts. In the home of family #3, Spanish and English are both spoken. The mother, Nora, was born in Chula Vista and grew up speaking Spanish with her parents, who moved from Mexico. Her husband, Miguel, moved from Tijuana to attend college; his parents also moved to San Diego. Alexa, 10, explains her experience with television in Spanish.

KM: Do you guys ever watch any TV in Spanish? Or movies in Spanish?
Alexa: Yeah, sometimes. I used to watch novelas.
KM: Oh you don't watch novelas anymore?
Alexa: Not that much anymore
Nora: Her grandmother died. She used to go to her [paternal] grandmother's house.
Alexa: She would only watch novelas and I used to get hooked on it and couldn't stop...
Nora: Tell her which one you used to watch all the time.
Alexa: It was called *Amigos para siempre*, which is like a teenage one.

The generational connection young Latina/os have through media is demonstrated by the ritual of watching the novela with grandparents, engaging in what Rios (2003) describes as "fortifying sociocultural glue among family members" (p. 62). But now that her grandmother has passed away and her own mother does not watch the novelas, Alexa has turned to mainstream programming. Currently, her preferences are for general market tween television, including shows on the Disney Channel and *America's Next Top Model*. Her brother, Miguelito, 11, is a fan of MTV and explained that he has outgrown Nickelodeon and Cartoon Network. He does not watch television in Spanish. Both children declared that their favorite media activity is going online to play interactive computer games such as Webkinz and Club Penguin. The experiences of these children as they approach their teenage years are much more connected to general market media than to anything tied to Mexican culture. While both children are bilingual and attend a bilingual school, they are, like most children, influenced by popular trends. Alexa announced her favorite celebrity is Miley Cyrus, who plays Hannah Montana on the Disney Channel. In fact, few of the young people in the families interviewed described watching Spanish-language television unless it was in a familial setting that included their first generation parents or grandparents.

As discussed earlier with family #13, Marisa wants her children to learn Spanish, and Sergio, 8, attends a Spanish immersion school and is bilingual. His brother, Pedro, 5, attends an English-language public charter school and announced his trepidation about learning Spanish.

> KM: Do you ever watch anything in Spanish?
> Pedro: I hate Spanish!
> KM: You don't like to speak Spanish?
> Pedro: Well when we were in Guadalajara we had to watch TV in Spanish.
> Sergio: I think we saw *Backyardigans* in Spanish.
> Marisa: You watch the ones with the tools... *Handy Manny*.
> KM: Do you like watching that show?
> Pedro: I love it!
> KM: [To Sergio]: Do you speak Spanish sometimes with your brother?
> Sergio: Almost never. I almost always talk to my mom in Spanish.

The children who are growing up with parents who want them to learn a second language do not easily articulate the lived experience of a bilingual environment. Many children resist being forced to anything, so the incorporation of Spanish needs to be seen as a natural part of the environment. According to Marisa,

Pedro will transfer to the Spanish immersion school for the upcoming school year.

Alejandro, 13, the son in family #7, speaks Spanish in the home and explained he prefers to be outside playing sports rather than watching TV or movies. When he does watch, he watches sports, which sometimes leads him to the Spanish-language channels for soccer.

> KM: What do you like to watch on TV when you watch TV?
> Alejandro: Um, I don't really know...sports.
> KM: What's your favorite sports team?
> Alejandro: My favorite sports team? Chargers.
> KM: Chargers? Who's your favorite player?
> Alejandro: Luis Castillo.

He then showed me an autographed jersey from a Mexican soccer team.

> Alejandro: This is signed from the whole team.
> KM: How did you get this?
> Alejandro: My cousin has a cousin that plays on the team...They don't have any soccer on English channels.

Although Alejandro was born in San Diego his family is still Spanish-language dominant; he speaks English at school and occasionally goes on MySpace to chat with friends. Similar to the other teens, the language of his television viewing is determined by the content.

In some ways it should be no surprise that the favorite TV shows of children in Latino families do not stray far from the mainstream top-rated general market programming. For many of the children, their favorites include *Spongebob Squarepants, Curious George,* Disney movies and, for older children, *iCarly, Hannah Montana* and the other popular programs. In family #17, Susana, 9, is a fan of the Disney channel, and while her father emigrated from Mexico, she does not speak Spanish.

KM: So what kind of stuff do you like to watch on TV?
Susana: I like to watch Disney channel, *Suite Life on Deck, Wizards of Waverly Place, Hannah Montana* but she is quitting. I mostly like *The Suite Life on Deck.*

Susana likes mostly tween programming and also watches *Cats 101* on the Animal Planet so she can learn more about cats. Susana has little connection to her relatives in Mexico, and while her father primarily speaks Spanish and watches television in Spanish, she tunes out the language. Her parents are divorced, but her father takes her to school most mornings. Her mother, a non-Latina Spanish speaker, most often communicates with Susana's father in Spanish, but exclusively speaks English with her daughter.

As children age, they begin to engage in more computer play, describing in the interviews their experiences with social network sites, online game sites, and other video games. While interviewing family #2, the television was on in the living room with the channel tuned to *iCarly* on Nickelodeon. When asked about television, Travis, 6, referred to the program on in the background and said that he likes *iCarly*. His brother, Timothy, 11, explains his television preferences.

KM: What do you like to watch on TV?
Timothy: A show called *Rob and Big.*
KM: What channel is that on?
Timothy: MTV 2.
KM: What do they do on that show?
Timothy: The skinny guy skateboards and the fat guy tries to skateboard and...
KM: Don't they do like random stunts and stuff?
Timothy: Yeah.
KM: That's funny. What other shows do you watch?
Timothy: Mm... *Drake and Josh...*
KM: Do you ever watch TV in Spanish?
Timothy: Not really.
KM: Not really?
Isabel: Movies you do.
KM: What movies do you watch in Spanish?
Timothy: Mm...
KM: Do you ever notice that there are Spanish stations on TV?

Timothy: Yeah. They are kind of funny because they talk really fast...I can understand them a little bit.

Although Timothy does not discuss watching programming in Spanish, Isabel, his mother, tells a story from when he was young:

Isabel: He had gotten a gift card to Toys-R-Us, he must have been about six, and he wanted to get the movie *The Fox and the Hound* and I was against buying kids movies and he picks up the Spanish version and I laughed and that's when I looked at it and I was like, "If that's what you want to spend your gift card on, go ahead!" He had no clue and he watched it two full times and the third time he started watching it he goes, "How come they're speaking in Spanish?"
KM: Did he continue watching it?
Isabel: Yeah, he would still watch it and then once DVDs came out we said, "let's look to see if they have a Spanish feature"...So we'd have them play in Spanish. I think we stopped doing that around last year. But with him [Timothy], there were times when he'd actually request the movie in Spanish.

Similar to other parents who are interested in non-native language acquisition, Isabel encouraged viewing in Spanish. As Timothy becomes more independent in his media use, he has abandoned Spanish and exclusively watches English-language fare. As the interview continued, it became clear that for these boys video games were a significant part of their media diet. Travis and Timothy explain their fondness for computer and video game time.

KM: What else do you like to do Travis?
Travis: Play on my computer.
KM: What do you like to do on the computer?
Travis: Play video games.
Isabel: When you open up your Internet, what's the first thing you see?
Travis: My Webkinz.
KM: What's that?
Travis: Like little stuffed animals that you can go online and play with. I like doing that also...you just have to win points by playing video games and then you go to the store and you buy them like ... stuff.
KM: What kind of stuff do you like to buy?
Travis: Clothes for them and food.
KM: When you go on the computer are you by yourself or do you play with other people?
Travis: Sometimes I play with other people, like my friends...

KM: But sometimes you do it by yourself?
Travis: Mmm...
KM: Do you ever play computer games with him [Timothy, 11]?
Travis: Mmm, usually... usually he beats a lot of levels on the Battlefield for me 'cause they're like too hard.
KM: So then he helps you win?
Travis: Mmm....Yeah.

As we continued the interview it became evident that video game playing was an activity that the males in the household enjoy doing together. The father, whose parents were both born in Mexico, was born and raised in Chula Vista. He was not present during the interview because he works at night as a police officer, but his wife Isabel explained his video game use.

Isabel: My husband has always been into the Halo types of games. Which I used to not even realize the ratings in the beginning, I thought "Oh, a cute little dinosaur." They have all these other games and the kids all play together. I thought, "Grand Theft Auto" is okay. They're not really doing the missions, they're just driving the cars and then there would be a time where my son would stumble across something and I'd say, "Hey, you're allowed to have this game as long as it's just to drive... And he's always done well as far as obeying the rules. I've never seen him sneak off to play... I think with video games we are more relaxed... I know they enjoy playing them together, so...So I have to see what system they want this year for Christmas. I was shooting for the Wii but they want the Xbox 360 cause that's the one that has Halo....My husband's youngest brother is a total computer geek, they'll pack up their hard drives and go to someone's house and hook them all up and play. There's been times where it's been like, "I'm going over to my mom's to play video games." "Okay hon, see you in about six hours." So for his family that was like a natural, everyday thing. In my family, my mom had a time limit for my brother when he played games, so this whole video game thing is new for me.

As Strasburger, Wilson, and Jordan (2009) detail, video games are now one of the most popular choices of leisure time activities for children and teenagers and, as demonstrated in this family, for some parents as well. The father grew up enjoying this activity and still uses it as a way to connect with his brothers. The boys and their father enjoy video game playing together, which can be compared to the multi-generational television viewing that occurs within families. Children's time spent with media is tied to the parents' media use. In this family, the father enjoys playing video games, and now this activity is being shared with his children. It is clear that even when their father is not at home the boys spend a lot of time using the computer and playing video games either by themselves or with each other. Video game playing is a natural part of this family's daily activity.

The older son, Timothy, 11, spends much of his free time on the computer in his room communicating with friends online and participating on MySpace. He tells me that he has his own MySpace page. His mother, Isabel, was concerned about what he was doing while online and tried to restrict his use by changing his password. After a few days when he did not say anything about not being able to log on, she questioned him. He replied that as soon as he could not log on, he requested his password and it was emailed to him. As many parents are learning, often the child can outsmart restrictions. Like many 11-year-olds, Timothy is adjusting from being a dependent child to one who relies more heavily on peer relationships and uses technology to stay connected with his friends. His mother also said that he had requested his own cell phone and was beginning to get phone calls from friends. Isabel confessed that Timothy's changing media habits are challenging her rules and forcing her to rethink how to manage his media use.

The boys in family #13, Sergio, 8, and Pedro, 5, had restrictions regarding time spent with television and video games, but expressed how much they like playing Wii.

Pedro: I love Wii!
KM: What do you like to play on the Wii?
Sergio: I like to play Wii Fit.
Pedro: I love Mario Cart!
Sergio: And Wii Sports.
KM: What sports do you like best?
Sergio: Baseball.
Pedro: I love baseball!

The children in family #3, Alexa and Miguelito, describe their preference for playing online over watching television.

KM: So if you guys had a choice between watching TV, watching a movie or going on the computer, which would you choose?
Alexa: Computer.
KM: What do you like to do on the computer?
Alexa: Club Penguin and Webkinz
KM: What sites do you like?
Miguelito: Umm, I'd say Club Penguin and then sometimes I go to YouTube and watch different things.

Susana, 9, likes using the social networking aspect of particular games such as Build-a-Bear. Susana's friend moved away from San Diego, and they are able to stay in touch through these sites.

Susana: I keep in contact with her. I call her up on the weekends and ask her if she wants to go on Build a Bear and she says yeah.
KM: What do you do on Build a Bear?
Susana: We play games together and go to each other's houses.
KM: So you're here and she is in Oakland and you can go into the same place on Build a Bear?
Susana: Yes. Sometimes we talk on the phone but sometimes we are talking on the Build a Bear on chat. There is a bar at the bottom of the screen and you can type in what you want.

In 2006, it was reported that one-third of American children access information online by the time they reach kindergarten (Rideout & Hammel, 2006). According to Rideout et al. (2010) 70% of young people between the ages of 8 and 18 use the computer every day. Latina/os spend nearly 1 hour and 50 minutes using the computer, which is more time than either white or black youth who spend less than 1 hour and a half. Certainly the youth in the households described here are spending much of their leisure time using some sort of gaming or networking device.

Santiago, 14, of family #12, lives in San Diego to attend a private high school, but his father spends part of his time in Mexico running his business. Santiago and his mother travel "home" to Ensenada often and his older half brothers attend university in Monterrey, Mexico. Santiago uses social networking sites to stay in touch with friends, and similar to other parts of life, his online experience is bilingual.

KM: So do you like to go on the computer?

Santiago: Yeah, for a while when I do get on I like YouTube, Facebook, stuff like that, Instant messenger.

KM: What do you do when you go on Facebook?

Santiago: I talk to friends and do little quizzes just for fun, stuff like that.

KM: And do you talk to friends from school or Mexico?

Santiago: Both. It's a good way to keep it touch.

KM: Do you use Facebook in Spanish or in English?

Santiago: English.

KM: When you talk to friends do you use mostly Spanish or English?

Santiago: When I talk to my friends here I use English and when I talk to my friends in Mexico I talk to them Spanish.

No longer are scholars concerned about online access issues related to ethnic differences. It appears that most children, regardless of race or class, find themselves using the computer. Nevertheless, there are discrepancies in the quality of that access; many lower income children access the Internet in public locations, changing the nature of the activity. Further, as Tripp and Herr-Stephenson (2009) discovered, because of the vast differences in computer expertise between parent and children, some Latino parents were resistant to the technology because of the perceived risks of encountering undesirable content.

The upper middle-class families interviewed for this project had high-speed Internet access in their home making Internet use possible for all family members. Pilar, 15, the daughter in family #10, is a sophomore at a public high school and describes her media use as "typical." She uses a variety of platforms and uses online media and her mobile phone as a way to connect with friends. Pilar explains that she often watches television programs *with* her friends; even when they are not in the same location they are together either on the phone or online.

Pilar: I don't know what category they go into, they're not really sitcoms but they're not reality TV. TV shows like *Whose Line Is It Anyway?*, it's not like scripted but it's planned out...I watch cooking shows on the Food Network. I watch Food Network a lot. I like to watch *Myth Busters.* ...I also watch *SVU Law & Order.* I think that's one of those shows that I watch with my friends sometimes. It will be 10:00 at night and I'll get a message from my friend and she'll be like *Law & Order SVU* is on and we'll watch it together and we'll talk about it as we're watching it. She's at her house...and we'll try and guess what's going to happen and stuff. And we'll sit there for a whole hour watching the show together and during the commercial we'll predict what's going to happen. It's just really fun.

KM: So do you go online much?

Pilar: On the Internet? I'm probably on it, the Internet, a lot more than I am watching TV.

KM: What do you like to do online?

Pilar: Usually when I'm on, all I do is talk to my friends from school or write emails or chat.

KM: What kind of programs do you use?

Pilar: MySpace, typical teenager. I also instant message with AOL or Yahoo and I use my email. I actually only use it for family that's in other places like my cousins in Argentina. I'll talk to them through email or my family in Mexico. But I don't really talk to my friends here in San Diego on email.

KM: Then you must do that on MySpace or instant messages.

Pilar: Instant messages. I'll talk to them through that.

Claudia (her mother): Or the phone.

Pilar: Or on the phone

Claudia: I think she's very multi-task[ing]. She's writing messages to several people at the same time and doing homework.

Roberto (her brother): That's like everybody in the world right now.

Pilar is typical in regard to her media use. She multitasks and spends time on social networking sites. Pilar reveals many elements that highlight teenage experiences with the media while also identifying connection to family in Latin America. Elements of her hybrid reality are articulated through her casual mention of her cousins in Argentina and Mexico. Her brother, Roberto, 18, also imagines a connection to the world as he sees himself as part of a broad global community of media users.

Jimena, 17, on the other hand explains, "I am just not really interested in those things" when I asked her about using MySpace or Facebook. While, she does not use the computer for social networking, she does enjoy using the computer for other purposes.

Jimena: I like to go on YouTube and see people playing songs from other artists like Taylor Swift. I just like how they perform. I just love looking at it. I like watching funny videos too. I like going to BestBuy.com and watching the videos and seeing the guitars that are really expensive.

Guitar playing is important for Jimena, and she says she spends most of her free time playing and writing music.

> Jimena: Yeah, I have been playing for five years and my dad taught me how to play and last year I took a guitar class at school.
> KM: Do you write songs?
> Jimena: Yeah I write songs.
> KM: When you write songs, do you sing in Spanish or English?
> Jimena: Both.
> KM: In the same song?
> KM: No, like one song in English and one song in Spanish.

Jimena describes the bicultural and bilingual reality she embodies by utilizing both languages in her songwriting, but unlike media produced for teenagers who are assumed to be like her, she does not mix the languages within the same song. The promotion for music on MTVtr3s, for example, uses code switching as a way to authenticate their product. Jimena sees through that and prefers "regular MTV." While she enjoys listening to popular artists from Mexico, she accesses the music through iTunes, where she can find what she likes.

> Jimena: I have seen MTV at my aunt's house who has direct TV. I love music and like watching music videos...I've just seen regular MTV.

The youth in the sample reflect emerging patterns of behavior that are not necessarily tied to their ethnicity, but certainly their engagement with multiple forms of media is from their position as a Latina/o youth. Parents are heavily invested in managing media exposure, especially for younger children, and see television as a tool for learning.

Latina/o youth embody a hybrid identity that is informed by their ability to navigate between cultures. While Ksiazek and Webster (2008) originally posit a pessimistic outlook regarding a media environment that is saturated by multiple media forms, they conclude that "English-Speaking Hispanics have a multicultural fluency" (p. 501) that supports the idea that given the varied media environment bilingual youth can easily move between Spanish and English content. Given the transnational environment of most households, traditional binaries of local vs. global and domestic vs. foreign should be revised. Within the United States, cultural proximity theory can be revisited by imagining two sights of local programming. The importation and production of Spanish-language media allow Spanish speakers access to a nuanced definition of local programming, which holds particular relevance. Further, living on the border families can directly access media from their native culture without any effort.

The context from which they view and interpret media is within a set of cultural practices that are influenced by multiple factors. The choices are not void of symbolic meaning. The preference to engage with Spanish-language media for an immigrant is purposeful; it is comfortable. The decision of a third generation parent to encourage Spanish-language acquisition is also purposeful; the parent is privileging elements of their cultural heritage to tell a story about their family. The children themselves are driven to make certain choices based on what they mean. A young girl sees the attraction of *Hannah Montana*, which is reinforced at school with her peer group as she participates in her social setting. The boys are watching ESPN so they too can fit in with mainstream habits. For the bilingual/bicultural child, however, watching ESPN to get information about their favorite team is coupled with watching *fútbol* on Televisa. The media consumption patterns demonstrate that for Latina/o youth their bilingual and bicultural reality affords them access to more cultural capital and opens up their worldview. The children who live in both worlds are better prepared to navigate a multicultural environment with ease; they practice this throughout their lives.

Chapter 4

Connecting to "Home"

During the family discussions, the participants in this sample explained that they access Spanish-language media primarily to watch programming that is unavailable in English. Not surprisingly, the most popular genre is telenovelas, which are part of the media experiences of many of the family members. Participants also access news in Spanish, preferring the channels directly from Mexico to Spanish-language news produced in the United States. Finally, a few of the participants mentioned watching Spanish-language media for sports information they cannot receive from the mainstream channels. The consumption patterns of Latina/o audience members included the use of Spanish-language media as a way to perform cultural maintenance (Rios & Gaines, 1998; Mayer, 2003a; Mato, 2005; de Block & Buckingham, 2008; Lemish, 2007) that is common among immigrant communities.

Family members articulate the ways in which media use is relevant for staying connected to elements of their culture while integrating into the U.S. dominant culture. More connection to a Latina/o heritage and proficient Spanish-language ability leads to more frequent Spanish-language media use. Often as families grow, older members will encourage younger members, who may have never lived outside the U.S., to access Spanish-language media. This serves as a way to maintain cultural awareness as well as ensuring that younger members feel connected to a Latina/o heritage while integrating into the larger Anglo culture (Subervi-Vélez, 1986). According to Diana Rios (2003), "Latinos may use media for selective acculturation to gain dominant cultural knowledge and learn cultural interaction and survival skills necessary in an Anglo American world" (p. 60). It is notable that although many families reported using mainstream English-language media, there is certain content some members preferred in Spanish—telenovelas and news.

Telenovelas: Entertainment from "Home"

Consistent with research on ethnic media use that illustrates how audience members watch television that reminds them of home, has cultural relevance, or allows for children to be connected to the homeland, in the interviews, Mexican and Mexican American participants describe watching telenovelas as a cultural experience (Rios, 2003; Barrera & Bielby, 2001; Mato, 2005; Mayer, 2003a; Moran, 2003). Vicki Mayer (2003a) focused on the way in which Mexican American girls in San Antonio negotiated their hybrid identity as they viewed *María Isabel*, a favorite novela at the time. Interestingly, the telenovela's story was centered on the main character's acceptance into Mexican society, which the girls found relevant to their own lives as they negotiated their place in relation to American culture. Mayer (2003a) explains that the telenovela became a "site for fantasies as well as criticism" (p. 492), whereby the girls read into the story an immigrant narrative that related to their own experiences. Rios (2003) interviewed viewers of serial dramas and found that for Latino participants, watching telenovelas provided a connection to their culture while offering familiar television.

During the past decade, more research has been conducted to uncover the bond audiences have with this quintessential Latin genre. Telenovelas, sometimes referred to as novelas, are drama serials that air daily with the most popular broadcast during prime-time hours. Often the word "telenovela" is translated into English as "soap opera," but the English term is loaded with connotations that do not apply to telenovelas. Daytime drama serials in the United States were developed as vehicles for household products to be pitched to women, the primary viewers during their early years on U.S. television. The genre has maintained its gendered position and is still thought of as a genre for female audiences. The evolution of telenovelas in Latin America is quite different. In a television format, Mexican producers envisioned the programs as high quality television, "inviting prominent writers to become part of developing the text" (Barrera & Bielby, 2001, p. 5). Finally, the primary objective was to reach a large audience, thus moving the telenovela to primetime ensuring the narratives would have mass appeal. The main distributors of telenovelas are Mexico's Televisa, Brazil's Rede Globo, and Venezuela's Venevisión. There is variety within the genre and among countries with major production sites. For example, the Mexican serials are more dramatic focusing more often on traditional romance stories (Fox, 1997), while Brazilian storylines tend to concentrate on social commentary through the narratives (Tufte, 2000). Venezuela is a site of production where telenovelas follow either a traditional romance trajectory, or those labeled *telenovelas de ruptura* include social and cultural issues (Acosta-Alzura, 2003). Colombia is also a center of telenovela production and has received much attention for the original *Yo soy Betty la fea (I Am Ugly Betty),* which has been adapted in many countries worldwide (Rivero, 2003).

The elements of the genre are consistent with episodic drama programs that often involve the search for true love, the search for true identity, revenge and vengeance, and all of the possible plots that keep audiences coming back for more. The transnational flow of telenovelas throughout the audiovisual market provides audiences with alternatives to Western modes of production and is evidence of a contra flow of programming that is not located within the U.S. or Europe (Thussu, 2006). The popularity of the genre has been explained by its broad use of melodramatic themes that appeal to audiences regardless of culture. Programs may be exported as an entire series rebroadcast in its original form or dubbed. The specific formats of particular programs, such as *Yo soy Betty la fea (I Am Ugly Betty),* have also been exported for localization. In this case, the local adaptation of the program uses local actors and often revises the script to include more culturally specific themes. In addition, the telenovela form has been copied in various countries, spawning new stories that loosely follow the genre conventions.

With an eye to the global market, Mexican telenovelas avoid specific cultural references and colloquialism to enhance their export potential (Casas Pérez, 2005). Joseph Straubhaar (2007) labels this process delocalization. Delocalization is beneficial as flows of television move across borders, but he warns that it should not be taken too far, "resulting in programming that is too bland and not appealing to anyone" (p. 171). What makes Latin American telenovelas appealing for most audiences is their Latin Americanness. The typical telenovela airs about 180 episodes with the final, most popular *capítulos* (episodes) garnering the largest audiences. Although the women in families often initiate viewing, it is common for prime-time novelas to be enjoyed by everyone, including the men. According to Nielsen, the prime-time telenovelas aired on Univisión are the highest rated programs among Hispanics in the United States. Viewers in San Diego, however, are able to watch the first run of the telenovela on Mexico's Televisa, while others farther away from the border must wait to view the exported version on Univisión affiliates. Telenovela fans articulate a sense of cultural caché associated with this first run access.

While telenovelas are not necessarily the favorite genre of all Latina/o audiences, they certainly are assumed, especially by U.S. marketers, to be viewed by most. According to Nielsen ratings, prime-time programs broadcast on Univisión reach, on average, 4 million viewers nightly. It is difficult to determine how many San Diegans are watching the Televisa feed. Telenovela viewing tends to be initiated by adult females, either a grandmother or a mother, and can become a family viewing ritual. Similar to previous studies, the participants in the sample enjoy watching novelas because they remind them of home, even if they have never lived in Mexico or did so only as a young child. In identifying a marker of Latina/o identity, or in this case Mexican, audience members use the Mexican television staple as a way to relax. The mother of family #6 explained her experience.

> Victoria: ...ahora estoy viendo las novelas no tanto por la drama pero por los personajes. Los actores, pues, muy guapos y que lo hacen muy bien y este. Bueno más o menos porque a veces no siempre son los mismos...divorcio y cosas así. No son buenas, en realidad no son buenas. No son buenas para los niños creo yo. Tal vez por otros no sé y ya estoy grande...Ya estoy grande y ya yo no me creo nada de eso.... No sé si Angela...lo que sea pasa allí. *(...right now I am watching the novelas not for*

the story, but for the characters. The actors, well, they are very handsome and they act really well and all that. But they are ok because they are all the same...divorce and things like this. They are not really very good. They are not good for children. For others, who knows? I am grown. I am grown and I don't believe in things like that. I don't know about Angela...whatever happens there.)

Angela: No, ya sé lo que va a pasar cuando empieza la novela, ya se que va a pasar. *(No, I know what is going to happen from the beginning of the novela, I know what is going to happen.)*

Victoria: Pero, yo pienso, tal vez es más entretenimiento. Está un rato allí y no pensar en otras cosas. No pensar en el dinero y qué vamos a hacer. Tal vez yo creo que ese es para entretenerse. *(But, I think, maybe it is just entertainment. It's a time when I'm there and not thinking about other things. I'm not thinking about money and what we are going to do. Maybe, I think it is for entertainment.)*

Victoria justifies her time watching the telenovela as an opportunity to escape the pressures of day-to-day life. She enjoys the predictability and allows herself this time. The same ideas are articulated in family #8. The mother is bilingual and does not work outside the home. She enjoys watching telenovelas and uses the time to relax. Her daughters, who moved to the United States when they were 11 and 12 and are now in their 20s, tease their mother for watching the programs.

KM: What do you like about the novelas?
María: It's just, there's good and bad, but they keep you like, "Oh, let's see what's going to happen with the bad guy or the good guy or if they're going to catch him or if they're going to kill him or...."
Diana: But you know!
María: You know he's going to die....
Diana: But you know how he's going to die. The moment you watch the first show you already know exactly what's going to happen. She's good and stupid. She's evil and smart. She's going to find a way to make it so that she's threatened and she's going to put her whole family in danger so that the stupid, good girl is going to cry, she's going to lose the love of her life, then they're going to kill the bad girl and everybody is going to be happy.
Jorge: That's true. Predictable of the same clichés. I'm sorry.
María: But anyways, it's my time, it's my hour. So don't ask me for dinner, nothing. It's my hour.
KM: It's okay that it's predictable?

María: Mmm hmm.

Diana is critical of her mother for watching what Diana perceives as low culture; her mother is purposeful in her enjoyment of her free time, which is consistent with other reception studies on telenovelas (Mayer, 2003a). The daughters did admit to the family getting hooked on what they consider to be "good ones." They describe a favorite, *El Clon*, produced by Brazil's TV Globo as *O Clone*, broadcast on TV Azteca in 2003, becoming a habit for the entire family.

Family #1 includes two young children ages 3 and 4 whose mother moved from Tijuana when she was one year old after her father died. The mother Lucia, a preschool teacher, is bilingual and does not watch a lot of television, but she and her husband (who emigrated from Guam) are fans of reality shows such as *Survivor*. When asked about telenovelas, Lucia admitted to watching them occasionally.

> Lucia: I see a huge difference between ... and I think I get caught up in the drama and what's going to happen–it's just different than the American soap operas.
> KM: Right.
> Freddie: Isn't there drama in those too?
> Lucia: There is but it's different, it's different cultures, it's different.
> Freddie: Oh, I see that.
> Lucia: You know, they have the señora who's cooking in the kitchen and they have these haciendas and it's...
> KM: Does it kind of remind you of Mexico?
> Lucia: Yeah, it brings me home a little bit because... I can't say it brings me home because I didn't grow up like that. But my family members now as adults, yeah, it feels real.

For family #3 telenovelas are not part of their media routine, but when thinking about them, the father, a marketing executive who immigrated to San Diego from Tijuana in 1984, explained his fondness for the novelas targeting children. His wife, who was born in San Diego, agreed that their daughter learned some Spanish:

Miguel: I like some of the programming that is in, like the novelas... *Amigos para siempre.* They had a healthy message, you know, the family and the kids having fun in a humble environment. I think that's something that us, on this side of the border, it's sort of what we miss, especially the parents. "Oh, look they are playing this game, that game, which we don't play here." So I think there's an identification of those elements, those cultural elements that they bring to the table and you go, "wow, that has a lot of cultural relevance for us."

Nora: Yeah because even with the novelas like *Rebelde* and *Amigos para siempre.* Alexa knew all the songs, all the words, it's not just the novela she watched, but you know, musically she enjoyed that as well. For me that was great because she was engaging in watching something in Spanish and developing her Spanish skills. There were other ones but they were when she was in school so she couldn't really watch those ones but she would come home and it's like, "Nana, it's 12 o'clock..." time for *Rebelde.* I even bought her the video set in Spanish.

Miguel: Those types of, like *Amigos para siempre* are for kids, but with those very grass roots, games and things that we used to do is probably what gained the interest of the kids. They'll say, "whoa, you used to do that?" or "that's so different," like breaking the piñata or playing with the kite, stuff like that.

The ability to share the heritage of the family with the children who have less firsthand experience with cultural elements echoes the findings of others who study the connections to home media by immigrant communities (Lemish, 2007; de Block & Buckingham, 2007). The families articulate that they feel connected to Mexico because they are able to stay updated on popular culture. Further, Mexican media instills a sense of nostalgia for home. Roberto, 18, and his mother, Claudia, of family #10, discuss telenovela viewing.

Roberto: And even when we do watch soap operas it's more to kind of laugh at them.

Claudia: naa.

Roberto: ...you know what's coming from miles away. So, it's not really for the thrill, maybe at one point in history they really were.

Claudia: But sometimes we were like "Oh, what's going to happen," but nowadays you kind of know. I mean you already know.

Roberto: You wish this would happen but you already know that's going to happen. Because they want to see it for another five seasons.

Claudia: I always say you have to watch the very beginning and the....you can miss a lot of things in the middle and then watch...a couple of things before the ending because the very, very ending is like also boring. Everything is like, as we expect it.

KM:...and when you watch novelas, does it make you feel closer to Mexico?

Claudia: ...yeah sometimes. I like that. And many of the gags and jokes and the things. I think we get them because it's part of the culture.

Roberto: I do think they kind of remind you of Mexico and that, for me, it's a good and a bad thing like you'll see something, I'll remember that part of Mexico then I'll miss that. But then you remember, the last time we watched I remember every other episode they had a scene where some mariachis came in and sang songs when they were eating the food. Then we're like "Oh, I'm glad I'm not in Mexico anymore cause we hate that." It reminds you of what you like about Mexico but it also reminds you of what you can't stand about Mexico.

While the family's telenovela viewing is downplayed, especially by Roberto, Claudia articulates her fondness for the genre and its ability to reinforce a sense of Mexicanness that is otherwise unavailable. The humor that is presented on Mexican television tends to reflect the culture of central Mexico (González Hernández, 2008), and that resonates with Claudia; she finds things funny because she is connected to culture. Her children are first generation, but not as connected to their Mexican heritage as their mother. For them, watching telenovelas functions to signal memories much in the same way that looking at photos from a trip might, rather than a longing for home. Claudia, on the other hand, misses Mexico and watching the novelas allows her to reminisce. Although the children were born in Mexico and have spent time there during childhood, they imagine it as a place they visit rather than as home.

The women in the sample, particularly those who would call themselves telenovela fans like those in families #6 and #7, Victoria, her daughter Angela, and sister Lola, all explained the importance of watching Televisa rather than Univisión for their favorite telenovelas. Due to international exportation and distribution agreement, Univisión must delay the broadcast until after Televisa debuts a program. There is a sense of cultural capital associated with being able to directly access media from Mexico. Telenovela viewing is a common cultural practice across Latin

America, and the genre has travelled well to other countries that have adopted the formula. The Spanish-language versions imported to the U.S. are popular among Latina/o audiences and are family entertainment. Despite their popularity, there exists a class bias associated with viewing that can be heard throughout the interviews. Members of higher status are less willing to admit to their telenovela viewing habit and are somewhat embarrassed to confess to getting hooked. Even those who readily admit to being fans are coy, often giggling when confessing their addiction acknowledging the perception of telenovelas as low culture. Some of the children were eager to tease their mothers for watching programs that are so predictable, but in their criticism they too express a connection to home by admitting that the programs remind them of their cultural heritage. Thomas Macias (2004) cautions not to overemphasize the ability of Spanish-language television to reinforce a Mexican identity. He concludes that "...the respondents' comments suggest that Spanish-language television works to reinforce Mexican ethnicity only to the degree that a prior connection to Mexican ethnicity, grounded in interpersonal relationships with other Mexican Americans, already exists" (p. 312). Diana Rios and Stanley Gaines (1998), however, discovered that connection to one's heritage can be a reliable predictor of media choice. In other words, the more connected one is to Mexico, by language or by culture, the more likely one is to choose Spanish-language programming.

Telenovelas in the U.S. Market

While it is evident that telenovelas are popular in Spanish, they have also made inroads in other areas of the U.S. market. In Spanish, they are delivered to Hispanic audiences through the Spanish-language networks and their cable affiliates. On a typical weekday, KBNT, the San Diego Univisión affiliate, airs six hours of novelas mostly imported from Mexico. Telemundo has adopted another strategy and that is to produce telenovelas in Spanish, but to produce and film in Miami. Further, there are various adaptations of the genre in English.

In an attempt to capitalize on the Latina/o audiences' affection for telenovelas, U.S. English-language networks have adapted specific stories for American audiences. While format adaptation is not new to the U.S. media marketplace, most adaptations have come from formats originating in the United Kingdom. Most notably reality programs such as *Survivor* and *Dancing with the Stars* and sitcoms such as *The Office* have been format adaptations. These formats require localization before entering the U.S. market by staffing the programs with American talent including script adaptations and the introduction of local humor. As a result of changing ownership patterns in 2006, a new network was created after the UPN and WB merged to become the CW. My Network TV, part of Rupert Murdoch's NewsCorp, entered the marketplace hoping to find its niche by adapting successful telenovelas to appeal to English-speaking audiences. The strategy had been successful in Eastern Europe and across South America. The network was launched featuring two serials: *Desire,* based on a Cuban series *Salir de Noche,* and *Fashion House*, adapted from *Mesa para tres*, a Colombian hit. The programs were filmed in San Diego by Stu Segall Productions and followed the traditional telenovela distribution model. They aired nightly (Monday through Friday) for 13 weeks at 8 p.m. and 9 p.m., respectively (McFarland, 2006).

The effort to capture the habitual viewing that is common in Latino households failed when the programs were adapted to the English-language market. The average rating rarely rose above a half of a rating point (Carter, 2006), far below what the network needed to ensure a long-term commitment to the genre. Many speculated about the failure of telenovelas for U.S. audiences. First, U.S.-born Latina/os are more likely to watch the novelas in Spanish in a family setting. Typically when they watch television in English, as demonstrated by the families interviewed for this project, they choose popular, general market programming. Second, the relentless production schedule, which demanded practically around the clock filming to keep pace with the 40 or so pages of script each day, was difficult and expensive to maintain (Carter,

2006). The fast-paced production schedule reduced the quality, resulting in a product that looked substandard in comparison to other programs. In the Latin American versions, this style has become a genre convention, but was not tolerated by U.S. audiences, who expect the production quality of the major networks. Further, English-speaking audiences are not accustomed to a prime-time schedule that offers new episodes nightly. The adaptations of telenovleas internationally mostly have been in markets with a history of the genre or in emerging media markets such as Eastern Europe where audiences are looking for programming with a history of success and can be localized to ensure cultural relevance. In emerging markets, these adaptations serve to provide jobs within the domestic industry, whereas in the United States, there are many production outlets. For audiences in the U.S. there are too many other programs from which to choose, making the production demands not worth the risk of additional failures.

The English-language telenovela story continues, however, with *Ugly Betty*, adapted from the Colombian *Yo soy Betty la fea*, which tells the story of a plain looking, hard working woman who is employed at a fashion magazine. With Salma Hayek as one of the executive producers and aired on ABC, *Ugly Betty* was positioned for a strong showing within the marketplace. ABC changed the distribution of its adaptation to bring it more in line with traditional network fare: *Ugly Betty* aired once a week and followed the traditional U.S. seasonal format. According to Nielsen ratings early seasons of the program were successful, but it never outperformed Univisión's *La fea más bella,* the Mexican version of *Yo soy Betty la fea,* which retained the traditional nightly broadcast schedule and drew more Spanish-speaking Latina/os while it was scheduled against ABC's *Betty*. Prior to the launch of *Ugly Betty*, ABC hired a Hispanic marketing agency to draw Latina/o audiences. ABC's version premiered to 1.26 million Hispanic viewers, nearly two and half times as many as the other English-language networks combined (de la Fuente, 2006). In September 2006 it was showcased in an 8:00 p.m. time slot before the network's hit *Grey's Anatomy*. For the October 2009 season premiere, the program was moved to Friday night at 8:00 and was fourth in its time slot (behind Major League Baseball playoffs and other popular series), rendering the long-term success of *Ugly Betty* unpredictable. In an effort to regain its audience, ABC moved it to Wednesdays at 10 p.m. in January 2010. The ratings in its new time slot were not enough to keep it on the air. On January 29, 2010, news broke that ABC would cancel the program after the completion of its fourth season (Wyatt, 2010). Despite its ultimately lackluster ratings, the program was honored by the ALMA Awards,[11] winning in 2008 for "Outstanding Television Series." Lead actress America Ferrera picked up the ALMA's 2008 "Outstanding Actress" award. As the show wrapped up its final season, much praise was given for its groundbreaking portrayals of Latina/o characters and for its treatment of issues such as illegal immigration.

Engaging in a textual analysis, Guillermo Avila-Saavedra (2010) examines the presentation of a U.S. Latino identity on the program. He determines that the inclusion of a Latino family "constructs a notion of U.S.-Latino identity as 'other' defined in opposition to non-Latinos" (p. 145). In the U.S. version of *Ugly Betty,* the immigrant storyline is presented in season one as audiences (and Betty and her sister) learn of the father Ignacio's illegal status. Betty and her family were positioned as both culturally assimilated and outside dominant culture with the secret of Ignacio's illegal entrance into the United States. The sympathetic treatment of Ignacio's storyline helped the audience understand his individual circumstances that concluded with his achieving legal status. *Ugly Betty* provided a strong representation of a Latino family on primetime broadcast television. The collectivist dynamic of the Suárez family was contrasted with the dysfunctional aspects of the other families on the program. According to Avila-Saavedra (2010) this strengthens the perception that Latino family values are in opposition to U.S. individualism, which appears to leave the Anglo characters unfulfilled. Even though this works to position the Latino family as enviable, it is from a position that is Othered.

The participants in this sample reflected the patterns of viewers across the nation. Spanish dominant viewers were more interested in watching the Mexican version available in San Diego, and when English dominant audience members watched television, they were not interested in the U.S. version of *Ugly Betty*. Family members in this sample did not report regular viewing and were more likely to watch telenovelas in Spanish because they offered them something different from the content choices on English-language television. The women in family #6, who describe themselves as telenovela fans, were not regular viewers of *Ugly Betty*.

> KM: Do you guys ever watch *Ugly Betty*?
> Angela: Well, we watch it in Spanish. *La fea más bella.*
> Rosa: ¿Y está en inglés? *(And it's in English?)*
> KM: Now it's in English, yeah, *Ugly Betty*.
> Angela: Esas novelas casi son comedias. Son chistosas. *(Those novelas are more like comedies. They are funny.)*
> KM: ¿Pero nunca ha visto *Ugly Betty* en inglés? *(But, you've never seen* Ugly Betty *in English?)*
> Angela: Una vez, no más. *(One time, no more.)*

Angela, a self-identified fan of telenovelas, had little interest in the English adaptation of the program. She is bilingual and watches programs in English, but for her the genre demands the qualities found in the Spanish-language version. She had not heard of other attempts to adapt the genre and had not viewed any other English-language adaptations. Mona, the daughter in family #8 who admitted getting hooked on *El Clon*, was familiar with *Ugly Betty*, but not a fan. Her sister and mother knew little of the American version.

> KM: Have you ever seen *Ugly Betty*, the American version?
> Mona: Yes.
> María: No.
> Diana: No.
> KM: Do you like it?
> Mona: I saw one episode with my very gay friend who is in love with the guy in the show because we wanted to watch something else and he was like "No! We're at my house, we're watching *Ugly Betty*." So we watched his episode of *Ugly Betty*, and it was, I mean it was okay but it wasn't anything particularly...
> Diana: Is it a movie now? *Ugly Betty*?
> KM: It's a TV show.
> María: There was one originally a long time ago, I think the name was *La fea más bella*.

Diana: *La fea más bella* is the Mexican one.
María: And then they took *La fea, o Betty La fea...*
Diana: The original one is *Betty la fea...*
Mona: With the girl from the pants, the *Traveling Pants*...It was okay.
KM: So you don't have any interest in watching it again?
Mona: Not particularly.

Jimena, 17, family #16, told me she enjoys watching telenovelas, but has to reserve time for homework and other activities. I asked her whether she watched *Ugly Betty*.

KM: Have you ever seen *Ugly Betty?* The U.S. version?
Jimena: No, I have seen the Colombian version and the Mexican version.
KM: What one did you like better?
Jimena: The Colombian version.

The assumption was that U.S. Latina/os would be eager to watch the program because of Latina/o casting, but there was no mention of the Latina/o cast of characters by the participants in this study. For the most part, the family members did not find *Ugly Betty* appealing in the same way as traditional telenovelas.

While family members did not specifically refer to Latina/o representation in reference to this program, many participants articulated a general desire for more diverse imagery in the media. As genre and format adaptations become increasingly more common in the global television market (Straubhaar, 2007), it would follow that the U.S. market will see more of this type of glocal[12] programming. As evidenced in earlier chapters, U.S.-born bilingual, bicultural Latina/os will continue to shape the direction of the media industry encouraging more programming that attempts to recreate the experiences they encounter on the Spanish-language channels hoping to lure them to the mainstream outlets. The evidence also shows that audiences who move between both television worlds are not eager for them to collide. When bilingual audiences want to watch a telenovela, they prefer the original version rather than the U.S. adaptation.

The telenovela style is not completely lost on English-language audiences, but in prime time audiences, have not supported a formula that demands nightly viewing. ABC's *Desperate Housewives* has been held up as an American example of a type of telenovela, incorporating lessons from Latin American favorites. In fact, ABC sold the adaptation rights, and local versions of the program can be found in Mexico, Argentina, Colombia, and Brazil. Further complicating the global/local dynamic, *Desperate Housewives* was adapted for Spanish-speaking audiences in the U.S. by Univisión, which broadcast the foreign/local version in 2008. The flow of telenovelas throughout the hemisphere provides insight into the changing dynamics of the television marketplace. Differentiations among programs based on their foreign or domestic status are out-dated, prompting consideration of cultural proximity theory em-phasizing communities that are not bound by geography but by cultural-linguistic spheres. As outlined elsewhere in the book, the United States is home to examples of specialized versions of do-mestic programs and networks, such as MTVtr3s, that are target-ed toward the Latina/o market assumed to be either Spanish dominant or bilingual and bicultural.

Getting News from "Home"

The sample family members revealed that their media con-sumption in Spanish is shaped by what they perceive to be missing in the English-language market and one of the areas that most members express that home media is superior is in the presenta-tion of news. Many participants feel the mainstream English-language news outlets do not cover issues relative to their inter-ests in meaningful ways. For many, Mexican news is better. Watching news is not a favorite pastime activity for many chil-dren, but the teenagers in the sample discussed the ways in which they receive information and were critical of mainstream English-language news. The parents, who were much more likely to have opinions about news, were critical of the news in the U.S. in both Spanish and English. Parents with higher levels of education and proficient Spanish skills were more likely to articulate a desire to watch news directly from Mexico. Again because of San Diego's geographical proximity to Mexico, even families who are not connected to satellite or cable are able to watch news directly from Tijuana and Mexico City.

For immigrant families, the desire to stay connected to news from home is evident. Families who are Spanish-language dominant also watch some local San Diego news in Spanish on KBNT. Spanish-language news media in the U.S. have traditionally centered on providing a service to their audience by introducing them to information relevant to the immigrant experience (Casteñda, 2008a; Moran, 2006). The type of coverage on KBNT is consistent with what Rodríquez (1999a) calls "service-oriented" journalism. "The Latino news audience is also understood as people in need of particular information about, and/or orientation to, dominant society institutions and practices" (Rodriquez, 1999, p. 108). Even though the Spanish-language news source provides a "how to" service to encourage democratic participation and provide information for new residents, few of the sample families articulated using news for that purpose.

The bilingual parents in family #7 described their preferences for news from Mexico City through channel 57, which is local news for Mexico City but has national distribution. I asked them to describe the news they watch:

> Lola: Las noticias sí son de Televisa. *[Yes, the news is from Televisa.]*
> Alejandro: Porque las noticias son nacional y aquí son regionales los de Tijuana, Baja California... *[Because that news is national and here it is regional...from Tijuana, Baja California]*
> KM: ¿Y cuál prefieres? *[And which do you prefer?]*
> Alejandro: Me gustan las nacionales *[I like the national news]*
> KM: ¿Por qué? *[Why]*
> Alejandro: Por que estamos enterrados de lo que está pasando. Fíjate en las nacionales...porque ellos también se enfocan mucho en la ciudad de México y qué pasa allí, lo que es el rol en su colonia, porque son de la ciudad de México, y pues verdad, pero no, no, no conoces que está pasando allí. Las noticias de allí son también locales aunque sean nacionales de canal. *[Because what is happening there is buried from us [in the San Diego news]. If you pay attention to the national news...because they also focus a lot on Mexico City and what happens there, the role in the colony, because it's from Mexico City,*

and well true you don't always know what is going on. The news from
there is also local even though it is the national news of the channel.]
KM: ¿A veces ven las noticias en inglés de San Diego? *[Do you ever*
watch the news in English from San Diego?]
Alejandro: A veces pero no mucho. *[Sometimes, but not much.]*

A more global outlook is desired on the part of some of the family members; many mentioned that Mexican news is better because it focuses on international viewpoints. The experiences of the immigrant families articulate a transnational perspective that was not present in the interviews with families who had been in the United States for multiple generations.

Manuel, family #4, came to San Diego as a child and explains that he remains connected to Mexico and Latin America through news and holds the opinion that English-language news is inadequate in its coverage of important events outside the United States. Further, he does not watch local Spanish-language news because of what he perceives as its bias toward a "Latino" perspective. He critiques the emphasis on the new immigrant experience and a political bias toward a democratic viewpoint.

Manuel: I try to watch Mexican news.
Jennifer: That's right, you watch a lot of Mexican news, every morning for like an hour.
Manuel: I like the one on Galavisión that comes straight out of Mexico City. I don't like the one side. It's just to me, I don't know I feel like there's something missing. The one that comes out of Mexico City, it covers more about the rest of the world, not just in the area, in general and unfortunately, I got to say, watching Univisión, it's very bias, in their political view and their agenda.
KM: Univisión, do you mean their national news or the local San Diego news?
Manuel: When it comes to local news I think it's very biased and very Latino oriented and I don't think they're putting out there, both sides of the story, so to me...I kind of march to a different drummer when it comes down to my beliefs. It kind of irritates me a little bit.
KM: Do you think it's biased to the Latino point of view?
Manuel: Correct, obviously, and I don't think they're fair, to me they, as democrats point of view as well, as big supporters. I'm independent and I come and go as, whatever fits my own world in my head. So, it's just very

biased to me, the one that comes out of Mexico City, it covers Europe a lot, it covers the Middle East, and it covers South America...
Jennifer: ...it covers South America and Central America really, really well. Because it's amazing to me because everything that's going on right now between Ecuador, Colombia, and Venezuela, there hasn't been any mention of it on ABC World [News Tonight], I haven't heard anything on KPBS in the morning.

Communication scholars critique U.S. English-language news for its ethnocentric focus and lackluster international reporting, which have been associated with the business imperative within a commercial system (Schudson, 1995). Journalists are connected to professional routines of news-gathering informed by professional rituals that impact the perceived newsworthiness. Further, the lack of diversity within the newsroom leads to the homogenization of news reporting focusing primarily on stories that are relevant to a white, middle class audience (Heider, 2003). "Black and Latino managers themselves may not feel comfortable pushing story ideas about underrepresented communities [because] these types of stories are not valued" (Heider, 2003, p. 86). Traditionally, news in the U.S. has a national focus privileging events that are perceived as entertaining to ensure audiences that are appealing to advertisers (Moran, 2006).

While many sample participants were critical of Spanish-language media and identified using media in English for entertainment purposes, family members praise news from Mexico. As members of a global society, the bilingual participants, even the teenagers, express a preference for international news sources. Again, elements of class were present in the discussion evidenced by the fact that the older children in homes with more cultural capital were more likely to pay attention to news. The parents, across the board, were critical of both the Spanish and English networks in the U.S.

Ernesto (family #10): I think, personally, in my experience... I have been of course all over the world...the U.S. is particularly parochial in the news. For example, I remember, still during the Soviet Era, the first time I went to Russia, at the time The Soviet Union, I was amazed to find the news and the newspapers had around 60% of their content was international news and they were very good. As a matter of fact, it was quite good. Quite objective. I don't think people knew about what was going on in the rest of the world. The U.S. in that sense is a microcosm. People don't know about what's going on in the rest of the world.

Ernesto continues to critique U.S. news coverage of Latin America and in particular Cuba. The interview occurred not long after Fidel Castro handed power to his brother Raul and the lifting of a number of restrictions on Cuban nationals.

Ernesto: I don't know if you guys are aware of this. Yesterday [March 30, 2008], the government of Cuba authorized Cubans to buy freely in all shops, including the famous people *tiendas* [shops] they can buy anything. They got to have cell phones. Cell phones were authorized like four days ago. And they can now access to every Cuban hotel without discrimination. The tourist hotels were only for tourists. And that was done, it was a sweeping move. It was, you know, it was one day the cell phones two days later the access to hotels and yesterday was the elimination of separated stores for Cubans and visitors. And it barely came out in the news here.

Claudia: I saw it in *Reforma*.[13]

Ernesto: In Mexico, in the Mexican newspapers it was like, eight columns. It was a big deal. Because I think it means a lot. It should mean more for the States because of economic interests at stake than for Mexico, but it didn't appear here.

Roberto: I think it is partly the fault of the American media, like CNN. All these other news outlets too they got this big ball rolling about Barack Obama and Hillary Clinton and what's going on with them and John McCain. I mean that's all you see today. In class during 4th period I have 24-hour fitness. I'll be on the bikes watching CNN; it's like, literally the only thing they talked about.

Claudia: It's kind of obsessive sometimes.

Roberto: ...and then it's like they have this huge ball rolling so like nothing they can talk about so they keep spewing out the same crap. But once they had this going all they, you know once they have this thing hooked on when something important did happen like what's going on in Cuba, they can't afford to switch to that because people are kind of already on this rail.

Pilar: I think that a lot of times, if I don't hear it at home, I don't hear about it at all. Because if I do watch the news on TV here in San Diego, I'm not going to hear about it and school, very rarely, will my classes or my peers talk about what's going on in Cuba. Like, really, honestly if I hear about things like that it's at home, at dinner, with my family, talking about it.

Roberto, 18, and Pilar, 15, have a broader awareness of international issues because of their family dynamic; they have travelled and have spent time in both the U.S. and Mexico. The father spends a lot of time reviewing international news sources online and relays much of that information to his children. The parents are ensuring that their children have a global perspective and encourage them to look past the mainstream news in the United States.

Latina/os have been woefully underrepresented in English-language news broadcasts and when Latina/os are featured, it is commonly in stories about crime or immigration issues. During 2005, of the 12,600 stories aired on the national news broadcasts of ABC, CBS, and NBC, 105 (0.83%) were about Latina/os (Montalvo, 2006). While family #10 is interested in international sources, others are critical of English-language news coverage of Latina/os and Latin America.

> Jorge: Did I tell you my perception of the *San Diego Union Tribune* on Mexico? Mexico has a lot of problems they need to fix, but there's obviously the stereotype about Mexico, which is most of the times, bad or folkloric. And I keep watching the same line perpetrate stereotypes on Mexico. That's what makes the *San Diego Union Tribune* a very provincial newspaper. Anytime they talked about Mexico, it's on a stereotype basis, mostly negative things. Decapitations, drug cartels, whatever. They never mention why the cartels are fighting or where the drugs are supposed to be distributed. But that's different. The classical double standard: what's in Mexico is terrible and what's here is just an error...that's the treatment the *San Diego Union Tribune* gives to Mexico.
> KM: What do you think would be helpful to reduce the stereotypes?
> Jorge: I want to reduce the stereotypes. I want to be objective. Stereotypes trace a line of judgment, or different objective, being objective in not only the quantity but the quality of the news. And I know that good things don't sell much, but, there are some positive things.

Both Jorge (family #8) and Ernesto (family #10) are well educated and are instilling a knowledge of global affairs in their children through modeling the importance of being well informed and also passing along the information through interpersonal channels. Santiago, 14, family #12, agreed that there should be more global coverage in U.S. news, a sentiment that was echoed by other participants. He also wanted to challenge the stereotypes that are perpetuated in national news programs.

> Santiago: Let's clear up that stereotype that we are not "raggy" people. That we are not poor, lazy and disheveled, and to clear up that all Mexicans are illegal because that is not true.

His mother interjects that news in Mexico is better because of its international coverage and because it presents positive stories about Americans while the U.S networks only report on the negative aspects of life in Mexico.

> Mariana: They [U.S. news programs] don't care about us and we are very close to the border and when there is news about us it is only bad news. So there is no balance between news. Over there we have news about the States, good and bad, but here you only get the bad news, and usually when that happens I don't really like it.
> KM: What is the bad news?
> Mariana: Poverty, violence and environment, how polluted the water is or the river is... but usually they don't take responsibility for what is going on in both countries.
> KM: Do you think the way the news covers Mexico impacts how people think about Mexico or Mexicans?
> Mariana: Yes, definitely Yes. We have BAs or Masters degrees and my son attends a good school where the people are more educated. But living here just 2 blocks up the hill there is a big big contrast and people who come to the States looking for a better future, I believe those are who suffer the most because of stereotypes. The news affects how people see us.

The teenagers who were first generation were most concerned about the negative imagery of Mexico in U.S. English-language news. Jimena, 17, family #16, spends a lot of time in Tijuana and feels the U.S. networks do a disservice by portraying Mexico as a dangerous place.

> Jimena: You hear "don't go to Mexico because everyone is dying over there," but not every single part of Mexico is a dangerous place to go. If you go to TJ, yeah, it is a dangerous place to go but if you go further to the south it's more calm.

Interestingly, she expresses the opinion that Tijuana is a dangerous place following into the same discourse she is critiquing.

The U.S. news coverage of Mexico in recent years has covered mainly crime, drug trafficking, and immigration, which according to the participants, limits the perceptions of the country for those who have little firsthand knowledge. In San Diego, border reporters work to provide a broader view of Mexico often travelling to Tijuana to gain access to Mexican sources, a strategy that is uncommon for national news. An example of this coverage is seen when *San Diego Union Tribune* journalist Sandra Dibble reports that as the July 2010 mayoral elections heat up in Tijuana, the topics on the agenda include public safety, public transportation and the economy (Dibble, 2010). Another example of this more balanced style is seen with Amy Isackson, border reporter for the local NPR affiliate, KPBS, who reports that in an effort to combat the representation of Tijuana as dangerous, city officials have engaged in a public relations campaign to change the perception to entice tourists to return to Mexico (Isackson, 2010) rather than only reporting on the release of the U.S. State Department's travel warning. This type of reporting is rare in most U.S. newsrooms, and even in San Diego, Dibble and Isackson are among only a handful of journalists who focus exclusively on this beat.

The coverage of Mexico and Latina/o issues does not change dramatically when considering domestic news in Spanish. For the most part, the coverage follows traditional news values and concentrates primarily on crime and conflict. Spanish-language news serves a purpose in the United States by providing much more information about issues facing a Latina/o community than English-language national or local news, but it is not alternative in the traditional sense of the word (Moran, 2006). The industry's structure demonstrates that it is not small, it is not outside corporate control, it must sell its audience to advertisers, and as such, functions in the same way as other mainstream mass media. Univisión and its local affiliates are appealing to a mass audience in Spanish using the lowest common denominator approach, which masks the diversity within the Latina/o community and relies on news stories that are entertaining, perhaps at the expense of information that is important to the diverse community of Latina/os living within San Diego County. Changing the language may be beneficial because it provides access to information for Spanish-speakers, but for the Spanish dominant families in this sample, they are more likely to access news in Spanish from Mexico. Family members also critique KBNT for following the journalistic conventions of mainstream reporting and feel like the news is dumbed down. From the industry perspective, this is done to attract the largest possible audience for advertisers. As Spanish-language news continues to outperform its English-language competitors in markets where there are large numbers of Latina/os, it is likely that this trend will continue and further rely on ways that produce content that is cheap, but profitable. The reliance on non-local, national programming on Spanish-language channels mimics the economic strategy of the English-language networks that create news that is repackaged and broadcast in a variety of cities (Castañeda, 2008a). As Latina/os search for news and information, they are looking toward international sources including websites that provide a more global outlook than the national news in either English or Spanish.

Television on the Border

The families interviewed offer insight into the use of television in a border context; their geographic location affords them a flexibility not seen in the interior regions of the United States or Mexico. The media system within the United States offers Latina/os many ways to stay connected to media from their native culture. The flexibility provides an opportunity for the development of a multilayered, transnational identity that informs the way in which they negotiate meanings as they interpret the images presented. As families spend more time in the U.S., it appears that they maintain their ties to programming that is culturally relevant. Even when they find problems with the content, first generation family members have a nostalgic view of their home productions. That is not to say they are not also consuming mainstream U.S.

programming as evidenced in Chapter 3. The family members, especially youth, consume media in ways that demonstrate their ability to navigate multiple systems.

In a study about on youth in Tijuana, David González Hernández (2008) discovered a similar pattern of cross border consumption. He found that *Tijuaneneses* youth were accessing U.S. television because they found it to be more appealing than local offerings. Bilingual youth in the border region demonstrate what González labels a "double competence...which serves as a basis for appraisal of two national television systems" (p. 230). The fact that the participants in the study can compare and contrast two national systems exemplifies their transnational status and identification with a hybrid identity. Further, the Mexican youth in Tijuana perceived U.S. television as symbolically modern and fun, whereas Mexican programming was seen as traditional and boring. This perception was also present within the families I spoke with although not articulated in the same manner. The parents were more likely to watch Mexican television voicing a desire for the traditional, while their children were more likely to watch U.S. programming. Young people in the border region have a fondness for the same type of programming reinforcing the creation of a global youth culture that transcends traditional borders. In fact, González states that access to international media systems can perform a "psychic mobility" (p. 231) where youth are not bound by their locality but move from place to place through their media consumption.

One can only imagine this symbolic border crossing happening more easily as young people utilize media in new ways to connect with friends regardless of physical space. The dynamics within the families show generational differences, both in terms of age and time spent in the country and between the parents and the children regarding their preference for and use of media from "home." The symbolic border crossing that is made possible through their exposure to multiple media has led to the creation of a transnational subculture that is not bound by political borders, but linked through their symbolic connections. Previous research into the creation of a third culture or a cosmopolitan class has been associated with high levels of cultural capital and often the movement of people through specific localities. What makes the border region unique is that travel, the hallmark of cosmopolitanism, is unnecessary as the youth in this region participate in symbolic border crossings almost daily. As media systems open up throughout the United States, this cosmopolitan identity, once reserved for the elite, has been made accessible across class lines. Cosmopolitans, as conceptionalized by scholar Ulf Hannerz (1990), are primarily those people who are able to travel throughout the world and experience the variations among cultures and when home inform the locals of the vast world. As transnational media systems make it possible for all members, regardless of mobility, to experience cultural difference through mediated channels, more people can become symbolically cosmopolitan. The families with lower levels of economic capital are able to acquire cultural capital through their exposure to international media sources. Jimena, 17, whose family #16 would fall on the lower end of the economic spectrum, finds herself better prepared to participate in this transnational culture because of her physical and symbolic border experience. The discourses of the first generation immigrant youth demonstrate this cosmopolitan outlook as their critiques of U.S. media include its ethnocentric focus. This global perspective was articulated by Santiago, 14 (family #12), when asked what he would change about U.S. television. He answered, "maybe make it more universal not just national so you can tell what is going on in the world not just the country." In many ways the children in Latino families are well prepared to participate in the changing dynamics of not just the border region, but of a broader global culture. The young people experience transnationalism in their daily lives by accessing media from many sources. Further, their family communication, influenced by their parents' immigrant status, reinforces the transnational experience, moving them into the cosmopolitan sphere.

Chapter 5

Concerning Representation: Latina/os in English-Language Media

As outlined in previous chapters, young people and their parents are careful and selective when deciding to engage with media. While discussing their media habits, most were critical of some form of content whether it was related to specific programs or more general topics such as stereotyping of Latina/o characters. Some participants were optimistic about the trajectory of Latina/os in the media industry, but remained worried about the relationship between the media images and audience perception. First generation immigrants had more direct concerns about the representation of Mexico specifically tied to drug trafficking, violence, and immigration while others were critical of the imagery of Latinas as either too sexy or as maids. As conversations emerged from the interviews, it became evident that the participants negotiate their understanding of the texts with which they interact. From a critical approach we can understand the readings articulated by the family members as part of the deconstructive process that contests a singular view of audience reception.

Latina/o Imagery

Historically, it has been well documented that Latino characters have been underrepresented in all types of English-language programming (Klein & Shiffman, 2006; Mastro & Behm-Morawitz, 2005; Mastro & Stern, 2003; Li-Vollmer, 2002; Subervi-Vélez, Berg, Constantakis-Valdés, Noriega, Ríos, & Wilkinson, 1994). In fact, Dana Mastro and Elizabeth Behm-Morawitz (2005) found that among prime-time TV show characters, Latina/os accounted for 3.9% and in prime-time TV commercials Latina/os accounted for only 1% of all characters (Mastro & Stern, 2003). In commercials broadcast during children's programming 2.4% were classified as Latina/o (Li-Vollmer, 2002). One might assume that representation has increased during the past few years given the industry's focus on the Hispanic market and the attention to census data, which reports Hispanic population growth, but that is not the case. It is true that since 1998 Latina/o representation has doubled in mainstream media, jumping from 3.5% to 6.4% in 2008, but that is still far below the numbers of Latina/os living in the U.S. In terms of proportional representation to the general population, the representation of Latina/os compared to other minority groups in the United States is problematic. For example, African Americans are holding steady at close to 15% of television roles while their percentage of population holds at approximately 13% of the total U.S. while Latina/o roles remain at 6.4% despite reaching close to 15% of the population (A Different America, 2007).

Although their overall percentage of roles is small in comparison to other groups, some notable Latina/o actors have enjoyed recent success, but as scholars point out, the new representations do not necessarily improve audience perceptions of Latina/os (Harewood & Valdivia, 2005; Markert, 2007; Martínez, 2007; Merskin, 2007; Lee et al., 2009) or alternatively lead audiences to believe that Latina/os have assimilated and no longer struggle with civil rights. Esteban del Río (2006) cautions that positive representations need to be examined as much as unflattering portrayals. As Latina/os enjoy more visibility in mainstream culture "...representations of Latina/o success, sexiness, assimilation, and acceptance by mainstream culture require...new questions" (del Río, 2006, p. 390) and the popularity of a few stars may mask the on going disparities that persist in Latina/o representation.

Latina/os have been present in the mainstream media from the early days of Hollywood and heyday of the network era. More often than not, however, they have been relegated to stereotypical roles including criminals or bandits, sexually aggressive and sexually desirable, and/or as buffoons (see, for example, Lichter & Amundson, 1997; Pieraccini & Alligood, 2005; Mastro & Behm-

Morawitz, 2005; Merskin, 2007; Lee, Bichard, Irey, Walt, & Carlson, 2009; Mastro & Ortiz, 2008; Rivadeneyra, 2006; Subervi-Vélez, et al., 1994). The imagery has become a point of contention as Latina/o audiences become frustrated with the lack of imagination and diversity associated with the portrayals.

Historic images of Latino men centered on the bandito or renegade of the "wild west." Similar to Native Americans in early Hollywood westerns, Mexicans represented a particular enemy encountered on the frontier of early California and other southwestern states. *Zorro,* an adventure program featuring the infamous swashbuckler, includes narratives about early California pitting the cultured Spaniards against the villainous Mexicans (Wilson & Gutiérrez, 1995). The bandito image became so commonplace that it was invoked in advertising campaigns including the "Frito Bandito" used to brand Fritos corn chips (Noriega, 2000). One of the most prevalent Latino television characters was Desi Arnaz who played Ricky Ricardo on the *I Love Lucy* show. "His Latin temperament, which exploded into a torrent of Spanish diatribe when Lucy's ill-fated activities were revealed, was classic stereotyped imagery" (Wilson & Gutiérrez, 1995, p. 100). As the folklore of the Southwest matured, the images of Latino men changed to include Latin lovers, laborers, criminals, and immigrants (Pieraccini & Alligood, 2005; Subervi-Vélez et al., 1994). Drug traffickers are also a common image that reinforces many of the stereotypes related to illegal drug trade (Shaw, 2005).

Latinas hold an exotic, tropical space highlighting their sexuality (Molina Guzmán & Valdivia, 2004; Aparicio & Chávez-Silverman, 1997) or alternatively as maids or other service workers (Rivadeneyra, 2006). Early images in film characterized Latinas as sensual and "firey" (Cortés, 1997), a stereotype that has stayed with Latinas into the contemporary era. Latina/o media scholars have described the impact of the limited imagery on audiences focusing attention on the discourses that surround particular texts and posit that one of the consequences of a stereotyped and limited imagery is the containment of a homogenized Latinidad that produces a singular notion of being Latina that is ripe for consumption by mainstream audiences. Debra Merskin

(2007) describes the representation of Eva Langoria's character on ABC's *Desperate Housewives* as furthering the "hot Latina stereotype" that remains uncontested in most mainstream portrayals. The consequences of stereotypical imagery "go beyond obvious manifestations such as name-calling or facile characterizations...[they] are, at least in part, responsible for the denial of opportunity for Latinas in their struggle for identity" (Merskin, 2007, p. 148).

Given the political economy of the mass media in the United States, the reliance on stereotyping is not surprising. Stereotyping has been a common practice across media as a tool for comedy and other genre conventions. Further, relying on stereotypes proves to be less economically risky because audiences know what to expect and since they are not challenged to reassess their own perspectives, they are less likely to change the channel. The networks have often canceled programs that have dealt with ethnic difference in significant ways. For example, *I Married Dora*, a short-lived series on ABC that premiered in the fall 1987 season, "dealt meaningfully with Latino immigration to the United States and the misconceptions the two cultures often have about one another" (Subervi-Vélez et al., 1994, p. 313). It was cancelled after 13 episodes.

Public television has made various attempts to promote ethnically diverse programming, and efforts in the late 1960s through the 1970s focused in part on programs that featured Latina/os. The Ford Foundation initiated a funding stream in response to the Kerner Commission findings indicating that media impacted audiences' racial attitudes. As a result of the Ford Foundation's grants, the PBS affiliate in Los Angeles (KCET) broadcast three programs aimed at "dealing with social issues facing the barrio" (Noriega, 2000). The success of the bilingual telenovela *Canción de la raza (Song of the People)* promoted its rebroadcast in other markets with a high number of Latina/os in the audience. The experiences depicted East L.A., but did not resonate with the diverse Latina/o population in other regions such as New York. Another pioneering effort at bilingual and bicultural programming is *¿Qué Pasa, USA?* funded through the Florida Department of Education and produced by the local PBS station in South Florida (WPBT), which has been repackaged and is now distributed through the Generation-ñ website (www.generation-n.com). Produced by PBS between 1977 and 1980, the complete series comprises 39 episodes that highlight the experiences of Cubans in Miami by centering the sitcom on the Peña family. These programs provide examples of Latino-themed programming that attempt to break down stereotypes many years before the 2000 Census spawned the current crop of Latino-themed shows. Of course, the difference between the programs offered on public television versus the efforts of the major conglomerates today lies in the latter's commercial motives.

Even within media produced for the Latina/o audience, research has found patterns of stereotyping that mimic the general market trends. For example, Dana Mastro and Michelle Ortiz (2008) discovered that the representation of women in Spanish-language television follows the patterns of gender representation in mainstream network fare emphasizing traditional gender roles as well as youth and beauty. Rocío Rivadeneyra (2006) studied adolescents' perceptions of Latina/o imagery and discovered that the participants rated Spanish-language media as less stereotypical than English-language programming, possibly because there are far more images overall. In audience research conducted by Viviana Rojas (2004), participants revealed their criticism of the sexualized representation of women on Spanish-language television commenting on the programs *El Show de Crisitina* broadcast on Univisión and *Laura en América* aired on Telemundo. Rojas (2004) explains: "On the one hand Latinas and Latinos appear misrepresented in Univisión and Telemundo, but at the same time these networks are also the most visible representation of their existence as a group within the U.S. society" (pp. 146–147). Studies related to Latina imagery in media targeted specifically to this group show a preference for lighter skin tones. Melissa Johnson, Prabu David, and Dawn Huey-Ohlsson (2003) found an overreliance on models with light skin in advertisements in Latina magazines published in the U.S. The authors explain: "To put it bluntly, out of 1,579 women's photos, 8 women were black-skinned, and more than 1,300 were light-skinned" (Johnson et al., 2003, p. 165). The representation of Latina/os in Spanish-language media, and more recently in Latino-themed media in English, follows similar patterns that have been identified in commercial media systems worldwide. Media organizations that rely on advertising revenue usually find the path of least resistance, and in the media industry that means sexualized, sensational, and stereotyped content. All commercial media in the U.S. can be critiqued from this perspective.

The patterns that emerge when studying the ways in which Latina/os have been characterized within the mainstream media are part of a broader ideological apparatus that functions to reinforce the logic of our social system. While some respondents resist the patriarchal and racializing discourses, resistance is not often modeled within the mainstream media (Thiel, 2005). More often than not, the younger participants have not been conditioned to resist; rather they have been interpellated by the mainstream media in ways that reinforce their position as Other, even as they see new opportunities. The industry has indeed created a space for Latina/os within the logic of the capitalist system, but the system will always function hegemonically to stabilize society rather than promote dissent.

Audience Response:
The Good, the Bad, and the "Spicy"

The participants in this study describe their perceptions of Latina/o imagery in the media by problematizing and contesting stereotypes. During the family interviews, the topic of Latina/o representation was addressed. The young adults in family #8 discuss the imagery. Mona, a 23-year-old fan of the Food Network, is not happy with a commercial that plays on the ethnic flavor of Mexico. Her sister, Diana, 22, agrees that the representation is annoying.

Mona: There was an obnoxious commercial on Food Channel. "Siempre delicioso."
KM: What makes it obnoxious?
Mona: Oh it's this lady trying to be Mexican and pretending to speak Spanish when really she does not. And she's like, "Oh salsa!" It's stereotypical.
Diana: Yeah that whole like, "Rrrra! Ole Mexico!" That stuff is pretty bad.
Mona: Like, they find the stereotypes and they stick to them.
Diana: Another thing is sometimes people won't believe me when I tell them there are blue-eyed Mexicans. They're like, "No way." That stuff, you know. It doesn't give you the full thing of what really, the entire culture, it just gives you the whole like "Oh Latino. Salsa. Spicy. Feisty women."

Both Mona and Diana articulate resistance to the common trope of describing Latin culture as "spicy" reinforcing the Otherness of not only the culture, but of the ethnic palate which is clearly coded as outside of the mainstream. Merskin (2007) finds the same elements used to describe Gabrielle Solis, Eva Langoria's character in *Desperate Housewives*, and code her as a Latina who makes a "spicy paella" (p. 139). Ironically, ABC clearly demonstrates the perpetuation of an unauthentic pan-Latinidad by assuming that one would make a paella—a traditionally flavorful, but not spicy, Spanish rice dish—*picante* (spicy). In the same vein, Mariana, family #12, who moved to San Diego so her son could attend a private school, laments the confusion that U.S. media have between Spain and Mexico explaining, "What I do not like is how U.S. TV relates Spanish music with Mexico. They use OLE for Mexican food and that is Spanish." The critiques by these women are grounded in what they perceive as an unauthentic portrayal of Mexican culture. While both examples are related to cooking shows and subsequent advertisements, the opposition to the imagery demonstrates a resistant positioning that can motivate them to actively change the minds of others.

Also of note in her critique, Diana articulates frustration regarding the perpetuation of the "Latin Look"—tanned (but not too dark) skin, dark hair and brown eyes—that has become the convention. In fact, Colombian actress Sofia Vergara, who plays Gloria Delgado Pritchett on the sitcom *Modern Family*, had to dye her hair darker to conform to the standard hot Latina style. Vergara's successful career in Colombia before crossing to the U.S. market demonstrates her varied hairstyles, most with a lighter hair color. Cameron Diaz, a San Diego native and Cuban American, is blonde and rarely situated within Latinidad in popular culture discourses. The look of Latinidad is reinforced through genre conventions in cast and costuming; the "hot" Latinas are most often shown in costumes that accentuate their busts and thin waists. Diana articulates that she combats these stereotypes when talking with her non-Latina/o friends who have been conditioned to internalize these images as accurate.

As discussed earlier, Latinas are commonly depicted as maids either in the home or in a service industry. Lucia, the mother in family #1 who moved to San Diego as a toddler from Tijuana, is frustrated with media images and commented on the housekeeper stereotype:

> Lucia: There's a few movies that have come out that have been inappropriate and I think that it sends a message of Mexican women in this country. It's so wrong.
> KM: Like what movies?
> Lucia: The J-Lo movie, I forget the name of it. [*Maid in Manhattan*] Oh, that was awful, that was awful and for her to play that role as... She's a high society role model in the United States. For her to play that role, and then- I just thought that was awful. I think that just sent the message that that's what the Mexican women do.
> KM: That they're maids...
> Lucia: Right. A rich man... it's just dumb. I watched it and I was so angry.
> Freddie: It's just a movie babe.
> Lucia: Well, it's not just a movie. I think it sends a bad message....

Lucia is upset because of Jennifer Lopez's decision to play the role of a maid in the film *Maid in Manhattan,* a typical Cinderella story where Lopez's character, a hotel maid, wins the heart of a wealthy senatorial candidate. Lucia almost feels betrayed because she sees Lopez as an important role model for Latinas. As she remembered the film, her tone became angry and her husband Freddie's response "It's just a movie babe" was an attempt to calm her down. She smiled, but it was clear that this representation was particularly troubling. Lucia's strong reaction may be explained by considering that Latina/os may see the success (or failure) of Latina/o celebrities as closely connected to their own place in society. In her analysis of editorial content in *Latina* magazine, Katynka Martínez (2004) found that articles that highlight the contributions of Latina/os in entertainment media worked to facilitate "cultural citizenship" by demonstrating that Latina/os, although marginalized, are an important part of the entertainment industry and further encourage readers to consume Latino-specific entertainment. Cultural citizenship describes ways in which marginalized groups claim identity within the dominant U.S. society while asserting difference (Martínez, 2004). The participants recognize the accomplishments of Latina/o celebrities in ways that suggest that they too are able to claim a legitimate space within the dominant culture.

Santiago, 14, family #12, lives a bicultural existence as he attends school in San Diego, but often returns to his family's home in Ensenada. His father commutes between the two countries while Santiago and his mother live primarily in the United States. Santiago is well aware of the stereotypes of Mexico and Mexicans on television and was concerned about the impact these images may have on others, but recognized the satirical use of stereotypes to make a point.

> KM: Do you see stereotypes on TV sometimes?
> Santiago: Yeah....Some stereotypes are that they are lazy or that they are really hard working.
> KM: What shows have those stereotypes?
> Santiago: *South Park,* but I don't take it personally. I think it is not good but it is funny that people think of us that way because we are not really like that....Well it's not good because people think we are lazy, and dance around sombreros and stuff like that... which we don't usually do...

One *South Park* episode, "Death Camp of Tolerance" (Season 6), follows the characters on an outing with their parents to the "Museum of Tolerance" to be "educated on the dynamics of racism and prejudice in America" as they are told by their tour guide. As the characters enter the "Hall of Stereotypes," the wax figures

highlight perceptions of different minority groups. As they reach
what appears to be the Mexican stereotype—a janitorial figure
sleeping on the job—their comments awaken the sleeping image
to reveal that it is in fact the janitor. The episode satirically critiques the hypocrisy of selective tolerance, but the most salient
experiences, especially for younger viewers, may be the recog-
nizable stereotypes that are not carefully contested (Greene,
2008). Santiago explains his own reading of the representation
from an insider perspective. He is aware of the reality so he can
laugh at the ridiculousness of the hyper-stereotypical representations on a program such as *South Park,* but does worry about
people who may not get the joke and internalize negative imagery. I asked him whether he has had any experiences with peers
who have demonstrated stereotyped thinking.

> Santiago: Sometimes, but I set them straight, no we don't do that, that
> is just a stereotype.
> KM: Do they ever say anything about you?
> Santiago: No not like that, but they ask 'do they have a lot of parties at
> ranches in Mexico?'... and no that's not true.
> KM: So where do you think they get that image from?
> Santiago: TV probably or other friends.

A typical trope of an upper-class Mexican lifestyle is highlighted through *hacienda* (ranch) living reinforced in movies and
television shows, particularly about the extravagant lifestyles of
members of the drug cartels (Shaw, 2005). Further, the history of
San Diego promoted at the core by Old Town State Park, reminds
San Diegans that when Mexican and Spanish settlers lived in the
region, they did so in *haciendas.* This architectural style has been
replicated in many San Diego buildings to highlight the city's cultural heritage. Santiago has trouble identifying any positive representations; when asked he continues to recall negative images
and is not familiar with programs or television that integrate
Mexican culture in positive ways. That is not to say this type of
imagery is altogether absent from the audiovisual landscape, but
clearly it is not the most salient. Strasburger, Wilson and Jordan
(2009) point out that as children age, they become more sophisticated in their interpretations of media content. While Rivaden-

eyra (2006) could not determine a significant relationship that predicted that as children age, they are more likely to identify stereotypes, but older teens in her sample saw more stereotypes. She explains, "...experience with stereotypes is connected to greater perceptions of them when presented with them" (Rivadeneyra, 2006, p. 409). In other words, as teenagers are faced with discrimination or other consequences of stereotypical attitudes in their real world experience they will be more likely to recognize them in the media. This age related trend was also present within the families who participated in this study, as older teens identified and contested what they recognized as stereotypical while younger teens were less likely to do so.

The teenagers in family #10 had varying opinions. The children moved from Mexico City when they were in elementary school. All the family members are bilingual and primarily engage with U.S. English-language media; family members turn to international sources for news. Pilar, 15, said she had never thought about the way Mexicans or Latina/os in general are represented in the media. Her brother, Roberto, 18, did have an opinion and was critical of the ways Spanish-language television represents Mexican culture.

> Roberto: I think definitely it sends off a bad [message], like of what they show here of what Mexican TV. It sends off a bad vibe. Like in fact there was this bad TV sketch that my friends were watching on YouTube, which by the way is the new TV. They were making fun of these Mexican game shows where it's just like random, there is like a penguin, then you see colors then you see a wheel rolling before you see what happens there and then they have this guy come out dressed in a black face and stuff like that. And they were making fun of that. I probably should have been offended but I can't blame them because that's what they're showing here, that's what sells here. If people here, if Mexicans here wanted to watch *Canal Once*[14] or other things they would show it here but there is a reason why they don't. So, I would like it if it was different but to be honest it doesn't bother me that much.

Roberto disassociates himself from the portrayals and the implications of the audience not demanding enough from the media by referring to "Mexicans" who are satisfied with this type of programming. Of course he is Mexican, but the implied target audience of the programming to which he refers are members of a different class. He negotiates his reading through a class position and sees himself outside of the audience that is hailed by Spanish-language media. His response resonates with Rivadeneyra's (2006) participants who found truth in some stereotypical portrayals because, as she quotes, "but *they* are like that" (p. 407) even though her sample was Latina/o teenagers. Most participants who were interviewed for this study had an easier time articulating problems with representation, but some parents were more optimistic in their outlook and saw a trajectory that includes more opportunities for Latina/os.

New Opportunities and Positive Thinking

Family #4 includes Jennifer, a non-native Spanish speaker. She is not Latina; she lived in Cádiz, Spain, as an undergraduate student and lived in Guanajuato, Mexico, for six months, where she taught English. She uses Spanish more since she met Manuel, who was born in Manzanillo, Mexico, and came to San Diego as a child. Currently, she and Manuel share a home in Chula Vista and share custody of his two daughters from a former marriage who are 6 and 4. Jennifer is pleased with the move toward including Latinas into television programming and the storyline of a popular Disney movie.

> Jennifer: I've noticed a change too in things like *Desperate Housewives*, Eva Longoria, who's a lead and in the movie that these girls watch all the time, *High School Musical*. The lead is played by a Latina, Gabriela. So you do see it actually a lot more. The leads are taken by Latinas and Latinos.
> Manuel: With roles that I think they have more substance in their role. It's not just the gangsters or like the housekeepers or anything like that, it's they have taken into the bigger roles which is an inspiration.
> Jennifer: And now I just remember being kind of shocked when I saw *High School Musical* thinking, Okay it's a Latina chic playing the lead against that and there's no, it's not a show about racial tensions or issues, it's just kind of normal.

The salient imagery for Jennifer, a non-Latina, is the interracial relationship, which mimics her own experience. Rather than using the *High School Musical* couple as a story about race relations, it is simply a story about teen romance.

Nora, the mother in family #3, pointed out that she went to high school with a cousin of Mario Lopez and that he is from the Chula Vista area of San Diego. Isabel, the mother in family #2, who was born and raised in Chula Vista, commented that Dr. Torres on *Grey's Anatomy* is played by a Latina from San Diego, Sara Ramírez. Ramírez moved to San Diego from Mazatlán at the age of eight. Participants are proud of Latina/o representation and stated that they would like to see more diversity in the types of roles given to Latina/o actors. While not lamenting any specific portrayal, Nora and Miguel, parents of family #3, would like to see more Latina/os on television.

> Nora: I like to watch *20/20, Dateline, 48 Hours... The Dog Whisperer.*
> Miguel: *The Dog Whisperer,* he's Hispanic.[15]
> Nora: I don't see too much of it, other than George Lopez.
> Miguel: I think we need more. I think we need a good balance...I think in overall TV they could gain by having more Latinos in their shows.

In the general market, some Latina/o actors have made a notable splash and have risen to fame that cuts across demographic characteristics of the audience. Mastro and Behm-Morawitz (2005) conclude, "While these results demonstrate noticeable improvements over previous decades, adherence to numerous unrealistic and demeaning depictions of Latina/os on primetime appears to persist" (p. 126). There is a sense that the portrayal of Latina/os in the media translates into real opportunities for Latina/os. There is pride among sample participants for Latina/o actors who have made it, especially those from the San Diego area. The participants mentioned George Lopez (*The George Lopez Show, Lopez Tonight*), Eva Longoria (*Desperate Housewives*), Vanessa Ann Hudgens (*High School Musical*), and Mario Lopez (*Saved by the Bell, Dancing with the Stars, Extra*) as examples of the presence of Latina/os in the mass media. Roberto's parents, family #10, are optimistic about the future possibilities for Latina/o actors.

> Ernesto: But, on a lighter note, don't you feel also, there is growing participation of people of Hispanic or specifically Mexican ancestry or Mexican origin or sometimes directing Mexicans in TV, in film industry, in media, in general?
> Roberto: Yeah, but do you mean like American shows with Hispanic actors?
> Ernesto: For example, the Mexican girl in *Desperate Housewives* [Eva Longoria].[16]
> Claudia: There's more integration now.

In spite of this optimism, it is imperative to evaluate positive representations to uncover their role in perpetuating the on going hegemonic discourse that keeps Latina/os positioned as the Other (Valdivia, 2008a; del Río, 2006; Jhally & Lewis, 1992; Gray, 1995).

One such case is *The George Lopez Show,* which was cheered for its entrance into the television landscape bringing with it Latino themes and an almost all Latino cast. Throughout the narrative, and more pointedly in his stand-up routines, Lopez jokes about the ingenuity of second generation Latina/os who are tough and fierce because of the many obstacles they face and ultimately overcome. Running jokes poking fun at white kids who are overprotected and handed opportunities are, in his opinion, weak and incapable of self-preservation. The constant us vs. them dichotomy hails Latina/os who identify with the stories, but also provides access to non-Latina/os who can metaphorically cheer for the underdog, evoking classic American mythology. This discourse works to unite Latina/os and non-Latina/os in critiquing the laziness of the bourgeois class while reinforcing the myth of meritocracy. The show finds itself squarely placed within a discourse of the underdog whereby George and his family are shown overcoming their challenges, being Latino in the U.S., and succeeding. On the program, George holds a managerial position, his family lives in a nice house, and his two children are college bound. According to Lopez, Latina/os are worthy of praise because of their hard work to make it against all odds.

The George Lopez Show provided new images of a Latino family, but as John Markert (2007) argues, the program both reinforces and challenges Latina/o stereotypes. In his research, Hispanic and non-Hispanic focus group participants responded to the program in ways that showcased their subject position. The show, broadcast on ABC, was carefully constructed to appeal to Latina/os while not alienating non-Latino viewers who could identify with general familial themes. *The George Lopez Show* resonates with Santiago, 14, of family #12, who enjoys the humor and finds it relevant. As a teen who is steeped in not only Mexican and American culture, but who also understands being Mexican American and/or Latino in the U.S. identifies with the show.

> Santiago: I like George Lopez...The show is about a Latino family and their daily struggle and it's funny at the same time, which is cool.
> KM: What makes him appealing?
> Santiago: I don't know, he is funny and he kind of gets the Mexican culture so even though he makes fun of himself sometimes it's funny anyways.
> KM: What are some the other things he gets, that he makes fun of?
> Santiago: That sometimes Americans are racist and stuff like that.
> KM: What part of Mexican culture does he tap into?
> Santiago: He speaks Spanish sometimes in the show and his mom tells stories about when she was in Mexico and basically yea that's it.

In the same way Santiago reads the stereotypes in *South Park* as an in-group member, he too finds elements with which to identify in *The George Lopez Show*. Teenagers and second generation and beyond were more likely to watch and enjoy the program. Lucia, of family #1, who grew up in San Diego, said this, "Well *The George Lopez Show*, that's a comedy show about a family. Some people could get offended but it's more comical because it's so true." Diana, a 22-year-old, who moved to San Diego as a young girl, worries that outgroup members will not be able to understand the subtle critique in the program's humor.

> Diana (family #8): I've seen his standup on YouTube and I think that it's really funny for Latinos because we identify with that but I don't think for Americans to watch that don't have the full idea of what it is, I think it's just helping to perpetuate stereotypes.

Michelle and her husband, Carlos, third generation parents of two, discuss *The George Lopez Show*.

> Michelle (family #9): I don't know. I've never been affected by anything like that. We think it's funny. I've never been really offended by the way it's [Latino culture] portrayed on T.V.
> Carlos: It's never an issue for me. I've never thought about it that way. Some people probably have. To me it's just...
> KM: It's just funny
> Carlos: Yeah
> KM: Does *The George Lopez Show* resonate with you?
> Carlos: Oh, definitely. Because he does say some stuff that you grew up, or you have heard or somebody has said. You know.
> Michelle: Or sometimes, we'll say it. And then we'll be like, Yeah. Cause it's usually when we're speaking Spanish it's to each other. So we think it's hilarious. I think it's hilarious.

Markert (2007) provides insight into audience readings dividing his focus groups into Hispanic and non-Hispanic, but what is missing in his analysis is a thorough investigation of the Hispanic audience. His claims are made with broad strokes without identifying other elements within the Hispanic group that go beyond ethnicity. What is clear from the families interviewed for this project is that generation is a strong factor mitigating readings of the program. John Fiske (1987) explains that "Readers will only produce meanings from, and find pleasures in, a television program if it allows for this articulation of their interests" (p. 83). In the case of *The George Lopez Show,* second generation and beyond are more likely to identify and find pleasure in this program, but not all appreciate the program's message. Nora is concerned about the way the family interacts and feels that the show does not model positive behavior. She argues that a program such as *The Cosby Show,* a program she watched as a youth, was a more appropriate example of a minority program because "It's a family oriented program, you're going to learn things that your mom and your dad are going to teach you, valuable lessons for future...George Lopez is funny, but is he really teaching what our family system is?" Nora would like to see more programs "geared toward Hispanics, but in a good way." Lopez's brash humor is problematic for Nora, but that is exactly what Santiago, Lucia, Michelle and Carlos find appealing. Discourses surrounding *The George Lopez Show* often highlight the success of the program with Latina/o audiences, but these family members demonstrate varied readings of the sitcom.

Children See Difference

Younger children can identify difference in their favorite programs; they recognize the characters' ethnicity and notice when they speak Spanish. Unlike older participants, however, they are rarely critical of the images they see, and they have not been socially conditioned to recognize difference as problematic. For younger children, ethnicity and language are nothing more than descriptive characteristics and are discussed without the cultural baggage associated with multicultural discourses from a teen's or an adult's perspective. One of the programs that stood out for the girls was Disney's *Wizards of Waverly Place* that features a Mexican American family. Marisol, 8, family #15, likes watching the show.

KM: Do you know where the mom is from on *Wizards of Waverly Place*?
Marisol: Mexico.
KM: Do you ever notice that the mom or the kids speak Spanish on *Wizards of Waverly Place*?
Marisol: I think there is one where the mom teaches Spanish one day.
KM: Did you like the episode?
Marisol: Yeah.
KM: Why do you think her mom wants her to learn Spanish?
Marisol: Because she was taking a Spanish class.
KM: Do you think her mom wants her to speak both English and Spanish?
Marisol: I think so.
KM: Does your mom speak Spanish to you?
Marisol: Yeah, I kind of only know a little Spanish and I am a Mexican person.
KM: Is your mom a Mexican person?
Marisol: Yes.

Marisol noticed that *Wizards of Waverly Place* is based on a family that is similar to hers. She can identify with the children learning Spanish and while it is struggle for the characters, it is a natural part of Marisol's life. Her mother often speaks Spanish and is interested in teaching her about Mexican traditions. Her mother explained that Marisol is already excitedly planning her *quinceañera*.

Susana, 9, family #17, is also a fan of *Wizards* and I asked her about the Russo family. Unlike Marisol, Susana does not speak Spanish, and although her father is from Mexico she is not strongly connected to Mexican cultural practices. She has a more difficult time identifying elements that would be coded as Mexican.

> KM: Do you notice anything about the parents that you don't usually see on TV?
> Susana: The dad gave powers to his brother so he could marry the mom.
> KM: What about the mom?
> Susana: She didn't have powers.
> KM: She is just mortal?
> Susana: She speaks in Spanish sometimes.
> KM: Why does she speak in Spanish sometimes?
> Susana: Because her mom taught her Spanish and so now she wants to teach it to her kids.
> KM: Did she grow up somewhere else?
> Susana: I don't know.
> KM: Why do you think she speaks Spanish?
> Susana: The mom?
> KM: Yeah.
> Susana: Because maybe her mom's husband likes to speak Spanish.
> KM: Why do they speak Spanish? Do you know where they are from?
> Susana: I don't know.
> KM: Do you remember any other things that brought in Spanish to *Wizards of Waverly Place*?
> Susana: They had the *quinceañera*.
> KM: Do you remember what happened on the episode?
> Susana: She used the spell to switch bodies with her mom because her mom did not have a *quinceañera* when she was a teenager.
> KM: Have you ever been to a *quinceañera*?
> Susana: No.
> KM: Do you think you will have a *quinceañera*?
> Susana: No.

Susana, although second generation, has not been introduced to Mexican cultural practices as much as Marisol. Both girls watch a lot of television and are fans of the Disney Channel, and while Marisol picks up elements within *Wizards* that are Mexican, Susana views it from a position that is not informed by Latina/o culture. Nevertheless, when I asked her about her ethnicity she described herself as "Jewish and Mexican." Many respondents did articulate specifically seeking programming featuring Latina/o characters or specific Latina/o cultural elements. As the discussions continued, it became clear that family members, especially parents, are appreciative of Latina/o imagery when it appears. Clara, Marisol's mother, thinks that incorporating more diversity into English-language shows is beneficial and is pleased when her daughter sees Latina characters.

Clara: Well I guess it would be so she could see it's not X and Y on the show and it's XYZ so more variety. Even the girl from *Wizards of Waverly* I think she is Latina. So when they have girls like that, it is good. I like her to watch that so I think it would be good.

Parents seemed hopeful that television programs would provide insight into their Mexican heritage. The introduction of U.S. programming featuring Latina/o casts and the Spanish language may be doing just that. When asked about children's programming, Carmen, the mother in family #5, remembered *Maya & Miguel*, a show on PBS that features a Mexican American family.

Carmen: Este sí representa la cultura mexicana, ¿no? *(Yes, in that one they represent the Mexican culture.)*
José: Hay un programa también en Disney Channel que se llama *Handy Manny* que sí salan la cultura hispana, caricatura cultura hispana americana y que se hagan palabras en español y palabras en inglés. *(There is also a program on Disney Channel called* Handy Manny *where you can see Hispanic culture, well Hispanic American, and they say words in Spanish and words in English.)*
KM: ¿Parece que es bueno para tú hijos ver cosas así? *(Do you think it is good for your kids to watch programs like that?)*
José: Pues en parte sí, por que lo que fijaba en estés programas en que llega *Handy Manny* en el Disney Channel, que sí sacan las culturas latinas. Como una piñata, como se vienen con una piñata a la fiesta, lo como

hablan ellos y me fijado que a los niños los han gustado y saben ellos qué es una piñata. Mismo los otros a qué traen los candies y todo eso. Y como digo es una cultura mucho de México que se rompen las piñatas. *(Well in part yes, because what I have noticed in those programs like Handy Manny on Disney Channel is that they do show the Latino culture...like a piñata, how they bring a piñata to a party, how they talk and what I have noticed that my children like the show and then they understand what is a piñata. The same thing with the candies and everything else. And like I said it is very much part of the Mexican culture to break open piñatas.)*

In maintaining a Mexican cultural identity in the home, the sample parents describe using some Latino-themed and Spanish-language programming to provide a window to their culture. Subervi-Vélez and Rios (2005) explain, "In sum, being Latino or having *identidad Latina* is not dependent on a person's skin color or other physical characteristics.... Culture is the most important factor that contributes to a person having an ethnic-based identity" (pp. 35–36). It became evident that some parents want to connect their children to elements of Mexico as a way to reinforce their cultural heritage, and many see the Latino-themed children's programs as a way to do this.

On the other hand, they are more concerned with the overall quality of the programs than with the ethnicity of the characters. It is apparent that the parents of preschool age children would not expose them to a program just because of the ethnicity of the characters. Marisa, family #13, who is careful about what her children Sergio, 8, and Pedro, 5, are exposed to, explains that the ethnicity of the characters is secondary to the quality of the program.

> KM: Do you think you would be more likely to have them watch a show that had Latino characters than not?
> Marisa: No, not necessarily. It depends entirely on what the show is about because a lot of stuff that is targeted towards a Latino audience is not something I would want them to watch.

Most parents agreed that programs should be perceived as educational, and if they also feature Latina/o characters and the Spanish language, then that is seen as an added benefit, but not the primary reason for choosing certain programs. Michelle, the mom of family #9, would like her children to learn Spanish, but at 4 and 5, they do not speak much Spanish. Her attitude demonstrates that Spanish language and Latinidad are not necessarily intertwined and in fact said that Dora's ethnicity does not matter, but the show's emphasis on language does. Lucia, the mother in family #1, whose children are 3 and 4, agreed that high quality children's programming is important, but the ethnicity is less important. When asked if she encouraged viewing of *Dora the Explorer* or *Go Diego Go* because they feature Latina/o characters she answered "no." The sentiments articulated by Michelle and Lucia dispute industry conventional wisdom that highlighted the characters' ethnicity in the promotion of the programs. Again, the desires of Latina/o parents are not any different than any other ethnic group—they want high quality and age appropriate educational programming. The fact that Dora is Latina matters little to the children who are watching the program. Moran (2010) found that 92% of parents of preschoolers regardless of ethnicity indicated that their child watched *Dora the Explorer* "often" or "sometimes." In assessing ethnic differences in children's identification with Dora, Calvert, Strong, Jacobs, and Conger (2007) discovered that Caucasian children were more likely to perceive Dora as like them and "there were no effects favoring Hispanic...identification with a Hispanic role model" (p. 438).

In family #3, Nora appreciates *Dora the Explorer* and *Sesame Street* teaching Spanish words, but when her children were younger they watched *Plaza Sésamo*, the Mexican version of *Sesame Street*, filmed as a co-production in Mexico City and broadcast on Tijuana's Televisa. Nora recounted a story of her cousin's criticism of Dora's Latinidad.

Nora: Oh, my cousin married a Caucasian and they had a daughter and we were talking one day. She wanted me to send her books in Spanish because she wants her to speak Spanish. My cousin was going to teach her to speak Spanish and he was going to speak English. And I don't even remember how we started talking about it but she said her daughter was NOT going to watch Dora. She does not like that show. I think I said, "Do you want me to send you some Dora books?" And she said, "no." But I did send her bilingual books, which are half in English. You turn it upside-down and one side is English and one side is Spanish. But she said, "No Dora." Because [she thought] that's not a true representation of what a Hispanic girl is. I'm speaking English and then Spanish....

This story can be compared to Susan Harewood and Angharad Valdivia (2005) and Nicole Guidotti-Hernández (2007) criticism of Dora's pan-Latina ethnicity, which hinders a deep understanding of the richness of a culture. Specifically, Harewood and Valdivia studied Dora's imagined space by analyzing discourses of parents in chat streams on the official Nick Jr. website. The authors conclude that Dora "in her myriad manifestations, is a graphic reiteration of tropicalist tropes" (p. 101) that further situate her experiences as exotic and outside of the dominant culture. What do children identify with if it is not Dora's ethnicity? Harewood and Valdivia (2005) explain that Dora "embodies the all-seeing, exploring, touring Western subject" (p. 100) and demonstrates a "first world media diet" (p. 100) that places her inside the dominant culture while maintaining the agreed upon social stereotypes that position her Latinidad as acceptable. The parents demonstrate these contradictions as they praise the programs' efforts at presenting Spanish, but are not attracted by the cultural elements that Nickelodeon sells as "Latino," maybe because they see them as unauthentic. More contradictions exist. Further in the interview discussion, Miguel, Nora's husband, explains that some images can be positive educational tools especially for children who have limited experiences with Latina/os in their daily lives.

> Miguel: And that's why I think the whole Diego and the Dora thing are for not only a marketing campaign but a learning tool for both White children and Latino children because it kind of bridges a lot of gaps. It teaches the White kids, the Caucasians, the English speakers, a little bit of Spanish and vice versa. I think Diego and Dora are really nice. I think they're nice for the population.

Noting the program's influence, Guidotti-Hernández (2007) states, "*Dora the Explorer* reminds us how we cannot forget that media and market forces of Latinidad do in fact have an effect on public life" (p. 229). The father in family #7, Alejandro, is frustrated that all young Latinas are referred to as Dora.

Alejandro: Las otras culturas...¿que pensará cuando los otros ve lo apoyemos y todo porque está simbolizando el Latino, verdad? Dora y el hombre, cómo se llama y todo...y corten el pelo y dicen, "Ay, ella es como Dora" a sí mismos. *[Other cultures...what do they think when they see that which supports it [stereotype], will it help?...and all of this because it symbolizes the Latino, right? Dora and the other guy, what is his name, and everything...and they cut their hair and say "Look, she is like Dora" and they do it to themselves.]*

Alejandro sees how Dora's identity is played out even within his community. He and his wife, Lola, operate a Head Start[17] daycare center from their home, and they each interact with parents of young children on a daily basis. They are both concerned that people who do not have firsthand experience with Latina/os will perceive Dora as representative of Latinidad.

Miguel, the father of family #3, explains that children of this generation do not see difference based on ethnicity, and if we expose them to programming that is diverse from young ages, it will impact their thinking about others.

Miguel: You know one of the things I have noticed in regards to television – television in a way has helped put also the Hispanic market on the map. At the same time to help kids to understand that being bilingual is cool. That speaking two languages is cool. Our generation has kids that are colorblind, so, they can be watching a program that is about African Americans or Asians, or a mix of them and for them they are all equal, they are all the same. And for my generation and my mother's – we see differences. But for them I think, I think we are only being enriched.

The contradictions between Miguel and Alejandro go to the very heart of issues about representation. Latina/os are becoming visible, but at what cost? For some the increased visibility is a necessary step to enter the mainstream, but others are less willing to sacrifice their diversity for the commodified version of Latinidad that is constructed by the media apparatus. Further, Miguel's optimistic outlook imagines a culture where racial distinction will be less pronounced, but the reality is that Latina/o children, especially those in lower income and new immigrant families, face much different experiences than those promoted on television. Latina/o children growing up in linguistically isolated households are more likely to do worse in school and drop out. Children in immigrant families are also at higher risk for asthma and childhood obesity and have limited access to social services such as food stamps (Barondess & Newhouse, 2007). Alejandro and Lola, the parents in family #7 who run a daycare, are concerned about the images of thinness promoted through animated characters and dolls such as Barbie as they interact with Latina/o children in their center who do not fit the dominant mold.

> Lola: Pero, por ejemplo las niñas les gustan los Barbies pero eso es para, como ante trece, y quieren su apariencia como los Barbies y..*(But, for example, the girls like Barbies, but those should be for girls who are around thirteen and they want their appearance to be like the Barbies.)*
> Alejandro: Bueno pero las niñas chiquitas pueden empezar con Barbies...*(And the little girls can start with Barbie.)*
> Lola: Sí, uh huh. Sí les gustan. Pero yo pienso que a las chicas les gustan y las niñas chiquitas les gustan pero ya viene el mensaje de las enfermedades que delgada delgada peso cero cero y también tomo ofendía a esto. *(Yes, uh huh, they do like them. But, I think for the girls they like them and the Little girls like them, but with them comes the messages that is the skinny skinny illness, they want to weigh zero, zero...that's what offends me)*
> Alejandro: Y te fijas, las princesas...son una princesas muy bonitas, muy marcados. Y como tú dices ahorita está de modo todo eso y qué pasa cuando una niña está sobre peso se encaja eso y no puede ser princesa porque no está como ellas. *(And if you notice, the princesses...they are very pretty princesses and very shapely. And like you say nowadays that is very popular and what happens when a little girl is heavier and she notices that and she thinks she can't be a princess because she doesn't look like that.)*

Alejandro points to what researchers have discovered in relation to the body image of characters in children's programming. Because of the international flow of children's television programming the Anglo-European body ideal has been established as the norm across the world (Lemish, 2007). Within the U.S. context the thin body with large breasts and a small waist is standard fare and even more pronounced in animated programming. The Disney Princesses repeat this narrow image in almost every product associated with them and when darker skinned bodies are presented they are drawn with the same body type as lighter skinned characters. Even Dora, who in her original form was presented with a stockier body, has been co-opted into the thin ideal with the release of the older Dora made to appeal to elementary school age children who may have grown beyond the preschool Dora. Of course, the older Dora still has dark hair to code her as Latina, but now she is presented with a narrow waist, long legs, and an obsession with appearance rather than exploring. Dora dolls are sold to be connected to the Dora Links website, where children can play interactive games that include changing Dora's hair and clothes as well as computer based adventures centered on "community, friendship, and mystery rather than outdoor adventures with talking animals" (Nisen, 2009). The website promotes a multicultural, idealistic world where Dora interacts with her friends and neighbors who are ethnically diverse. The main characters share common interests, demonstrating a world that moves to post-racial discourses where tensions and difference are ignored.

The presentation of racial inclusion that is found in much of children's programming follows Herman Gray's (1995) analysis in what he calls an assimilation discourse. He explains that assimilationist programs, or in this case websites, construct worlds where social and cultural difference has been erased and replaced with a "universal similarity" (p. 85), which may be as troubling as the stereotypes referred to by the parents in this study. Scholars should interrogate the propensity of children's programs to gloss over racial difference by showing everyone getting along in a mostly middle to upper class environment where Anglo values are dominant. Parents wanted to see diversity incorporated into programs in a way that would fit with Gray's multicultural discourse rather than a "pluralist or separate but equal" (Gray, 1995, p. 87) frame. Media for children in either English or Spanish have yet to provide a realistic portrayal of the varied experiences of children in the United States. Children's programming need not be lesson heavy, but could include realistic tensions that may occur as a result of cultural difference with a focus on healthy resolutions that do not deny that problems exist, but provide an opportunity for children to see conflicts resolved in ways that are beneficial to all. As indicated by the children in the sample, there is little difference between the types of media accessed by Latina/o children and the rest of the child audience. All children would be better served by a media system that was less reliant on commercial motives and more willing to risk opening up the representations to truly reflect the lives of all children in the United States.

Representation Matters

Overall it appears that Latina/os, especially adults, are aware of the common stereotypes associated with their group and fear that the stereotypes indeed impact people's perceptions. There is optimism that new opportunities are on the horizon and that mainstream media are moving away from the same old story. We should be cautious not to allow optimism to obscure the hegemonic power of television and be ready to interrogate the media images especially if they continue to situate Latina/os outside of the dominant culture.

The responses to media imagery by the Latina/o respondents demonstrate how audience members resist and contest the imagery of mainstream media. But, do these articulations translate into a real resistance of the status quo? The success of Latina/o performers within popular culture is offered as evidence for a new era of representation where Latina/os have been offered more opportunities. While it is certainly true that since 1998 the number of Latina/os working on screen has increased, the number is still significantly lower than what would be expected based on the proportional makeup of the audience. Further, it is often forgotten that Latino-themed programs and networks are not just a response to the "Latin pop explosion" of the late 1990s, but have been sporadically produced by networks for varying reasons since the 1970s. When PBS entered the marketplace as the first national public television channel in 1969, it offered programming in part to respond to the information that had been released by the Kerner Commission, the Surgeon General's Scientific Advisory

Committee on Television, and other reports showcasing evidence collected in the 1960s demonstrating links between media exposure and attitudes about race, violence, and subsequent behaviors (Noriega, 2000; Baran & Davis, 2006). As a result, PBS offered the first television programs that dealt with issues facing U.S.-born Latinos. However, market forces shifted to a neo-liberal perspective under an FCC appointed by Ronald Reagan that deregulated the media industries in a way that systematically privileged private interests and shifted regulatory power away from the government (McChesney, 2004). As a result, we have a media system that focuses on profit as the ultimate measure of success so that we are left with programming that titillates rather than educates or enlightens. It is within this capitalist logic that the images of Latina/os can be found to hegemonically reinforce an outsider's position. The young Latina/os in the families represented here are not necessarily motivated to move beyond complaining about media stereotypes, but the first step of recognition may provide a sense of empowerment that inspires those who are eager for change. If we are in agreement with those participants who feel that a new era is on the horizon as more Latina/os are offered positions both on and off the screen, then we can imagine a media system that includes Latina/os in ways that integrate their experiences into the stories that are told. One thing is unmistakable, representation matters because what audiences see is part of the social system that teaches them about who they are.

As youth engage with media, it is important to see the ways in which they negotiate their own identity. The process of identity formation is a complex web of testing and experimenting with elements in a social environment that teaches what to value and devalue. Family structure is a key element in shaping the identity of children, but also the media to which children are exposed present a blueprint for acceptable behaviors. "It is through the pervasive cultural value patterns—as filtered through the family and media systems—that the meanings and values of identity are differentiated and defined" (Moran & Chung, 2008).

For members who find themselves engaging with media from within the Mexican diaspora (Rinderle, 2005) the process is influenced by global, transnational, and local forces (Straubhaar, 2007). Convincingly, Susana Rinderle (2005) describes the characteristics of diasporic communities through a Mexican lens, painting a picture of a group of people who experience geographic and/or cultural displacement. The cultural dislocation that occurs through the process of colonization leads to a hybrid identity, which has been exemplified by many of the youth in the families described here. Whether actual migration has taken place or not, many Latina/os find themselves connected to two cultural practices that are reinforced by multilingual national and transnational media. For example, in family #10, Roberto, 18, sees himself as a global citizen. He has high levels of cultural capital, which he has attained through travelling with his family, his bilingual ability, his education, and his family's social class. This translates into his own identity as a member of a broader social group that transcends traditional borders and political boundaries.

Working from Isabel Molina Guzmán and Angharad Valdivia's (2004) definition of Latindad, which explains it as "an imagined community of recent, established and multigenerational immigrants from diverse cultural, linguistic, racial, and economic backgrounds" (p. 207), Latinidad is constructed in part by audiences' exposure to media texts. We see how young children very early on recognize difference in the representation of characters, but that difference is not defined by social connotations. As they age, who they are becomes contained within the limits of the culture. For most young people, peer groups, family, and the mass media are very influential as they transition through their teen years. The representations of Latinidad within the commercial system sets a strict definition of who is accepted as part of the group. Nevertheless, the discourses about how the family members choose to participate in their own media use points to the fractured and contested notion of being part of the group identified by the industry as Latina/o.

Latina/o children are learning to navigate what it means to be a member of their family within the structure of the U.S. that positions Latinidad as outside dominant culture. Younger children in the sample articulated a sense of identity that was descriptive, detailing what their parents told them about who or what they are, while older children and teens articulated their identity by recognizing how it fits into the broader social structure. Jimena, 17, family #16, who moves between Tijuana and San Diego on a regular basis, discusses her identity.

> KM: If someone asked you to identify yourself in terms of your identity, what would you say?
> Jimena: I would say I am a Mexican American.
> KM: Yeah. What do you think your parents would say?
> Jimena: My parents would say Mexican.
> KM: So if your parents identify more with Mexico, do you think since you have been here for a while that you identify more with American culture?
> Jimena: A little bit, I would say, I like celebrating the days we celebrate here. So, yeah.

In Jimena's behaviors she seems to be closely connected to her Mexican identity, but envisions future opportunities in the U.S and articulates what she sees as the best part of being American. It is in the details of daily life that she sees American culture most specifically, but her worldview as a 17-year-old is absolutely transnational.

In the imaginations of children we can see the beginning of what media products may look like through the logic of Latinidad. Media conventions that are utilized hail Latina/o audiences within a limited range of inspiration, repeating common stereotypes and narrative tropes. The Latina/o look is easily identified, but the way in which the audience members describe their own patterns of exposure, there appears to be little reason to keep the possibilities constrained by replicating overused conventions. Producing programming from the logic of Latinidad does not necessarily mean creating Latino-themed programming, but it might mean that Latina/o experience is always already part of the construction of the text. When asked to describe a media product they would create, most young children stayed within the mainstream framework, but older children were more interested in seeing programming that reflected their experiences.

Jimena, 17, family #16, a music fan and guitar player, wants a program that reflects her interests.

KM: If you could make your own television program or movie what would you want it to be about? What would you put in it?
Jimena: That is a good question. Well, it would have to be something related to music. I love music. Like a MTV show but focused on music.
KM: Do you think it would be important to have the characters be Latina or from Mexico or it doesn't matter that much?
Jimena: I would love to have Latinos more recognized in American culture. That would be nice.

Although I had to prompt her to articulate her desire for more Latina/os, when she paused to think about it a smile crossed her face, indicating the moment that she realized that the audiovisual landscape could be different. Younger children had more difficulty thinking up alternative possibilities. Lupe, 6, of family #11, who watches television in both languages and is a fan of Disney princesses, explains her idea.

KM: If you could make a TV show what would you make it about?
Lupe: Princess and the Frog Valentines Day!
KM: If you made a princess would your princess speak Spanish or English?
Lupe: English.
KM: Why would she speak English?
Lupe: Because the princess does not speak Spanish just English.

Lupe has been trained that English is the important language to learn and envisions princesses as English speakers. She was not alone in telling me that all princesses speak English. Mercedes, 5, of family #14, and I had a conversation about her favorite princesses.

KM: Have you ever seen any princesses that speak Spanish?
Mercedes: No.
KM: Why do you think that is?
Mercedes: Because the movies are made in English.
KM: That would make sense. Do you think there are princesses in the world that speak Spanish and they are just not in the movies?
Mercedes: Yes, probably.

Mercedes' family embodies a transnational perspective and has worked hard to incorporate the Spanish language and their cultural heritage—both Spanish and Mexican—into their life. Mercedes understands that the movies of the princesses are in English, so naturally they speak English, but she also understands that that is a limited representation, indicating her knowledge of alternatives by stating that indeed there may be some princess out there who speaks Spanish.

Santiago, 14, family #12, is more specific in his criteria. He would like to see more diverse characters but in ways that seem natural and authentic. He is critical of the way in which U.S. television represents the experiences of Latina/o youth.

> KM: Would you like to see teen shows or kid shows that have bilingual characters?
> Santiago: It depends. If it is extremely *pocho* that would be annoying. If it were a little bit of Spanish and a little bit of English it would be interesting to watch.
> KM: Would it be like how you experienced your life while you are here?
> Santiago: Yeah, a little bit... because I speak English and Spanish a lot.
> Mariana: What is *pocho* language?
> Santiago: When you mix one Spanish word in a sentence of English that is it, so finish the sentence in Spanish or start one in English.
> Mariana: Do you think that happens because they do not know the Spanish language well.
> Santiago: Yeah, I think that is mostly it.
> KM: Do you think they sometimes do it or at least television executives do it to make it seem more realistic?
> Santiago: Yeah I think that is what they think is realistic.
> KM: Is that what you think is realistic?
> Sergio: No, not really.

After Santiago explains to his mother, Mariana, the meaning of *pocho,*[18] which is also used to refer to someone who is Latina/o but does not speak Spanish, it is evident that the mother and son have different views on what is "realistic." Throughout the interview, Mariana was concerned about preserving proper Spanish and is critical of the second generation and beyond moving away from the language. Santiago is more forgiving of the changes in the language, but still perceives attempts by some programs as unauthentic.

Even though I prompted the younger participants to develop ideas that would break from conventional productions, it was difficult for them to think of examples. It has been shown that even when children complete a media literacy curriculum, they have a difficult time producing alternative narratives. For example, Jesse Gainer (2010) designed a critical media literacy project for middle school students. The school is in the Southwest and of the approximately 1,000 students, 65% are Latino, 20% white, 14% African American and 1% other. The students were exposed to issues of representation and could readily identify when they saw stereotypes presented. For example, Gainer showed clips from the movie *Dangerous Minds*[19] and the students contested the image of the Mexican students as troublemakers. After Gainer instructed the students in media production and other lessons, they were left to design their own short movies. While the students' own work challenged some conventional notions, they easily slipped into using traditional media conventions that they had earlier critiqued (Gainer, 2010).

Audiences, including children, actively negotiate meaning and use their own experiences to understand the images they see. They are adept at recognizing and challenging problematic representation, but at the same time it is apparent that there is a chasm between contesting imagery to imagining an alternative. The relationship between audiences and imagery is seen in not only the ways that audiences process the information, but in the ways they explain their own identity. The family members, including the children, were eager to discuss examples of Latina/os who had become successful in English-language media, but were critical of stereotypical representations. Nearly everyone interviewed would like to see more diverse narratives that include realistic portrayals that reflect their experiences.

Chapter 6

(Re)Imagining a Latina/o Audience

As evidenced by the participants in this study, it is unmistakable that there is no one way to define the Latina/o audience. Audience members are conditioned by multiple layers of influence that manifest in a myriad of ways when they make decisions regarding media consumption. Latina/os in the United States find themselves pulled in several directions since the media may position them as immigrant, outsider, Spanish speaker, or as a hot commodity and the "it" ethnicity. Media producers interested in capitalizing on this audience have been ferociously creating products that are thought to be appealing to this group. With those productions, however, comes the assumption that Latina/os are so different from the dominant culture that they require something unique, and thus niche programming has become the norm. One of the most significant lessons learned from the family members in this study is that their tastes are diverse and it is more effective to think of them as part of a larger multicultural audience rather than as a separate group that desires its own programming.

Complexities and Contradictions

Echoing Federico Subervi-Vélez (1999), Angharad Valdivia (2008c) continues the call for more research focusing on the relationship between Latina/o youth and popular culture. The past few years have seen tremendous growth in the literature that investigates Latina/o media and audiences, but there is still much more terrain to cover. The findings presented here contribute to the discussion regarding Latina/o media consumption by exposing trends among Latino families and by emphasizing the experiences of youth while highlighting the diversity of audience. The participants' responses point to what Joseph Straubhaar (2007) has identified as a multilayered identity process in which global, transnational and local processes interact to form a concept of self. Audience members who find themselves connected to a variety of identities, such as immigrants to their former home and new culture, attach meaning to media products in ways that make sense from their unique perspective (Barrera & Bielby, 2001; Casa Pérez, 2005; Dávila, 2002; Hall, 1980; Jhally & Lewis, 1995; Radway, 1984). It became apparent that the youth in this sample see the binaries of Latino/dominant and Mexican/American not as two competing forces but rather as "dialogical counterpoints" (Kraidy, 2005, p. 127), a conclusion that was also drawn by Lucila Vargas (2008), who interviewed Latina teenagers about their perceptions of themselves. Youth articulate these two positions, but do not feel the need to choose between one or the other. Consistently, research that investigates Latina/o youth finds that they identify with both the dominant culture and their more specific (native) culture.

Identity is fluid and informed by the context in which audience members find themselves. At times Latina/os may adopt elements of the dominant culture (Kriady, 2005; Molina Guzmán, 2006; Dávila, 2002) but still maintain a traditional core that is evident in interactions with family members (Barrera & Bielby, 2001) or even by watching television from "home" (Rios, 2003; Rojas, 2004; Mayer, 2004). As the migration patterns of Latina/os become more intricate and intertwined within the American fabric, the characteristics that define a traditional Latina/o identity become outdated. Straubhaar (2007) points out that as identities become more complex and informed by multiple sources—gender, culture, geography, language—predictable media use patterns are less apparent. As Valdivia (2008c) notes, the multiple subjective positions open to bicultural (or multicultural) youth "can be both enabling and restraining" (p. 105). This multiple subjectivity can be seen as a hybrid identity informed by the immigrant experience. Douglas Massey and Magaly Sanchez (2007) explain that the movement of people, popular culture, objects, and ideas across transnational networks "produces a hybrid identity [that] incorporates elements of both settings while standing apart from each one" (p. 83). Marwan Kraidy (2005) interrogates the concept of hybridity within the logic of transnational or "translocal" (p. 155) spaces. If Latina/o youth are considered as part of a translocal space created by their unique subjective positions informed by family experience and interactions with popular culture, we can see that even if they do not experience immigration firsthand, they are rendered part of the *trans*national culture without ever leaving their local space. The hybrid identity is imposed and therefore becomes part of what it means to be Latina/o in the United States.

Hybridity, as part of larger global processes of migration and access to foreign media content, can be seen as the cultural specificity of globalization. The way Latina/o youth negotiate their identity and meaning associated with mass media is a process informed by global and local forces that are not two ends of a continuum, but elements that are intertwined to inform everyday experiences. Some of the sample families included here are traditional candidates for the discussion of transnational forces— they have moved from Mexico to the United States. On the other hand, the youth and their parents who are U.S. born also live hybridity because of the outsider status imposed by the social structure. It is useful to consider how media construct a transnational experience for audiences even when they have not experienced it firsthand.

Kraidy (2005) proposes the use of a framework that he describes as "critical transculturalism," encouraging scholars to emphasize the link between hybridity and agency. Critical transculturalism exposes the inequality of intercultural relations moving beyond cultural pluralism discourses that imply a step toward multiculturalism that is celebrated without interrogating power differentials. Critical transculturalism, on the other hand, explains hybridity not as resistance outside power relationships, but as negotiated within the primary social structure. Hybridity, as a concept, should not restrain the ever-changing cultural environment, but push us to remain comfortable in the tension that is created through intercultural interactions. As articulated by the young people in this sample, authentic expressions of hybridity are most powerful when they are embraced as part of what it means to grow up in the Unite States in 2010.

Latino-themed networks such as MTVtr3s position the audience as distinctively hybrid and outside of the general market and thus outside mainstream U.S. culture. The hybrid status is imposed by the production of programming that sees the audience as immersed in transnational experiences that have most often been defined as the ability to speak Spanish or engaged in family rituals that are seen as foreign. It appears that within the families represented in this study, Latina/o youth are developing a hybrid identity that is multilayered and influenced by their family histories and personal experiences. The lived experiences of Latina/o youth may elicit an authentic connection to a hybrid identity. If that identity is co-opted by popular culture, however, the representation of hybridity turns into a way to hail audiences evoking a reading that defines their subject position as outside of mainstream culture. Cynthia Bejarano (2005) suggests, "Mass marketing and mainstream appropriation of Latina/o identities symbolically strips youths of the integrity of their cultures" (p. 97). The market forces that have identified a hybrid identity channel it through the logic of capitalism whereby the youth are rendered consumers rather than citizens.[20] Hybridity as exemplified by Latino-themed programming and advertising does not provide an outlet for authentic agency; rather it limits youths' possibilities by co-opting cultural elements as a way to imitate authentic experiences.

Viviana, the mother of 5-year-old twins in family #14, describes how she negotiates her identity.

> KM: If you could identify your family with a name what word would you use?
> Viviana: We are Mexican American. That is what I would say.
> KM: It is interesting you identify as Mexican American even though you are 50% Spanish.
> Viviana: Right because that is how other people identified me. Meaning that okay, growing up in Texas my father was a Spaniard, and a lot of people did not know what that was. If you speak Spanish, Spain must be in South America for all intents and purposes; second of all, people talk about being biracial. Technically, I mean my father is White but somehow Spain is not White. Portugal might be White but Spain is not White.

It was a big identity issue. If you say you are half Spanish and half Mexican they go..."Really?" My dad is from Spain and people think you are making it up. A lot of Mexican Americans, if you speak to them, they will say, "oh my father is from Spain." Oh really, where from? But oh not really. So there is this whole big thing and everyone thinks you're making it up.

She emphasizes her hybrid identity between a Mexican and Spanish space that has been imposed upon her by other people. In the U.S. she is seen as Mexican American even though her family is from Texas and has been there for generations. Her father is an immigrant from Spain, a much closer connection to a homeland that is outside the United States, but her identity is Mexican American. She continues:

Viviana: But growing up where I grew up, there were not that many immigrants, they were Tejano they were a Texas Mexican as opposed to my husband's kind of Mexican, the immigrant kind of Mexican. The interesting thing is that culturally my family should have forgotten their "Mexicanness" and Mexican heritage a long time ago, but I think it is because of discrimination issues in Texas that kept it so preserved.

Viviana's husband was born in Los Angeles where his grandparents emigrated from Mexico. She wants to maintain a strong connection to her Mexican heritage defined first in her early years living in Texas and now infused with being a Mexican American in California.

Positive Representations and Other Possibilities

The producers of Latino-themed children's programming created in the United States have worked diligently to portray Latina/os positively. Sesame Workshop and Nickelodeon, among others, have engaged in extensive research to ensure that the images of Latina/o children diversify the television landscape in an attempt to eliminate stereotyped perceptions. Characters across children's programming are found using Spanish phrases, embracing customs from countries such as Mexico and Cuba, and making friends with children who do not necessarily look like them. While these efforts have been critiqued here and elsewhere (Harewood & Valdivia, 2005; Guidotti-Hernández, 2007), it cannot be denied that improvements have been made since the era of Frito Bandito (Noriega, 2000). For example, *Sesame Street* segments show characters of different ethnicities interacting in a variety of contexts. Nickelodeon's *El Tigre* showcases Mexican American cultural practices in its animation. The participants in this study describe Latina/o celebrities who have found success in network and cable programming as part of ensemble casts. Family members applauded these efforts and were optimistic about the future where they imagined more Latina/os excelling in the media industry. At first glance, it does appear that the representation of Latina/os has shifted dramatically, but in fact the percentage of Latina/o actors in English-language programming is far below a representation proportional to the population.

The success of shows such as *Dora the Explorer* point to the fact that children's programs featuring Latina/o casts can be economically viable; scholars must now consider how these images get rearticulated into the broader societal landscape. Herman Gray (1995) eloquently cautions that positive representations can be as problematic as stereotyping or invisibility and may function hegemonically to distract audiences from the complexities of racism. How can a Latina child reconcile the happy go lucky nature of her favorite *Wizards of Waverly Place* episode, where the most challenging cultural dilemma manifests itself as needing to learn a few Spanish phrases, with the anti-Latina/o sentiment that is associated with discussions about immigration? While I am not suggesting that children's programming is the place for a serious discussion about discrimination, I am confident that given the space, creative and talented writers will come up with clever ways to acknowledge the challenges that young Latina/os deal with in their daily lives. Growing up Latina/o in the United States can be difficult as spotlighted in the 2009 CNN special *Latino in America*. Reporter Soledad O'Brien's treatment of the challenges facing Latina/os centered on teen pregnancy, access to education, and even media representation (del Río, 2009). The CNN program, as described by its own promotion, "explores how Latinos are reshaping our communities and culture and forcing a nation of immigrants to rediscover what it means to be an American" (www.cnn.com/ SPECIALS/2009/latino.in.america/). Esteban del Río (2009) concludes, however, that the ways in which Latina/os have been depicted in programs such as these "yield productive but highly limited possibilities for Latino agency." The rearticulation of the American Dream as now defined through a brown lens leaves the U.S. landscape unchanged because Latina/os become merely the next immigrant group to make the United States home. This story is more complicated because market forces in both Spanish and English work for and against authentic agency.

Children growing up in an environment that reinforces white privilege do not need to be sheltered from reality but should have their experiences validated so that they are comfortable taking ownership of being American. During the course of the family interviews, Carmen, the mother of family #4, remembered a specific instance that she connected to the media portrayal of Latina/os.

> Carmen: Bueno, hay veces que hay programas que burlan de la gente mexicanos y también hay los programas que burlan de los americanos. Lo que me pienso es que...hay gente que ve la televisión como racistas, ¿no?...y un día, saliendo con mí niño, y era por aquí, por esta calle, había una señora en un carro y estaban mirando y hablando de eso en las noticias y comentando de los papeles y iba caminando y va a echarme con su carro ya vi que me va a tropear...diciendo "¡fuera de aquí!" Yo lo que veo es la televisión y eso influye mucho a la gente. Y si es una persona que es racista, la televisión pone un granito de arena y está metiendo cosas a la gente. *[Carmen: Well, there are progams that make fun of Mexicans but also there are programs [in Spanish] that make fun of Americans. What I think is that...there are people who watch television who are racists right?...well one day, going out with my son, and it was right here, in this street, there was a woman in her car and she was watching me and talking about the things that had been in the news [immigration issues] and commenting on the newspaper and she was walking and got back in her car and I saw that she was trying to hit us [with her car] yelling "get out of here!" What I see is that the television and those things can influence people. And if a person who is racist sees the television, it puts in a grain of sand and it is giving people ideas.]*

Carmen's story exemplifies the on going struggles that Latina/os face as a result of discrimination, and children are not immune to this treatment. The media may be a place where children can learn that everyone counts and that a young Latina/o child has every right to the opportunities society has to offer if the stories move beyond the benign multicultural narratives that are the traditional hallmark of children's programming. There are "high stakes in the articulation of Latinidad" (del Río, 2009) demanding a careful eye on the media industry, which continues to render these issues invisible by creating superficial programming that depicts everyone getting along. As Cynthia Bejarano (2005) notes, "...appropriating pan-ethnic Latino customs and fashions into American pop culture does not mean that racism and discrimination against Latina/os have been exterminated" (p. 97). Although Latino-themed programming provides new images for children, they have not been exposed to lessons that will help them negotiate their complex reality. It is not sufficient to add a bit of Spanish to a catch phrase and/or include a storyline about a *quinceañera* to claim that the United States is a place where discrimination is a moot point. The industry is betraying its audience by not engaging with issues that are facing the community. Latina/o youth deserve more than fantasy; they should be thought of as viewers who require and demand information that is relevant to their own lives.

One approach that has been used to elicit social change has been the entertainment/education approach outlined by Miguel Sabido that explains how social issues can be incorporated into entertainment programming (Singhal & Rogers, 1999). Sabido's strategy was based on a multi-disciplinary theoretical framework involving elements from Bandura's social learning theory. The approach has been widely adopted in countries with on going development goals (Goldstein, Usdin, Scheepers, & Japhet, 2005) and even in preschool programming in the United States, but it has not been adopted consistently in programming aimed at older youth. In youth programming, the approach has not been systematic, and the attempts to incorporate on going storylines created to persuade attitudes have been met with resistance from industry personnel who believe that American youth will not tolerate preachy television (Wilkin, Valente, Murphy, Cody, Huang & Beck, 2007). There are a few notable exceptions, mainly concerning health information. In 2003, Telemundo collaborated with health communication experts to create a breast cancer storyline as a way to improve awareness regarding cancer detection and treatment.

The telenovela *Ladrón de corazones (Thief of Hearts)* has utilized the entertainment/education approach, and audience research concluded that among viewers there was an increase in knowledge and behavioral intent (Wilkin et al., 2007). There are other mainstream examples of programming that address health issues and, in particular, teen and unplanned pregnancy. Storylines have been included in programs such as *The Secret Life of the American Teenager* (ABC Family) and *One Life to Live* (ABC), among others, but there are few, if any, examples that focus on the Latina/o experience. The entertainment/education model has proven to be effective with specific types of knowledge gain, but where the model has fallen short is in dealing with the more complex issues. For example, there have not been programs that expose the multiple reasons why there is a difference in teenage pregnancy rates between Latinas and other teen populations. Even though entertainment/education has addressed the symptoms of the issues facing Latina/o youth, the ideas behind using media for social change and awareness prove that the industry can do more to encourage new ways of thinking among audience members.

Questions of Language

As noted by the participants in the study, many bilingual audience members watch programming in both Spanish and English. Family members with less English proficiency use mass media in Spanish more frequently, and because of San Diego's proximity to Mexico, many are able to access Mexican television stations. The use of Spanish-language media by immigrants has raised a number of questions about its role in the process of acculturation. On the one hand, Spanish-language media, especially news, provides vital information for a significant portion of society in a language they can understand. Further, for audience members interested in issues pertaining to the Latino community or to Latin America, Spanish-language media provide these stories, which are typically absent from English-language news (Moran, 2006; Montalvo, 2006; Brown, 2009). On the other hand, some critics maintain that the availability of so much information and entertainment in Spanish becomes a stumbling block for immigrants' English-language acquisition. In 2007, Arnold Schwarzenegger, speaking to the National Association of Hispanic Journalists at their annual convention in California, expressed his view that using Spanish-language media has a negative impact on learning English and said "turn off the Spanish television set" as advice to English-language learners, fueling the already heated debate about language. He cited his own experiences learning English as an immigrant to justify his position.

Members of family #9 are Mexican American; the parents were both raised in California. In the home, the family speaks English, although both parents describe themselves as bilingual and use Spanish in their professions. Michelle is an admissions counselor at a local community college, and Carlos is a maintenance worker at a local high school. Although both parents speak Spanish, as a family they mostly watch television in English. Their favorite family shows include *American Idol* and *Dancing with the Stars*. The parents enjoy *The George Lopez Show* because they find the humor relevant to their own experiences. Their children, 5 and 4, never watch television in Spanish.

> KM: Do you ever watch any Spanish-language television?
> Michelle: I don't, he likes to watch movies.
> Carlos: I do, I watch maybe western movies, stuff like that, that I kind of grew up watching. As for me, I was raised to speak English. Spanish was a second language for me. I actually learned on my own. I learned to write it and read it.
> I still watch [Spanish-language television]....When I was at my grandma's house we used to watch wrestling and boxing, you name it, so I did watch that in Spanish too.

For Carlos, watching Spanish-language television performs the task of reinforcing a cultural marker, Spanish, as a way to connect to his family history. Throughout the interview he did not expressly lament not learning Spanish as a first language, but he explained he worked hard as an adult to learn to speak Spanish. Carlos' experience is common among U.S. born Latina/os who are learning Spanish as a second language. "Recently...a growing minority of Hispanic youth [are] expressing a preference for Spanish over English, underlining a renewed pride in their Hispanic heritage" (Callow & McDonald, 2005, p. 285).

Carlos and Michelle were critical, however, of immigrants who come to California and do not try to learn English. Carlos recounted a story about trying to order at a fast food restaurant and the employee did not understand English and asked him to speak Spanish. He refused because he thought it was important for the transaction to be conducted in English. Carlos concluded, "Well finally I got pissed off and had to call Jack in the Box... I called them up and told them he was the rudest you know what. I said I eat there...daily. The point is he should learn some English." Michelle's perspective was similar, and in her work at a local community college she encourages all students to speak English with her.

> Michelle: There's only me and one other person that speaks Spanish so we get a lot of people that are coming to the ESL program, which is fine, obviously they are there to learn English. They're taking the program but sometimes it's hard when you need instructions to register them, stuff like that, so I'll talk to them in Spanish. But there was this one girl that came and wanted to speak Spanish and then I heard her talk to one of our other co-workers in English....if you're here and you're taking, hello, ESL, you need to practice. You need to learn or at least try. She clearly didn't want to.

Nevertheless, both Carlos and Michelle were in favor of television programming in Spanish, especially for entertainment purposes. They also pointed out other stations broadcasting in a variety of languages including Arabic. Michelle concluded, "TV is not going to matter. It's what they know and what they like.... It's for entertainment. I think out in the real world that they're going to need to learn English."

The responses from Carlos and Michelle point to the complexities of the Mexican American perspectives on English-language acquisition. They demonstrate affection for the Spanish language by maintaining its use, but they highlight the tenuous relationship between Spanish-speaking Latinos and English-proficient Latinos. Some of the most avid English-only proponents are immigrants who have mastered English. Arnold Schwarzenegger, governor of California and an immigrant from Austria who learned English, is a member of the advisory board for U.S. English, Inc., an organization "dedicated to preserving the unifying role of the English language in the United States" (www.us-english.org/view/2). English-only rhetoric is mounting in the face of the perceived threat of Spanish and other languages. Confirmation of the perspective is echoed throughout popular culture as evidenced by a Facebook fan page "THIS IS AMERICA...I SHOULDNT HAVE TO PRESS 1 FOR ENGLISH" with a profile picture of a button that reads "Press 1 for English. Press 2 for Deportation." Language is intimately bound with cultural heritage, and while the debates about English-language acquisition rage on, the media industry is not interested in the politics of language, but in the ability to use the appropriate language to appeal to consumers. The tension reveals itself in the ways new immigrants discuss the desire to learn English and also in the ways second generation and beyond participants discuss the desire to maintain Spanish.

Questions of language and media use are central to the experiences of Latina/os in the United States. For those living on the border, a bicultural and bilingual reality is made possible not just from U.S.-based Spanish-language media, but from the availability of Mexican media. People can physically move north across the border, yet remain tightly connected to Mexico. There has been a push from marketing initiatives to create U.S. programming that will appeal to these families, but it will be a difficult task to create something that will compete with the allure of authentic Mexican programming. For families living in the borderlands the broadcast signal from home will remain strong. As the children in these families spend more time in the U.S., they will become entrenched in the mainstream. They shared their opinions about language. Marisol, 8, family #15, explains the benefits of bilingualism, which is echoed by her mother, Clara.

> KM: Do you think it helps you to speak Spanish and English?
> Marisol: Yep. Because you are learning a lot.
> Clara: Because there are more opportunities later on in life, more job opportunities. It is just good for her to know her culture.

There is cultural capital to be gained with bilingual ability. Clara explains that she feels she provides a valuable service to her employer because of her ability to speak Spanish. However, she is in a non-management service position and receives no added pay or benefits for providing additional services. The irony of her bilingualism is that it is useful to her employer, but not materially valued. Viviana (family #14), a lawyer, also explained that her colleagues rely on her bilingual ability, but she does not feel that it gives her much advantage when considered by her superiors. She says, "People are happy I speak Spanish being an attorney but in other places, if I go to another law firm and they need a translator, they are happy to bring in the janitor or someone who works in the kitchen."

Certainly, based on immigrant data alone, we can conclude that many Californians speak Spanish and many more are bilingual. The politics of language, however, are complicated when individuals negotiate their own language abilities. As noted in earlier chapters, immigrant parents want to improve their English skills and also ensure that their children are proficient English speakers. What is a bit different from previous generations is that as the children acquire English, most are still connected to the Spanish language, even beyond the second generation.

Learning a new language is difficult, and it is true that the more one is immersed, the more likely a person is to become proficient. That begs the question: do Spanish-language media do more harm than good? Since English is the de facto official language of the United States and is one of the common international languages, it is to every resident's benefit to be able to read, write and converse in English with an accomplished level of proficiency. Many of the parents interviewed agreed that it is important for their children to speak both English and Spanish, and of the first generation immigrants all of them were trying to improve their English skills. By the second generation, 98% of Latina/os have English-language proficiency, and 79% remain fluent in Spanish (Pew Hispanic Report, 2009). It may be that the use of Spanish-language media functions more as a way for second generation and beyond to maintain their Spanish rather than to keep them from learning English.

Youth oriented media outlets commonly use Spanglish[21] in their programs, on websites and in advertising. Latina/o marketing campaigns have used Spanglish as a shorthand way to hail Latina/os by tapping into their supposed authentic understanding of the market. According to Callow and McDonald (2005) "[Marketing] Researchers have suggested that this code-switching behaviour reflects the perceived importance of the individual's ethnic heritage and his or her adopted culture" (p. 291), and the authors point out the success of Latino-themed media that use this strategy as evidence of its power to appeal to Latina/o audiences. According to the 2009 Pew Hispanic Report, using Spanglish is common among Latina/o youth; an average of 70% use this form of speaking some or most of the time. In October 2009, the *Los Angeles Times* reported on the growth of Spanglish in media directed to U.S.-born Latina/os (Villarreal, 2009). Alex Pels, the general manager of mun2, was quoted as saying, "Networks like ours are a one-stop destination for the bicultural viewer." On mun2, many of the hosts use their bicultural status to appeal to viewers, and the use of Spanglish establishes credibility or authenticity for the young viewer. Yarel Ramos is the host of *Reventón,* a program that showcases the "regional Mexican music scene" as a way to connect U.S.-born Latina/os with their heritage (Villarreal, 2009). Ramos is bilingual and was raised speaking Spanish at home, and while hosting the program she engages in the code-switching practices that are the hallmark of Spanglish. Katynka Martínez (2008) in describing the use of Spanish and English in letters to the editor in *Latina* magazine concludes, "*Latina* readers' use of Spanish emphasizes the fact that their manners of expressing themselves may be English-language dominant but their experiences are bicultural" (p. 147). Some parents, including Viviana, the mother in family #14, found this strategy unauthentic or, worse, annoying.

> Viviana: You should just speak Spanish or English just one or the other. I don't know, I think it depends on who it is coming from, I don't like to see it in written format, I don't like to see it on television because I think it perpetuates a stereotype that people don't speak English and they don't speak Spanish well. That is the other thing that is more common living in California, I run into Mexicans from Mexico who think the worst of Mexican Americans just because of this Spanglish going on out here.

Parents were more critical of Spanglish than their teenage children. Young people were more concerned with how Spanglish was used and whether its use was realistic.

After reviewing the programming aimed at young Latina/os, it becomes apparent that the use of Spanglish can hail certain audience members in a way that defines their connection to the Latina/o identity. Spanglish has become central to the construction of Latinidad, especially for young people who are comfortable negotiating the two languages. Cynthia Bejarano (2005) noted that young people living in the borderlands used Spanglish frequently. "Chicanas/os forked tongues and code-switching were pervasive in the school setting" (p. 147) illustrates her conclusion that their hybrid identity forces them to adopt both languages, especially among the second generation. An important discrepancy between the media representation of Spanglish and the lived experience of Latina/o youth can be found in the reactions to the code switching practices. In Latino-themed media that use Spanglish, it is situated as fun and hip to establish credibility as authentically Latina/o. There are never moments when the hosts or characters are chastised for using Spanglish or code-switching. Further, there are no sideways glances indicating the inappropriateness of this practice or their bilingual status. The lived experience may be much different; the youth in Bejarano's (2005) study describe feeling alienated as a result of their language preferences. While the youth in the families interviewed in this sample did not describe any specific instances of discrimination as a result of speaking Spanish or

Spanglish, they did indicate that they mostly speak English with their friends.

It should also be noted that differentiated language use among youth is nothing new. Slang terms that indicate ingroup status among subgroups are common, and most youth understand when and how to use this style of language and gage its appropriateness given the context. Journalist Ed Morales (2002) discusses the notion of Spanglish and describes its roots as much more than a combination of English and Spanish. He uses the term to describe the complexities of Latina/o identity in the United States. He writes: "But Spanglish is altogether something else—it expresses something much broader and interesting than just a glitch in language" (p. 6). He argues that the spoken Spanglish is the "verbal manifestation" of the changing nature of the U.S. landscape. Anyone can live Spanglish, even if it is never manifested through language.

Latina/o celebrities can become the center of the debate about living Spanglish. Actress Selena Gomez, who stars on the Disney Channel in *Wizards of Waverly Place* and is featured as Beezus Quimby in the film adaptation of Beverly Cleary's *Ramona and Beezus* released in the summer of 2010, presents an opportunity to interrogate the relationship between language and Latinidad. Gomez was born in Texas; her father is from Mexico. In February 2008 Selena Gomez was interviewed for *Twist* magazine, a celebrity gossip source aimed at teenagers also available online at www.twistmagazine.com. The interview titled "Selena Gomez Talks About Being Mexican" elicited a range of viewpoints on her ability to speak Spanish. Comments posted on a weblog titled Gossip Chic (http://gossipchic.com/selena-gomez-talks-about-being-mexican/) showcase these sentiments: on March 4, 2008, Ronald asked "Does she speak Spanish cause [she] seems to be happy about her heritage but I never heard her speak Spanish." Ruby (8/12/08) posted "selena, i want to ask you one question, do you speak Spanish. becuz i never heard u speak Spanish." Others commented on her body as the site of Latinidad. Many of the posts disclosed that they are proud to be Mexican and xmnmx1011 (5/24/09) posted "...i love selena cuz she has taught me to keep believing and be proud of who i am." Travis (5/26/09) commented,

"Although i love the U.S.A. I always wear Mexican soccer jerseys and i will always be proud to be Mexican no matter what people say. I have lots of love for the beautiful motherland and its people. I applaud Selena for not becoming too Americanized like some other Mexican girls who are stupid and buckle with the pressure and are ashamed. That's one of the reasons I love Selena Gomez. She stays true. Viva Mexico!"

The posters responding to Gomez's heritage describe salient features of Latinidad, whereby Gomez looks Mexican because of her dark hair and eyes and many encourage her to be proud of her heritage. Gomez was featured on the cover of *Latina* magazine in April 2009 (distributed March 17, 2009 and posted on the *Latina* website March 12, 2009), where she was described as being proud of her Latino heritage. She was quoted as saying, "it's pretty neat to be Mexican." The choice to present her as a cover feature indicates her move into greater stardom. As a result, more publicity provides further opportunities for audiences to deliberate her Latina status. After the *Latina* article, on a celebrity gossip blog, Just Jared (http://justjaredjr.buzznet.com/), many posted comments on her role model status and again focused on language. Flawed_perfection wrote, "I'm glad that we can have a really, good young Latina to represent what it's all about. I'm proud that I have someone that my nieces can look up to and show them that anything is possible." Love2Flaughter (3/15/09) agreed, "I absolutely Love Selena Gomez. She is a true person. She is young. She is beautiful. I am proud that she is a young Mexican girl that is blossoming into a strong woman that my girls look up to." Others were critical about her authentic Latina status. Chrys wrote (3/12/09), "I like Selena and all but come on, I'm Latina and I would not be calling myself that if I wasn't fluent in the language. If she wants to be taken seriously (as a Latina) she should take some classes and learn the language more." Coolio defends her (3/21/2009), "Um, Selena has every right to call herself a Latina. I mean come on! She's MEXICAN for goodness sakes. Do you expect her to call herself white?! It doesn't matter if she speaks Spanish fluently or not, she's a Latina whether you like it or not."

These selected comments are not a representative sample of all the perceptions of this young Latina star, but they do exemplify the contradictions of audiences who engage with popular culture. Some fans are adamant in defending her as Mexican, when in fact she is U.S.-born, highlighting the constant negotiation of an identity that is always already informed by multiple, although not necessarily competing, forces. Selena Gomez has the making of a Latina superstar following in the footsteps of other success stories such as Jennifer Lopez, who, as Valdivia (2004) points out, became successful in part because of her ambiguous body that allows her to play a variety of characters that have widespread appeal. Gomez, like the U.S. Latina stars before her, will become part of the pattern of representations that enable audiences to identify and question Latinidad.

As immigration from Spanish-speaking countries continues to impact the demographic makeup of the United States, questions of language will be pondered. The economic incentive to create media in Spanish to appeal to Spanish-dominant speakers will be the determining factor for the media industry regardless of any social or political initiatives. In other words, if it is profitable to make domestic media in Spanish, it will be made. As more Latina/os are born in the U.S. using English as their primary language, bilingualism may indeed become more common.

Considering the Future

Reflecting on the first decade of the 21st century when marketing efforts and subsequent Latino-themed media became the hot commodity, it becomes clear that the trend of bilingual and bicultural programming is not fading away. As the 2010 Census numbers are released, there is even more attention devoted to this market. It is therefore incumbent on scholars, especially those in communication and media studies, to continue serious inquiry into the production practices that privilege certain types of representation. As marketing executives seek to placate advertiser need, further differentiating audiences based on stereotyped assumptions about what they desire, it should be noted that for the young members of the families included in this study, there is a preference for more inclusive narratives rather than being relegated to a niche. The general consensus among the participants is for programming with cast members who engage fully in the stories that are told, but are seen as unique because of their Latina/o heritage. Within the field of communication, Latina/o media studies research should become a central component to understanding the ways in which the mass media shape the audiences' perceptions of themselves and others. Media scholars, including those who focus on children and teens, should incorporate Latina/o youth into every study because they are central to understanding the ways media impact this generation. Racial categorizations typically used by social scientists limit the possibility of assessing the true complexity of the experiences of young Americans. Studies that compare children's media use by ethnicity have found it difficult to uncover significant findings related to the experiences of Latina/o children (see, for example, Bickham, Vandewater, Huston, Lee, Caplovitz, & Wright, 2003; Anand & Krosnick, 2005) however, when language is used to differentiate between groups, significant differences emerge (Thompson, Sibinga, Jennings, Bair-Merritt, & Christakis, 2010). The lesson learned for scholars is that the hybrid nature of the audience, demonstrated by the ways in which Latina/o family members describe their media use, points to the complexity of the category, which may ultimately render the ethnic classification useless. Instead future studies should pay closer attention to language and nativity when studying media habits for Latina/o audience members.

The choice to view television in either Spanish or English is much more about the content than the language. Even though it might be in the industry's best interest to utilize Spanish-language programming as a way to diversify the media landscape, it should not be assumed that Latina/os who speak Spanish will watch more Spanish-language programming. What is appealing to audience members, especially those second generation and beyond, is programming within English-language media that showcases the heterogeneity of their generation. The industry should recognize and reflect the bicultural or multicultural reality of American youth and explore representations in responsible ways. One approach to diversifying the marketplace is by having more Latina/os in positions of power throughout the industry. Actor Edward James Olmos, interviewed for a Turner Classic Movie special series on *Race & Hollywood: Latino Images in Film* in reference to the progression of representation, indicated that when given the opportunity, Latina/os have produced successful films. He stated: "When they [mainstream producers] have tried to exploit the culture it has not been successful, but when Latinos have been allowed to use the medium, it has been successful" http://www.tcm.com/2009 /lif/index.jsp), indicating the efficacy for more opportunities for Latina/os behind the scenes as a way to create more inclusive narratives on the screen. One organization involved in facilitating more opportunity in the entertainment industry is the National Association of Latino Independent Producers (NALIP), which describes itself as an "organization that addresses the professional needs of Latino/Latina independent producers" (http://www.nalip.org/ nalip/NALIP-About.html). Founded in 1999, the organization is committed to supporting the production of film and media arts by Latina/os in all genres. While Latina/o productions do not guarantee authentic, inspiring or problem free portrayals, the narratives are at least informed by being read as Latina/o. It is not the case that non-Latina/os should not engage in the creation of stories for or about the Latina/o lived experience, but that all storytellers need to be mindful of the consequences of representation.

Latino families engage with the mass media from their own subject position. Parents who are new to the United States are more likely to stay connected to the native culture through the use of Spanish-language media outlets, but their children are quick to adopt mainstream media practices. Spanish-language television has enjoyed growth spurred on by the assumption that even English-dominant Latino families prefer Spanish-language media, but listening to the sample family members, it is obvious that this assumption needs to be interrogated. Advocacy groups have questioned the accuracy of the Nielsen rating system that consistently places Univisión programming atop all else and Nielsen's ability to account for U.S.-born Latina/os' media preferences. Listening to Latina/o youth demonstrates that young people are not bound by the traditional dualities that shaped previous generations. They recognize their bicultural position, but are not necessarily interested in being defined as outside mainstream culture. As one participant explained, she's just a "typical teenager." What is changing is the definition of typical. For many, typical used to mean white and middle class; now it is more common and therefore typical to be something else.

Data consistently show that non-white youth outnumber their Caucasian counterparts and, as a result, growing up in the United States is a much different experience than it was even 30 years ago. While changing demographics are nothing new to the landscape of the U.S., what is different is the speed at which these changes are occurring. Further complicating the social process is the role that mediated messages play in the audiences' construction of self. Latina/o youth spend a significant amount of time interacting with technology. The most recent study by the Kaiser Family Foundation released January 20, 2010 found that young people in the United States spend a total of 7:38 hours per day using media, and much of that time includes media multitasking (Rideout, Foehr, & Roberto, 2010). According to the 2010 report, Hispanic youth have increased their daily total media use by 4:08 hours since the 2004 report. The authors note that the increase in time has mainly come from new media platforms such as handheld video game devices. As outlined, more media outlets across platforms have been created for this audience, and obviously they have responded. The Kaiser study is good news for industry professionals who are looking to exploit the Latina/o market by showcasing their success in appealing more broadly to Latina/o youth, but may serve as a warning for those concerned with the relationship between media and youth. The availability of media products coupled with the knowledge of the amount of time Latina/o youth spend with media underscores the urgency to understand this phenomena.

As a group, Latina/os are young; of second generation 37.5% and of third generation and beyond 29% are younger than ten

years old indicating that Latina/o youth will play a significant role
in shaping the future of U.S. society. Their tastes, style, and language are already incorporated into U.S. popular culture, but
many more stories are waiting to unfold. This new generation of
Americans will shape U.S. culture in unprecedented ways and reveal the complexity of multicultural hybrid identities. As scholars
address the actions of media producers looking to target youth
markets, we can encourage new modes of representation that do
not follow predictable patterns. We have seen too few examples of
sustainable, quality productions that provide rich imagery of the
diverse Latina/o experience. It appears that media are at a cross-
roads. What kinds of representations and narratives can give audience members more agency? How might young Latina/os achieve
power and freedom outside the logic of consumption? When will
stories be told without being driven by Latina/o marketing? Af-
fordable, cutting-edge technology provides access to a range of
voices and youth are responding by engaging in new conversations
and taking ownership over representation, but there is not widespread distribution of these alternatives. Websites provide alternative choices for Latina/o youth, but one must actively seek out such
sites. Mainstream media producers should be held accountable for
representations and be encouraged to create more responsible portrayals, especially in the context of diversity and difference. One of
the perplexing challenges of media representation is that as the
market drives more media targeting the Latina/o audience, it
strips Latina/o youth of their ability to enact an authentic voice.
Programs such as *LatiNation* have taken up the challenge to represent Latina/o youth by emphasizing the variation of their experiences. Questions remain, however, about whether a program that
places itself within the current logic of the mainstream media industry can promote an alternative outlook. Some media outlets are
representing Latina/o youth, but do they provide opportunities for
youth to represent themselves?

The media are an integral part of children's daily lives, and as
such, we can demand more from the producers who look to profit
from youth. By listening to Latina/o youth, we have learned that
the interplay of language and culture impacts the way media im-

agery affects the formation of identity. The Latina/o youth market has been recognized as an important part of the media industry and more U.S. products incorporating Latino themes and/or characters are likely. If the industry continues to promote an essentialized Latina/o identity by creating more products that repeat standard media conventions that are based on stereotypes of the Latina/o experience, Latina/o audiences will not be satisfied. If we accept that many Latina/o youth in this country are living a hybrid experience conditioned by their experiences with the mass media, we have to remember that it is a hybridity without guarantees. We should not blindly celebrate the dynamic changes occurring among American youth without interrogating the on going systems of power that limit or expand opportunities. As parents, critics, and scholars, it is our responsibility to keep the industry in check by demanding more comprehensive programming that is not focused solely on economic gain, but instead support alternative modes of production that open up possibilities for young people across the nation and throughout the world.

Appendix A

The following descriptions of the participating families are included to provide information about the demographics of the members. The first group of families was interviewed in February and March of 2008. The families were numbered in the order in which they were interviewed, and there was no strategy to the order. I interviewed families according to their schedules. The names of the family members have been changed to protect their identities. A second round of interviews was conducted in March 2010 to increase participation from children and to provide a more nuanced understanding of the ways in which children navigate their media use.

Family #1

Family #1 was interviewed in their home in the evening after dinner. Lucia, the mother, is a teacher who works at a preschool on a university campus. She is in her early 30s and moved to San Diego when she was a toddler. She met her husband, Freddie, in high school in Chula Vista (south San Diego County) and they continue to live there. Freddie is a title officer and his family is from Guam. They have two children, Ian, 4, and Emma, 3. The family speaks English in the home, although Lucia speaks Spanish with her family and does encourage her children to speak Spanish. The interview was conducted in English.

Family #2

The second family interviewed also lives in Chula Vista. The mother and children were interviewed in the evening in their home. The father, a police officer, works at night. Isabel graduated from UCSD with a communication degree. She currently works as a substitute teacher. Isabel's maternal family is from Mexico and her mother immigrated to California as a young child. Her mother and aunts enjoy watching telenovelas. Isabel's husband grew up in Chula Vista, and both his parents emigrated from Mexico. She and her husband are both in their 30s. Their children, Travis, 6, and Timothy, 11, Isabel's son from a previous relationship, live with them. The family speaks English in the home although both parents speak Spanish with family members. The children are enrolled in Spanish immersion programs and use Spanish daily in school, but communicate with friends and each other in English. The interview was conducted in English.

Family #3

Family #3 also lives in Chula Vista and was interviewed in their home in the early evening. Nora, born in San Diego, works at a bank as a loan officer and met her husband while attending San Diego State University. Her parents are from Mexico. Her husband, Miguel, immigrated to San Diego from Tijuana with his parents when he was 18 so he could attend college. Miguel owns his own marketing firm, which specializes in the Hispanic market. The parents are in their 40s and have two children, Miguelito, 11, and Alexa, 10. The children attend a Spanish emersion school and can speak both Spanish and English with equal ease. In the home, the family interacts more often in English, but uses Spanish occasionally. When they are with their paternal grandparents the primary language is Spanish. The interview was conducted in English.

Family #4

Family #4 lives in the Eastlake neighborhood in south San Diego County and was interviewed in their home on a weekend afternoon. Jennifer and Manuel live together and share custody of Manuel's young children with his first wife. Jennifer is Caucasian and works in the international studies office of a university. She speaks Spanish; she lived in Cádiz, Spain, as an undergraduate student, majored in Spanish in college and lived in Guanajuato, Mexico, for six months, where she taught English. Jennifer uses Spanish more since she met Manuel, who is from Manzanillo, Mexico, and immigrated to San Diego as a child. She speaks both Spanish and English with the girls who are 6 and 4. Manuel is a chef and is opening his own restaurant in downtown San Diego. Both adults are in their 30s. The mother of the children speaks primarily Spanish and Jennifer explained that the girls speak Spanish, and watch Spanish-language TV when they are with their mother. The interview was conducted in English.

Family #5

Family #5 was interviewed in their apartment in the Clairemont neighborhood of San Diego in the evening. José moved from Mexico to San Diego 18 years ago and his wife, who he met in an English class, immigrated 8 years ago. They have two children who were born in San Diego, Jaime, 6 (who has low spectrum autism), and Juan, 2. Jaime is in first grade at the local elementary school, where he speaks English. The parents use Spanish in the home, although they have a desire to become more proficient English speakers. José works as a cook in a chain restaurant, and Carmen cleans houses. José is in his 40s, and Carmen is in her 30s. The interview was conducted in Spanish.

Family #6

I interviewed family #6 in their home in the Barrio Logan neighborhood of San Diego in the afternoon. Five members of the household were present during the interview and the grandmother was home, but due to health reasons did not participate in the interview. Victoria, the mother, moved to her grandmother's home from Tijuana when she was 25 and has lived there ever since. Her husband, Esteban, moved into the family home after their marriage. They have two children who were born in San Diego, Angela, 21, a college student, and Pablo, 17, a senior in high school. Their cousin, Rosa, in her 30s, immigrated to California less than a year

ago. Victoria is a housekeeper, and Esteban works at a manufacturing plant and volunteers at their church. At home, the family
primarily speaks Spanish. Victoria is shy about her English skills,
but she can understand and speak competently. Esteban uses English at work, and the children are bilingual. The interview was
conducted primarily in Spanish, but with some discussions in English.

Family #7

I was introduced to Family #7 because the mothers of Family #6
and #7 are sisters. Lola moved with her sister from Tijuana when
she was in her early 20s and lived with her grandmother. She is
now nearing 40, and she and her husband, Alejandro, operate a
Head Start daycare program in their home. Lola primarily speaks
Spanish, and most of the children in the daycare are from Spanish-
speaking families. I conducted the interview in the evening in their
home in Chula Vista. They have a son, Alejandro, 13, who attends
private school, and while they speak Spanish in the home, the son
is bilingual. The interview was conducted primarily in Spanish.

Family #8

Family #8 moved to San Diego in 1996 when Jorge, the father, was
offered a job through the Mexican consulate. He now works for the
state of California in educational assessment. His wife, Beatriz,
cares for their home. The parents are in their 50s and have two
daughters, Mona, 23, and Diana, 22. The girls had little English
proficiency when they arrived, but after a year in an English as a
Second Language (ESL) program they moved to the mainstream
classroom. Mona now lives in Orange County and works at Disney-
land, and Diana attends art school in Guadalajara, Mexico. The
daughters were visiting their family at the time of the interview,
so all members participated. The interview was conducted in both
English and Spanish.

Family #9

The parents in Family #9 grew up in California and now live in La Mesa in east San Diego County with their two children Sofia, 5 and Clara, 4. Michelle, in her 30s, grew up speaking Spanish with her parents, who emigrated from Mexico. She works as an admissions counselor at a local community college. Her husband, Carlos, was raised in the Imperial Valley of California and explained that his grandparents are Spanish and lived for some time in Mexico. His parents are both from Arizona. Carlos spoke English as a child, but learned Spanish as he got older. He works at a local high school as a member of the maintenance staff. The children attend a local public elementary school and speak very little Spanish. The interview was conducted in English in their home on a weekend afternoon.

Family #10

Family #10 came to San Diego in 1998 when the father, Ernesto, was offered a position as a research scientist at the San Diego Natural History Museum. Ernesto, originally from Buenos Aires, Argentina moved to Mexico City where he met Claudia who left her job with Televisa when they moved to San Diego. She now does freelance translation work. They have two children who were born in Mexico, Pilar, 15 and Roberto, 18. The children learned English quickly and are bilingual and attend a local public high school. Both parents are bilingual, but speak to each other in Spanish. They have travelled extensively and have lived in Europe. The interview was conducted in their home in La Mesa in the evening and was mostly in English.

Family #11

The two older children in family #11 were the primary interview subjects, but their stepmother and younger half-brother were also present. Lupe, 6, and her brother Armando, 9, immigrated to Chula Vista about one year ago from Puerto Escondido, Oaxaca, Mexico, after their father, also from Mexico, married Linda. The parents are in their 40s. Linda is second generation Mexican American and is from Chicago, where she attended the University of Illinois before becoming a journalist. She is now a professor at a community college. The family is bilingual. The interview was conducted in English on a weekend afternoon in the family home in Chula Vista.

Family #12

The family members are natives of Ensenada, Baja California, Mexico, and travel between San Diego and Ensenada regularly. The father is a mechanical engineer and owns a winery in Baja California while the mother takes care of their son and home. The parents are in their 40s. The son, Santiago, 14, attends a private middle school in San Diego, so he spends most of his time in San Diego. The family speaks Spanish in the home, but all members are bilingual. Santiago speaks English at school although admits to using Spanish strategically with his friends, who sometimes want to keep secrets from non-Spanish speakers. His mother, Mariana, explains that they are willing to be in San Diego to ensure a better education for Santiago, and they have the resources to move freely between the two countries and to finance his private education. The interview was conducted in the afternoon primarily in English in the family's San Diego home.

Family #13

The family lives in San Diego and includes two boys who are 5 and 8 years old. The children, born in San Diego, were the primary focus of the interview. Their mother, Marisa, is from Texas, and her parents are from Mexico. The parents are in their late 30s. The mother was present during the interview and offered some comments. The older son, Sergio, attends a Spanish immersion school and is bilingual. He communicates with his mother in Spanish, but as a unit, the family speaks English. The younger son, Pedro, is in kindergarten at an English-language charter school. The boys do not watch television or movies in Spanish. The interview was conducted in the afternoon in their home in English.

Family #14

I interviewed 5-year-old twins, Marcos and Mercedes, in their home in San Diego. Their mother, Viviana, was present during the interview. The children are in their final year of preschool and are eager to attend kindergarten next year. The family identifies as Mexican American; their father is from Los Angeles and identifies as Mexican American. Viviana, the mother, is from Texas; her mother is Texan with Mexican ancestry, and her father is from Spain. The parents are in their late 40s. The interview was conducted in English in the family home.

Family #15

An 8-year-old girl, Marisol, was the primary subject of this interview. She lives in Spring Valley, in San Diego County, with her mother and aunt. Marisol attends an English-language elementary school and is in second grade; she is third generation. Her mother, now in her late 20s, grew up in Chula Vista, and her grandparents are natives of Mexico. Marisol speaks English with her friends and her family, although her mother often gives her directions in Spanish. The interview was conducted at my home in La Mesa and was conducted in English.

Family #16

The focus of the interview was Jimena, a 17-year-old senior who attends a public high school in south San Diego County. The family lives in National City but travels to Tijuana nearly every weekend and is still very connected to family members in Mexico. The parents, in their 40s, immigrated to ensure educational opportunities for the children. Jimena has a younger brother who is in seventh grade, and he declined to be interviewed. The interview was in English and took place in Jimena's home.

Family #17

Susana, 9 years old, was interviewed in her home in La Jolla, California. Her father emigrated from Mexico, and her mother is American. Her parents are divorced. Susana does not speak Spanish and is not close to her relatives in Mexico. Her father wants to improve that connection and would like her to speak more Spanish and learn about Mexican culture. Her mother, in her 40s, is English-language dominant, but learned Spanish and continues to primarily speak Spanish with her ex-husband.

Notes

1. Much has been written about the labels associated with the group I am describing, and as the book unfolds the reader will understand the diversity of the audience that marketers refer to as "Hispanic" and academics sometimes refer to as "Latina/o" as well as a variety of other cultural signifiers that include "Chicano" and "Mexicano" (Rinderle, 2005). Based on Spanish grammar, the "o" ending is gender neutral, but the trend within critical approaches is to foreground the inclusion of women by using Latina/o. Therefore, I have chosen to use Latina/o when referring to the group, with more specific references to nationality when appropriate. I do not want to promote an essentialist image of the group and will carefully foreground Mayer's (2004) warnings about "panlatinidad" and del Río's (2006) call to "problematize" the category in order to ensure that the diversity of the group is recognized.
2. Telemundo, owned by NBC/Universal, is a Spanish-language U.S. network.
3. Telenovelas are Spanish-language drama serials discussed in detail in Chapter 4.
4. *CHiPs* was a police drama broadcast on NBC between 1977 and 1983 starring Erik Estrada, who is of Puerto Rican descent.
5. The California Proposition 187 was on the ballot in November 1994. The measure sought to deny all state-funded benefits to "illegal aliens" including health care and public schooling. The proposition passed with 59% of the vote. Los Angeles-based U.S. District Judge Mariana Pfaelzer issued a temporary restraining order against the measure to prevent Prop 187 from taking effect (Federal Judge, 1997). After years in legal limbo, Prop 187 was deemed unconstitutional in 1998.
6. Hispanic is the label used by the Census to identify those with a heritage from Latin America or Spain. It includes racially "white" Hispanics while the category for Caucasians reads "White, non-Hispanic."
7. While it is important to be cognizant of the diversity among the group, the following description is provided to ensure a common base of understanding to contextualize the interview responses in later chapters. I do

not intend to claim that these characteristics are true for all Latino families.

8. Tween is the name given to in-betweeners: those children who have aged out of preschool/educational programming, but are not quite ready for older teen programming such as shows on MTV.

9. In 1990, the U.S. Congress passed the CTA, which stated that all television license holders must serve the "educational and informational" needs of children. In 1996, Congress revised the Act to specifically state that license holders must provide at least three hours per week of programs that are defined as having a significant purpose in educating child audiences and file quarterly reports describing the station's compliance, as well as make those records available to the public. These programs are defined as "core programs" and must be identified on a quarterly report filed with the FCC.

10. A *quinceañera* is a Mexican tradition that began under the presidency of Porfirio Díaz as a coming of age ceremony for fifteen-year-olds. It has become a rite of passage for many Latina girls and an important cultural tradition in many Latino families. For Roman Catholics the ceremony has a strong religious element that precedes a reception. In recent years these parties have become, for some, lavish affairs supporting ancillary industries.

11. The National Council of La Raza, the largest national Latino civil rights and advocacy organization in the U.S., created the ALMA Awards in 1995 to recognize the contributions of Latina/os in the entertainment industry.

12. Glocal refers to programs that have a global format, e.g., the telenovela, and localize in a particular market to make it culturally appealing.

13. *Reforma* is a Mexican newspaper. It was unclear whether Claudia had read the print or electronic version.

14. *Canal Once* is the public television station in Mexico.

15. *The Dog Whisperer* is broadcast on the National Geographic Channel and stars Cesar Millan, who is from Mexico and moved to California as a young adult.

16. Eva Longoria is from Texas, where her family has lived for generations.

17. According to their website, the Head Start program allocates grants to provide assistance for child development services to economically disadvantaged children and families.

18. *Pocho* is typically used for a person of Mexican descent who does not speak Spanish and is not connected to the culture.

19. *Dangerous Minds* stars Michelle Pfieffer as a teacher who motivates a group of mostly minority high school students to succeed.

20. I want to emphasize that I am not using citizen to refer to legal status, but in the more general sense to refer to youth as members of an informed civil society.

21. Spanglish is an informal combination of Spanish and English. For example, using both languages in one sentence or in one conversation.

References

Acosta-Alzuru, C. (2003). Tackling the issues: Meaning making in a telenovela. *Popular Communication, 1,* 193–215.

A Different America on Screen. *Screen Actor,* Winter, 2007, 55–59.

Alban, D. (2009, 21 October). An uphill battle to combat Latino childhood obesity. Retrieved on March 11, 2010, from http://www.cnn.com/2009/HEALTH/10/21/childhood.obesity/index.html.

Anand, S. & Krosnick, J. (2005). Demographic predictors of media use among infants, toddlers, and preschoolers. *American Behavioral Scientist, 48,* 539–561.

Anderson, K. & Cavallaro, D. (2002). Parent or pop culture? Children's heroes and role models. *Childhood Education, 78,* 161–169.

Aparicio, F. (2003). Jennifer as Selena: Rethinking Latinidad in media and popular culture. *Latino Studies, 1,* 90–105.

Aparicio, F. (1999). The blackness of sugar: Celia Cruz and the performance of (trans)nationalism. *Cultural Studies, 13*(2), 223–236.

Aparicio, F. & Chávez-Siverman, S. (1997). (Eds.). *Tropicalizations: Transcultural representations of* Latinidad. Hanover, NH: Dartmouth College.

Avila-Saavedra, G. (2010). A fish out of water: New articulations of U.S.-Latino identity on *Ugly Betty. Communication Quarterly, 58*(2), 133–147.

Ayala, N. (2007, June 5). TNS Report: Hispanic TV, magazines ad spend grows, print suffers setback. Retrieved November 10, 2009 from http://juantornoe.blogs.com/hispanictrending/2007/06/tns_report_hisp.html.

Baent-Weiser, S. (2007). The Nickelodeon brand: Buying and selling the audience. In S. Banet-Weiser, C. Chris, and A. Feitas (Eds.), *Cable visions: Television beyond broadcasting* (pp. 234–252). New York: New York University Press.

Bandura, A. (1986). *Social foundations of thought and actions: A social cognitive theory.* Englewood Cliffs, NJ: Prentice Hall, Inc.

Baran, S. & Davis, D. (2006). *Mass communication theory: Foundations, ferment, and future,* 4th edition. Belmont, CA: Thomson Wadsworth.

Barondess, H. & Newhouse, C. (2007, June). The unique challenges to the well-being of California's border kids. Report prepared for Children Now.

Barrera,V. & Bielby, D. (2001). Places, faces and other familiar things: The cultural experience of telenovela viewing among Latinos in the United States. *Journal of Popular Culture, 34,* 1–18.

Bastien, T. (Director). (2010). The twisty turn twist [74]. In. P. Lehn (Executive Producer). *Handy Manny.* Disney.

194 *Listening to Latina/o Youth*

Bednarski, P.J. (2003, October). PBS toon targets bilingual Latinos. *Broadcasting & Cable.* Retrieved on June 8, 2006 from http://www.broadcastingcable.com.

Bejarano, C. (2005). *¿Que Onda? Urban youth cultures and border identity.* Tucson, AZ: University of Arizona Press.

Beltrán, M. (2009). *Latina/o stars in U.S. eyes: The making and meanings of film and TV stardom.* Chicago: University of Illinois Press.

Bickham, D., Vandewater, E., Huston, A., Lee, J., Caplovitz, A., & Wright, J. (2003). Predictors of children's electronic media use: An examination of three ethnic groups. *Media Psychology, 5,* 107–137.

Blosser, B. J. (1988). Ethnic differences in children's media use. *Journal of Broadcasting and Electronic Media, 32,* 453–470.

Bourdieu, P. (1998). *On television.* New York: The New Press.

Brown, C. (2009). Immigration in the news. FlowTV, 11, 4. Retrieved on January 6, 2010, from http://flowtv.org/?p=4633.

Brown, D., Davis, P. & Stoffel, N. (2010, 13 April). Hispanic population has strong buying power [radio broadcast]. In N. Stoffel (producer), *KPBS Morning Edition.* San Diego, CA: National Public Radio.

Brown, S. (2004, June). Latina's media are bilingual. *MediaWeek, 14,* 8.

Bryant, J. & Oliver, M.B. (2009). *Media effects: Advances in theory and research,* 3rd edition. New York: Routledge.

Calbreath, D. (2002, June 13). Clout of Hispanic media: U.S. TV giant Univisión to pay $3 billion for nation's largest Latino radio network. *San Diego Union Tribune.*

Callow, M. & McDonald, C. G. (2005). The 'spanglification' of advertising campaigns in Hispanic media? A comparison of approaches in Spanish-only and dual language magazines. *Journal of Marketing Communications, 11,* 283–295.

Calvert, S. (1999). *Children's journey through the information age.* New York: McGraw-Hill Companies, Inc.

Calvert, S., Rideout, V., Woolard, J., Barr, R. & Strouse, G. (2005). Age, ethnicity, and socioeconomic patterns in early computer use: A national survey. *American Behavioral Scientist, 48,* 590–607.

Calvert, S., Strong, B., Jacobs, E., & Conger, E. (2007). Interaction and participation for young Hispanic and Caucasian girls' and boys' learning of media content. *Media Psychology, 9,* 431–446.

Carter, B. (2006, 25 December). Sizzling a year ago, but now pfffft....*The New York Times.* Retrieved on October 29, 2009, from http://www.nytimes.com/2006/12/25/business/media/25telenovela.html.

Carter, B. & Elliot, S. (2009, August 14). Media companies seek rival for Nielsen ratings. *The New York Times.* Retrieved on August 25, 2009, from http://www.nytimes.com/2009/08/15/business/media/15ratings.html.

Casas Pérez, M. (2005). Cultural identity: Between reality and fiction: A transformation of genre and roles in Mexican *telenovelas. Television & New Media, 6(4),* 407–414.

Castañeda, M. (2008a). The importance of Spanish-language and Latino media. In A. Valdivia (Ed.), *Latina/o communication studies today* (pp. 51–66). New York: Peter Lang.

Castañeda, M. (2008b). Rethinking the U.S. Spanish-language media market in an era of deregulation. In P. Chakravartty and Y. Zhao (Eds.), *Global communications: Toward a transcultural political economy* (pp. 201–215). Lanham, MD: Rowman & Littlefield Publishers, Inc.

Cauce, A.M. & Domenech-Rodríguez, M. (2002). Latino families: Myths and realities. In J. Contreras, K. Kerns, A. Neal-Barnett (Eds.). *Latino children and families in the United States: Current research and future directions* (pp. 3–26). Westport, CT: Praeger Publishers.

Cepeda, M.E. (2008). Survival aesthetics: U.S. Latinas and the negotiation of popular media. In A. Valdivia (Ed.), *Latina/o communication studies today* (pp. 237–255). New York: Peter Lang.

Clemens, L. (2006, February 13). Next-Gen Hispanics reshape the market: Cable nets cater to young Latinos with telenovelas, music, wrestling. Multichannel News. Retrieved on June 8, 2006, from http://www.multichannel.com/article/122097Next_Gen_Hispanics_Reshape_the_Market.php.

Cohn, D. & Bahhrampour, T. (2006, May 10). "Of U.S. children under 5, nearly half are minorities: Hispanic growth fuels rise." (www.washingtonpost.com). Retrieved on May 31, 2006, from http://www.washingtonpost.com/wp-dyn/content/article/2006/05/09/AR2006050901841.html.

Condit, C. M. (1989). The rhetorical limits of polysemy. *Critical Studies in Mass Communication, 6*(2), 103–122.

Consoli, J. (2008, March 31). Univision opens up, *MediaWeek, 18,* 6.

Cortés, C. (1997). Chicanas in film: History of an image. In C. Rodriguez (Ed.), *Latin looks: Images of Latinas and Latinos in the U.S. media* (pp. 121–141). Boulder, CO: Westview Press.

Cortés, C. (2000). *The children are watching: How the media teach about diversity.* New York: Teachers College Press.

Dávila, A. (2008). *Latino spin: Public image and the whitewashing of race.* New York: New York University Press.

Dávila, A. (2002). Talking back: Spanish media and U.S. Latinidad. In M. Habell-Pallán and M. Romero (Eds.), *Latino/a Popular Culture* (pp. 25–37). New York: New York University Press.

Dávila, A. (2001a). *Latinos, Inc.: The marketing and making of a people.* Los Angeles, CA: University of California Press.

Dávila, A. (2001b). The Latin side of Madison avenue: Marketing and the language that makes us "Hispanics." In A. Laó-Montes and A. Dávila (Eds.), *Mambo montage: The Latinization of New York* (pp. 411–424). New York: Columbia University Press.

Dávila, A. (2000). Mapping Latinidad: Language and culture in the Spanish TV battlefront. *Television & New Media,* 1, 75-94.

de Block, L. & Buckingham, D. (2007). *Global children, global media: Migration, media and childhood.* New York: Palgrave Macmillian.

de la Fuente, A.M. (2006, October 9). Battle of the "Betty" beauties. *Variety.*

de la Garza, R., DeSipio, L., Lee, J. & Pachon, H. (2004). A policy review paper assessing the Nielsen and Rincón Study on Latino Television Viewing. Policy paper. Claremont, CA: The Tomás Rivera Policy Institute.

del Río, E. (2010a). Consuming and contesting Latinidad: Audience research and cultural capital. *Participations: Journal of Audience & Reception Studies.* http://www.participations.org/Volume%207/Issue%201/delrio.htm.

del Río, E. (2010b). Remembering Latina/o Television. *FlowTV, 11,* 5. Retrieved January 8, 2010, from http://flowtv.org/?p=4676.

del Río, E. (2009). Tall, dark, and American: Latino authenticity and appropriation in general market television. *FlowTV, 11,* 1. Retrieved on January 6, 2010, from http://flowtv.org/?p=4484#discussion.

del Río, E. (2006). The Latina/o problematic: categories and questions in media communication research. *Communication Yearbook 30,* 387–429.

del Valle, E. (Ed.) (2005). *Hispanic marketing & public relations: Understanding and targeting America's largest minority.* Boca Raton, FL: Poyeen Publishing.

Denzin, N. & Lincoln, Y. (Eds.). (2003). *Collecting and interpreting qualitative materials* (2nd Ed.). Thousand Oaks, CA: Sage Publications.

DeSipio, L. (2003). Latino viewing choices: Bilingual television viewers and the language choices they make. Research report. Claremont, CA: The Tomás Rivera Policy Institute.

Dibble, S. (2010, June 20). Tijuana's mayoral candidates focus on city issues: Two hopefuls emerging in popularity out of five. Retrieved on June 22, 2010, from http://www.signonsandiego.com/news/2010/jun/20/citys-mayoral-candidates-focus-on-border/.

Dora saves the prince [120]. (2001). In C. Gifford (Executive Producer). *Dora the Explorer.* Nickelodeon.

Elias, N. & Lemish, D. (2008). Media uses in immigrant families: Torn between 'inward' and 'outward' paths of integration. *The International Communication Gazette, 70,* 21–40.

Elliot, S. (2009, August 14). Another challenge to Nielsen, with some big names attached. The New York Times Media Decoder. Retrieved on August 25, 2009, from http://mediadecoder.blogs.nytimes.com/2009/08/14/another-challenge-to-nielsen-with-some-big-names-attached/.

Elsmar, M. (2003). An alternative paradigm for conceptualizing and labeling the process of influence of imported television programs. In M. Elsmar (Ed.), *The impact of international television: A paradigm shift* (157–179). Mahwah, NJ: Lawrence Erlbaum Associates.

Engstrand, I. (1998). The impact of the U.S.-Mexican war on the Spanish southwest. In I. Engstrand, R. Griswold del Castillo & E. Poniatowska (Eds.), *Cul-*

ture y cultura: Consequences of the U.S-Mexican war, 1846-1848. Los Angeles, CA: Autry Museum of Western Heritage.

Ethnic trends in media (2009, March). Report prepared for Nielsen Media Research. Retrieved on November 10, 2009, from http://blog.nielsen.com/nielsenwire/media_entertainment/looking-towards-2050-ethnic-trends-in-media/.

Fall Colors: 2003-04 Prime-time diversity report. Prepared for Children Now. http://publications.childrennow.org/publications/media/fallcolors_2003.cfm.

Federal Judge Mariana Pfaelzer will formally invalidate California Prop 187. (1997, 28 November). *Human Events, 53*, 6.

Fernández, C. & Paxman, A. (2000). *El Tigre: Emilio Azcárraga y su imperio Televisa.* Mexico City: Editorial Grijalbo, Miguel Hildalgo.

Fernández, I. (2005, October). Go, Diego Go. *Hispanic, 18*(10), 68.

Fiske, J. (1987). *Television culture.* New York: Methuen.

Flores, J. (1997). The Latino imaginary: Dimensions of community and identity. In F. Aparicio and S. Chávez-Siverman (Eds.), *Tropicalizations: Transcultural representations of* Latinidad (pp. 183–193). Hanover, NH: Dartmouth College.

Fox, E. (1997). *Latin American broadcasting: From tango to telenovela.* Luton, UK: University of Luton Press.

Frutkin, A. J. (2006, 11 September). Domestic drama: Telenovelas hit prime time. *Mediaweek.* Retrieved on May 24, 2010, from http://www.mediaweek.com/mw/departments/features/article_display.jsp?vnu_content_id=1003119348.

Fry, R. (2002). Latinos in higher education: Many enroll, too few graduate. Retrieved on June 13, 2008, from http://pewhispanic.org/reports/report.php?ReportID=11.

Gainer, J. (2010). Critical media literacy in middle school: Exploring the politics of representation. *Journal of Adolescent & Adult Literacy, 53*(5), 364–373.

García Canclini, N. (2001). Hybrid cultures, oblique powers. In M.G. Durham & D. Kellner (Eds.), *Media and cultural studies: Keyworks.* Malden, MA. Blackwell Publishers, Inc.

Garvin, G. (2007, February 12). Prime-time soaps sizzle in Spanish but fall flat in English. *The Miami Herald.* Retrieved May 24, 2010, from http://democraciausa.org/en/headlines/021207en3/.

Gerbner, G. (1998). Cultivation analysis: An overview. *Mass Communication & Society, 3/4*, 175–194.

Gibbons, K. (2009, May 18). Upfronts 2009: Telemundo hopes to ride ratings, Hispanic growth: NBCU-owned Latino network adds new original primetime telenovelas. Multichannel News. Retrieved on October 20, 2009, from http://www.multichannel.com/article/232888upfronts_2009_Telemundo_Hopes_to_Ride_Ratings_Hispanic_Growth.php.

Goldstein, S., Usdin, S., Scheepers, E., & Japhet, G. (2005). Communicating HIV and AIDS, what works? A report on the impact evaluation of *Soul City's* fourth series. *Journal of Health Communication, 10*, 465–483.

González Hernández, D. (2008). Watching over the border: A case study of the Mexico-U.S. television and youth audience. In A. Valdivia (Ed.), *Latina/o communication studies today* (pp. 219–233). New York: Peter Lang.

Gray, H. (1995). *Watching race: Television and the struggle for blackness.* Minneapolis: University of Minnesota Press.

Greenberg, B., Burgoon, M., Burgoon, J. & Korzenny, F. (1983). *Mexican Americans and the mass media.* Norwood, NJ: Ablex Publishing Corporation.

Greene, B. (2008). *Politics and the American television comedy: A critical survey from* I Love Lucy *through* South Park. Jefferson, NC: McFarland & Company, Inc. Publishers.

Gregor, A. (2003). What's Spanish for big media? *Columbian Journalism Review* (www.cjr.org/issues/2003).

Guidotti-Hernández, N. M. (2007). *Dora the Explorer,* constructing "Latinidades" and the politics of global citizenship. *Latino Studies, 5,* 209–232.

Hakimzadeh, S. & Cohn, D. (2007, November 29). English usage among Hispanics in the United States. Report prepared for the Pew Hispanic Center.

Hall, S. (1980). Encoding/Decoding. In S. Hall, S. Hobson, A. Lowe, & P. Willis (Eds.), *Culture, media, language: Working papers in cultural studies 1972-79* (pp. 128–138). London: Hutchinson.

Hannerz, U. (1990). Cosmopolitans and locals in world culture. In M. Featherstone (Ed.). *Global culture: Nationalism, globalization and modernity* (pp. 237–251). London: Sage Publications.

Harewood, S. & Valdivia, A. (2005). Exploring Dora: Re-embodied Latinidad on the web. In S. Mazzarella, (Ed.), *Girl wide web* (pp. 85–103). New York: Peter Lang.

Harrington, C.L. & Bielby, D.D. (2005). Flow, home and media pleasures. *The Journal of Popular Culture, 38*(5), 834–854.

Hasinoff, A. A. (2008). Fashioning race for the free market on *America's Next Top Model. Critical Studies in Media Communication, 25*(3), 324–343.

Hayes-Bautista, D., Chameline, C., Jones, B., Cornejo, J.C., Cañadas, C., Martinez, C. & Meza, G. (2007). Empowerment, expansion, and engagement: Las Juntas Patrióticas in California, 1848–1869, *California History,* 85, 4–23.

Heider, D. (2003). Black, brown, and poor: Who you don't see on local TV news and why. In D. Ríos & A.N. Mohamed (Eds.), *Brown and black communication: Latino and African American conflict and convergence in mass media* (pp. 81–91). Westport, CT: Praeger Publishers.

Hernández, R., Siles, M. & Rochin, R. (2000). Latino youth: converting challenges to opportunities. In M. Montero-Sieburth and F. Villarruel (Eds). *Making invisible Latino adolescents visible: A critical approach to Latino diversity* (pp. 1–28). New York: Falmer Press.

Hispanics at Mid-Decade. Pew Hispanic Center. Retrieved on January 3, 2008 from http://pewhispanic.org/reports/middecade.

Holmes, G. (2007, August). Nielsen to generate national ratings for both English- and Spanish-language television from the same panel. Nielsen Media Research Press Release. Retrieved on August 29, 2007, from http://www.nielsenmedia.com/nc/portal/site/Public/.

Houpt, S. (2006, December 11). Producer battles Nielsen over missing Latinos. *The Globe and Mail*, R6.

Humphreys, J. (2008). The multicultural economy 2008. Report prepared for the Selig Center for Economic Growth. Terry College of Business, The University of Georgia. Retrieved on November 10, 2009, from http://www.terry.uga.edu/selig/buying_power.html.

Isackson, A. (2010, February 22). US state department updates travel alert on Mexico. Retrieved on June 22, 2010, from http://www.kpbs.org/news/2010/feb/22/us-state-department-updates-travel-alert-mexico/.

James, M. (2007, August 27). Nielsen ends separate Latino TV survey. *Los Angeles Times*. Retrieved on January 9, 2009, from http://articles.latimes.com/2007/aug/27/business/fi-nielsen27.

Jhally, S. & Lewis, J. (1992). *Enlightened racism: The Cosby Show, audiences, and the myth of the American dream.* Boulder, CO: Westview Press.

Johnson, M. (2000). How ethnic are the U.S. media: The case of Latina magazines. *Mass Communication & Society*, 3, 229–249.

Johnson, M., David, P. & Huey-Ohlsson, D. (2003). Beauty in brown: Skin color in Latina magazines. In D. Ríos & A.N. Mohamed (Eds.), *Brown and black communication: Latino and African American conflict and convergence in mass media* (pp. 159–173). Westport, CT: Praeger Publishers.

Jordon, A. (2004). The role of media in children's development: An ecological perspective. *Developmental and Behavioral Pediatrics, 25,* 196–206.

Just the Facts: Poverty in California. (2009, March). Report prepared for the Public Policy Institute of California. Retrieved on October 24, 2009, from http://www.ppic.org.

Kaplan, D. (2009, July). Now you're speaking my language. Consumer Insight Report prepared for Nielsen Media Research.

Key facts about childhood obesity in the Latino community. (2006). Report prepared by the National Council for La Raza. Retrieved on March 11, 2010, from www.nclr.org/files/41691_files_FS_childObesity_FNL.pdf.

Klein, H. & Shiffman, K. (2006). Race-related content of animated cartoons. *The Howard Journal of Communication, 17,* 163–182.

Kotler, J., Wright, J. & Huston, A. (2001). Television use in families with children. In Bryant, J. & Bryant, J. A. (Eds.), *Television and the American family,* 2nd edition (pp. 33–48). Mahwah, NJ: Lawrence Erlbaum Associates, Inc.

Kraidy, M. (2005). *Hybridity or the cultural logic of globalization.* Philadelphia: Temple University Press.

Ksiazek, T. B. & Webster, J. G. (2008). Cultural proximity and audience behavior: The role of language in patterns of polarization and multicultural fluency. *Journal of Broadcasting & Electronic Media, 52,* 485–503.

Labaton, S. (24 February 2007). Record fine expected for Univision. *The New York Times.* Retrieved on February 26, 2007, from http://www.nytimes.com/2007/02/24/business/24fcc.html.

La Pastina, A. & Straubhaar, J. (2005). Multiple proximities between television genres and audiences: The schism between telenovelas' global distribution and local consumption. *Gazette: The International Journal for Communication Studies, 67,* 271–288.

LazyTown, V-me, Tycoon Entertainment to bring *LazyTown Live!* to U.S.: International hit is first-ever live family show to tour U.S. nationally in Spanish (2009, June). V-me press release. Retrieved on September 2, 2009, from http://www.vmetv.com/press_room/.

Learmonth, M. (2006, 30 July). MyNetwork turns up heat on spicy telenovelas: Each 'Fashion' episode costs just $200,000. *Variety.* Retrieved on May 24, 2010 from http://www.variety.com/article/VR11179 47630.html ?categoryid=14&cs=1.

Lee, M., Bichard, S., Irey, M., Walt, H., Carlson, A. (2009). Television viewing and ethnic stereotypes: Do college students form stereotypical perceptions of ethnic groups as a result of heavy television consumption? *The Howard Journal of Communications, 20,* 95–110.

Lemish, D. (2007). *Children and television: A global perspective.* Oxford, U.K.: Blackwell Publishing.

Lichter, S. R. & Amundson, D. (1997). Distorted reality: Hispanic characters in TV entertainment. In C. Rodríguez (Ed.), *Latin looks: Images of Latinas and Latinos in the U.S. media* (pp. 57–72). Boulder, CO: Westview Press.

Liesse, J. (2007). The Latino identity project: Understanding a market. *Advertising Age, 78,* A5–A8.

Lindlof, T. (1991). The qualitative study of media audiences. *Journal of Broadcasting & Electronic Media, 35*(1), 23-42.

Lisotta, C. (2004, September). PBS Sets Diversity Curve. *Television Week, 23,* 36.

Livingstone, S. (2008). Engaging with media—a matter of literacy. *Communication, Culture & Critique, 1,* 51–62.

Li-Vollmer, M. (2002). Race representation of child-targeted television commercials. *Mass Communication & Society, 5,* 207–228.

Lugo Steidel, A., Ikhlas, M., Lopez, I., Rahman, R., & Teichman, J. (2002). The challenges and rewards of conducting ethnic minority research. In J. Contreras, K. Kerns, A. Neal-Barnett (Eds.), *Latino children and families in the United States: Current research and future directions* (pp. 253–264). Westport, CT: Praeger Publishers.

Lull, J. (1995). *Media, communication, culture: A global approach.* New York: Columbia University Press.

Luna, D. & Peracchio, L. (2005). Advertising to bilingual consumers: The impact of code-switching on persuasion. *Journal of Consumer Research, 31,* 760–765.

Macias, T. (2004). *Imaginanadose Mexicano*: The symbolic context of Mexican American ethnicity beyond the second generation. *Qualitative Sociology, 27,* 299–315.

Marín, G. & Marín, B.V. (1991). *Research with Hispanic populations.* Newbury Park, CA: Sage Publications.

Markert, J. (2007). *The George Lopez Show*: The same old Hispano? *Bilingual Review, 28,* 148–165.

Martín-Barbero, J. (1995). Memory and form in the Latin American soap opera. in R. Allen (Ed.), *To be continued...soap operas around the world.* New York: Routledge.

Martínez, K. (2004). *Latina* magazine and the invocation of a panethnic family: Latino identity as it is informed by celebrities and *Papis Chulos. The Communication Review, 7,* 155–175.

Martínez, K. (2007). Monolingualism, biculturalism, and cable TV: HBO Latino and the promise of the multiplex. In S. Banet-Weiser, C. Chris, and A. Feitas (Eds.). *Cable visions: Television beyond broadcasting* (pp. 194–214). New York: New York University Press.

Martínez, L. (2008, December). Univisión stars in its own soap opera. *Broadcasting & Cable,* retrieved January 9, 2009, from http://www.broadcastingcable.com/article/CA6620356.html?industryid=47168 &.

Massey, D. & Sanchez, M. (2007). Latino and American identities as perceived by immigrants. *Qual Sociol, 30,* 81–107.

Mastro, D., Behm-Morawitz, E. & Kopacz, M. (2008). Exposure to television portrayals of Latinos: The implications of aversive racism and social identity theory. *Human Communication Research, 34,* 1–27.

Mastro, D. (2003). A social identity approach to understanding the impact of television messages. *Communication Monographs, 70,* 98–113.

Mastro, D. & Behm-Morawitz, E. (2005). Latino representation on primetime television. *Journalism & Mass Communication Quarterly, 82,* 110–130.

Mastro, D. & Ortiz, M. (2008). A content analysis of social groups in prime-time Spanish-language television. *Journal of Broadcasting & Electronic Media, 52*(1), 101–118.

Mastro, D. & Stern, S. (2003). Representations of race in television commercials: A content analysis of prime-time advertising. *Journal of Broadcasting and Electronic Media, 47,* 638–647.

Mato, D. (2005). The transnationalization of the *telenovela* industry, territorial references, and the production of markets and representations of transnational identities. *Television & New Media, 6*(4), 423–444.

Mayer, V. (2004). Please pass the pan: Retheorizing the map of panlatinidad in communication research. *The Communication Review, 7,* 113–124.

Mayer, V. (2003a). Living *telenovelas/telenovelizing* life: Mexican American girls' identities and transnational *telenovelas*. *Journal of Communication, 53*(3), 479–495.

Mayer, V. (2003b). *Producing dreams, consuming youth: Mexican Americans and mass media*. New Brunswick, NJ: Rutgers University Press.

McAnany, E. (1993). The telenovela and social change: Popular culture, public policy and communication theory. In A. Fadul (Ed.), *Serial Fiction in TV: The Latin Amercian Telenovelas*. São Paulo: University of São Paulo Press.

McAnany, E. & La Pastina, A. (1994). Telenovela audiences: A review and methodological critique of Latin American research. *Communication Research, 21*(6), 828–849.

McChesney, R. (2004). *The problem of the media: U.S. communication politics in the 21st century*. New York: Monthly Review Press.

McFarland, M. (2006, 2 September) My network TV will be awash in a new brand of soaps. *Seattle Post-Intelligencer*. Retrieved on November 1, 2009, from http://www.seattlepi.com/tv/283530_tv02.html.

Merskin, D. (2007). Three faces of Eva: Perpetuation of the hot-Latina stereotype in *Desperate Housewives*. *The Howard Journal of Communications, 18,* 133–151.

Meskill, C. (1998). Commercial television and the limited English proficient child: Implications for language development. In K. Swan, C. Meskill, and S. DeMaio, (Eds.), *Social learning from broadcast television* (pp. 61–85). Creskill, NJ: Hampton Press, Inc.

Molina Guzmán, I. (2006). Mediating *Frida*: Negotiating discourses of Latina/o authenticity in global media representations of ethnic identity. *Critical Studies in Media Communication, 23*(3), 232–251.

Molina Guzmán, I. & Valdivia, A. (2004). Brain, brow, and body: Latina iconicity in U.S. popular culture. *The Communication Review, 7*, 205–221.

Montalvo, D. (2006). Network brownout report 2006: The portrayal of Latinos and Latinos issues on network television news, 2005. Report prepared for the National Association of Hispanic Journalists.

Morales, E. (2002). *Living in Spanglish: The search for Latino identity in America*. New York: St. Martin's Griffin.

Moran, K. (2003). A reception analysis: Latina teenagers talk about *telenovelas*. *Global Media Journal, 2,* 2. http://lass.calumet.purdue.edu/cca/gmj/sp03/gmj-sp03-moran.htm.

Moran, K. (2004). The development of Spanish-language television in San Diego: A contemporary history. *The Journal of San Diego History, 50* (1 & 2), 42–54.

Moran, K. (2006). Is changing the language enough? The Spanish-language "alternative" in the United States. *Journalism: Theory, Practice and Criticism, 7*(3), 389–405.

Moran, K. (2007). The growth of Spanish-language and Latino-themed television programs for children in the United States. *Journal of Children and Media, 1*(3), 296–302.

Moran, K. (2010). Parents' perceptions of preschool television: Exploring differences between Spanish- and English-speaking families. *Journal of Children & Media, 4*(4) 467–482.

Moran, K. & Chung, L. (2008). Global or local identity? A theoretical analysis of the role of Viacom on identity formation among children in an international context. *Global Media Journal, 7*, 12 http://lass.calumet.purdue.edu/cca/gmj/sp08/gmj-sp08-moran-chung.htm.

Morley, D. (1993). Active audience theory: Pendulums and pitfalls. *Journal of Communication, 43(4)*, 13–21.

Morley, D. (2006). Unanswered questions in audience research. *The Communication Review, 9*, 101–121.

National Association of Latino Independent Producers http://www.nalip.org/nalip/NALIP-About.html.

Naughton, S. & Love, M. (2006). A snapshot of children on the San Diego-Mexico border. Report prepared for Children Now.

Navarro, M. (2005, 6 November). The prime time of the telenovela: A global audience for campy drama shows its force. *The New York Times*. Retrieved on November 3, 2009, from http://query.nytimes.com/gst/fullpage.html?res=9F07E4DD163EF935A35752C1A9639C8B63.

Newhouse, C. (2007). Children in immigrant families: A California data brief. Report prepared for Children Now.

Nisen, J. (2009, 29 September). Dora links doll revealed; Mattel releases photo, details. Retrieved on November 30, 2009 from http://www.hispanicbusiness.com/news/news_print.asp?id=162180.

Noriega, C. (2000). *Shot in America: Television, the state, and the rise of Chicano cinema*. Minneapolis: University of Minnesota Press.

O'Brien, E. (2008). *The racial middle: Latinos and Asian Americans living beyond the racial divide*. New York: New York University Press.

Olympusat buys Sorpresa: Hispanic children's TV network joins distributor Hispanic pack (2009, 4 August). Multichannel News. Retrieved on August 27, 2009, from http://www.multichannel.com/article/326445-Olympusat_Buys_Sorpresa.php.

Parker, T. (Writer & Director). (2002). The death camp of tolerance [6,16]. In A. Garefino, M. Stone, T. Parker (Executive Producers), *South Park*. Comedy Central.

Percoa, N., Murray, J. & Wartella, E. (2007). (Eds.), *Children and television: Fifty years of research*. Mahwah, NJ: Lawrence Erlbaum Associates.

Perreira, K., Chapman, M., & Stein, G. (2006). Becoming an American parent: Overcoming challenges and finding strength in a new immigrant Latino community. *Journal of Family Issues, 27*(10), 1383–1414.

Pew Hispanic Center. (2009, 11 December). *Between two worlds: How young Latinos come of age in America*. Report Prepared for the Pew Hispanic Center: Washington, D.C.

204   *Listening to Latina/o Youth*

Pieraccini, C. & Alligood, D. (2005). *Color television: Fifty years of African American and Latino images on prime-time television.* Dubuque, IA: Kendall/Hunt.

Radway, J. (1984). *Reading the romance: Women, patriarchy, and popular literature.* Chapel Hill: University of North Carolina Press.

Rideout, V., Foehr, U. & Roberts, D. (2010, January). Generation M2: Media in the lives of 8- to 18-year olds. Report prepared for the Henry J. Kaiser Family Foundation.

Rideout, V. & Hamel, E. (2006, May). The media family: Electronic media in the lives of infants, toddlers, preschoolers and their parents. Report prepared for the Henry J. Kaiser Family Foundation.

Rinderle, S. (2005). The Mexican diaspora: A critical examination of signifiers. *Journal of Communication Inquiry, 29*(4), 294–316.

Ríos, D. (2003). U.S. Latino audiences of "telenovelas." *Journal of Latinos and Education, 2*(1), 59–65.

Ríos, D. & Gaines, S. (1998). Latino mass media use for cultural maintenance. *Journalism and Mass Communication Quarterly, 75,* 746–761.

Rivadeneyra, R. (2006). Do you see what I see? Latino adolescents' perceptions of the images on television. *Journal of Adolescent Research, 21,* 393–414.

Rivadeneyra, R., Ward, L.M., & Gordon, M. (2007). Distorted reflections: Media exposure and Latino adolescents' conceptions of self. *Media Psychology, 9,* 261–290.

Rivero, Y. (2003). The performance and reception of televisual "ugliness" in *Yo soy Betty, la fea. Feminist Media Studies, 3*(1), 65–81.

Roberts, D., Foehr, U. & Rideout, V. (2005, March). Generation M: Media in the Lives of 8–18 year-olds. Report prepared for the Henry J. Kaiser Family Foundation.

Rodríguez, A. (1999a). *Making Latino news: race, language, class.* Thousand Oaks, CA: Sage Publications.

Rodríguez, A. (1999b). Creating an audience and remapping a nation: A brief history of Spanish-language broadcasting, 1930–1980, *Quarterly Review of Film and Video, 16,* 357–375.

Rojas, V. (2004). The gender of Latinidad: Latinas speak about Hispanic television. *The Communication Review, 7,* 125–153.

Romano, A. (2003, March). Latino kids net fills market hole. *Broadcasting & Cable, 133,* 10.

Sanchez, L. (2007, February 8). Hispanic TV network extends PBS franchise. Retrieved on April 16, 2007, from Hispanic Business.com http://www.hispanicbusiness.com/news/news_print.asp?id=55330.

Sass, E. (2007, February 26). Hola! Kagan predicts $5.5 billion Hispanic Ad Market. Retrieved on November 9, 2009 from http://www.mediapost.com/publications/index.cfm?fa=Articles.showArticle&art_aid=56051.

Schudson, M. (1995). *The power of news.* Cambridge, MA: Havard University Press.

Selznick, B. (2008). *Global television: Co-producing culture.* Philadelphia: Temple University Press.

Seiter, E. & Mayer, V. (2004). Diversifying representation in children's TV: Nickelodeon's model. In Hendershot, H. (Ed.), *Nickelodeon nation: The history, politics and economics of America's only channel for kids,* (pp. 120–133). New York: New York University Press.

Shaw, D. (2005). "You are alright, but...": Individual and collective representations of Mexicans, Latinos, Anglo-Americans, and African-Americans in Steven Soderbergh's *Traffic. Quarterly Review of Film and Video, 22,* 211-223.

Sigler, E. (2003, September). A girl named Dora. *Hispanic, 16*(9), 42–45.

Sigler, E. (2004, December). Maya & Miguel. *Hispanic, 17*(12), 68.

Sinclair, J. (1999). *Latin American television: A global view.* New York: Oxford University Press.

Singhal, A. & Rogers, E. (1999). *Entertainment-education: A communication strategy for social change.* Mahwah, NJ: Lawrence Erlbaum Associates.

Statistical Portrait of Hispanics in the United States, 2006. Report prepared for the Pew Hispanic Center. Retrieved on June 13, 2008, from http://pewhispanic.org/factsheets/factsheet.php?FactsheetID=35.

Stelter, B. (2009, August 31). 'Wizards' help Disney. *New York Times.* Retrieved on September 8, 2009, from http://www.nytimes.com/2009/08/31/arts/television/31arts-WIZARDSHELPD_BRF.html.

Strasburger, V., Wilson, B. & Jordan, A. (2009). *Children, adolescents, and the media,* 2nd edition. Thousand Oaks, CA: Sage Publications.

Straubhaar, J. (2003). Choosing national TV: Cultural capital, language, and cultural proximity in Brazil. In M. Elsmar (Ed.), *The impact of international television: A paradigm shift* (pp. 77–110). Mahwah, NJ: Lawrence Erlbaum Associates.

Straubhaar, J. (2007). *World television: From global to local.* Thousand Oaks, CA: Sage Publications.

Subervi-Vélez, F. (2005, November 30). Declaration to the FCC.

Subervi-Vélez, F. A. (1999). The mass media and Latinos: Policy and research agendas for the next century. *Aztlán, 24,* 131–147.

Subervi-Vélez, F. (1986). The mass media and ethnic assimilation and pluralism: A review and research proposal with special focus on Hispanics. *Communication Research, 13,* 71–96.

Subervi-Vélez, F. A., Berg, C. R., Constantakis-Valdés, P., Noriega, C., Ríos, D. I., & Wilkinson, K. T. (1994). Mass communication and Hispanics. In F. Padilla (Ed), *Handbook of Hispanic cultures in the United States: Sociology* (pp. 304–357). Houston, TX: Arte Público Press.

Subervi-Vélez, F. A. & Colsant, S. (1993). The television worlds of Latino children. In Berry, G. & Asamen, J. K. (Eds.), *Children and television: Images in a changing sociocultural world* (pp. 215–228). Newbury Park, CA: Sage Publications.

Subervi-Vélez, F. & Rios, D. (2005). Latino identity & situational Latinidad. In E. del Valle. (Ed.), *Hispanic Marketing & Public Relations: Understanding and targeting America's largest minority* (pp. 29–46). Boca Raton, FL: Poyeen Publishing.

Swan, K. (1998). Social learning from Saturday morning cartoons. In Swan, K., Meskill, C., & DeMaio, S. (Eds.), *Social learning from broadcast television* (pp. 87–112). Creskill, NJ: Hampton Press, Inc.

Taveras, E., Hohman, K., Price, S., Gortmaker, S. & Sonneville, K. (2009). Television in the bedrooms of racial/ethnic minority children: How did they get there and how do we get them out? *Clinical Pediatrics, 48*(7), 715–719.

Thiel, S. M. (2005). "IM Me": Identity construction and gender negotiation in the world of adolescent girls and instant messaging. In S. Mazzarella (Ed.), *Girl wide web* (pp. 179–201). New York: Peter Lang.

Thompson, D., Sibinga, E., Jennings, J., Bair-Merritt, M., Christakis, D. (2010). Television viewing by young Hispanic children: Evidence of heterogeneity. *Archives of Pediatrics & Adolescent Medicine, 164*(2), 174-179.

Thussu, D. (2006). *International communication: Continuity and change.* London: Hodder Arnold Press.

Trevino, J. (1999, October). Bilingual television grows an audience. *Hispanic,12*, 68.

Tripp, L. & Herr-Stephenson, R. (2009). Making access meaningful: Latino young people using digital media at home and at school. *Journal of Computer-Mediated Communication, 14,* 1190–1207.

Truglio, R.T., Lovelace, V.O., Seguí, I., & Scheirner, S. (2001). The varied role of formative research: Case studies from 30 years. In S. Fisch & R. Truglio (Eds.), *G is for growing: Thirty years of research on* Sesame Street (pp. 61–79). Mahwah, NJ: Lawrence Erlbaum Associates.

Tufte, T. (2000). *Living with the rubbish queen: Telenovelas, culture, and modernity in Brazil.* Luton, UK: University of Luton Press.

Turegano, P. (2002, June 13). News director uses her job to fulfill a mission. *San Diego Union-Tribune.*

Turegano, P. (2002, October 28). Two Spanish-language stations go head-to-head across border. *San Diego Union Tribune.*

Turegano, P. (2004, July 9). Spanish-language KBNT touts growth in young adult viewers. *San Diego Union-Tribune.*

Turner Classic Movies: Race & Hollywood: Latino Images in Film (http://www.tcm.com/2009/lif/index.jsp).

Umaña-Taylor, A., Gonzales-Backen, M., & Guimond, A. (2009). Latino adolescents' ethnic identity: Is there a developmental progression and does growth in ethnic identity predict self-esteem? *Child Development, 80*(2), 391–405.

Univisión San Diego outperforms the competition in July 2009. (2009, July). Report prepared for Entravision Communications Corporation from NSI July 09.

Univisión San Diego Turns Up the Heat in July 2009. (2009, July). Report prepared for Entravision Communications Corporation from NSI July 09.

Valdivia, A. N. (2008a). Is my butt your island? The myth of discovery and contemporary Latina/o Communication studies. In A.N. Valdivia (Ed.), *Latina/o communication studies today* (pp. 3–26). New York: Peter Lang Publishers.

Valdivia, A. N. (2008b). Mixed race on the Disney Channel: From *Johnnie Tsunami* through *Lizzie McGuire* and ending with *The Cheetah Girls*. In M. Beltrán and C. Fojas (Eds.), *Mixed race Hollywood* (pp. 269–289). New York: New York University Press.

Valdivia, A.N. (2008c). Popular culture and recognition: Narratives of youth and Latinidad. In N. Dolby and F. Rizvi (Eds.), *Youth moves: Identities and education in global perspective* (pp. 101–114). New York: Routledge Taylor & Francis Group.

Valdivia, A. N. (2007). Is Penélope to J. Lo as culture is to nature? Eurocentric approaches to "Latin" beauties. In M. Mendible (Ed.), *From bananas to buttocks: The Latina body in popular film and culture* (pp. 129–148). Austin: University of Texas Press.

Valdivia, A.N. (2005). The location of the Spanish in Latinidad: Examples from contemporary U.S. popular culture. *Letras Femeninas, 31*(2), 6–78.

Valdivia, A. N. (2004). Latinas as radical hybrid: Transnationally gendered traces in mainstream media, *Global Media Journal, 3,* 4. Retrieved on December 3, 2009 from http://lass.calumet.purdue.edu/cca/gmj/sp04/gmj-sp04-valdivia.htm.

Valero, R., Villaseñor, G. & Román, D. (2008). *The third culture and mass media in-between Mexico-USA border*. Mexicali, Baja California: Ago Litográfica.

Vargas, L. (2009). *Latina teens, migration, and popular culture*. New York: Peter Lang Publishing Inc.

Vargas, L. (2008). Media practices and gendered identity among transnational Latina teens. In A.N. Valdivia (Ed.), *Latina/o communication studies today* (pp. 187–218). New York: Peter Lang Publishers.

Vargas, L. (2006). Transnational media literacy: Analytic reflections on a program with Latina teens. *Hispanic Journal of Behavioral Sciences, 28*(2), 267–285.

Vázquez García, H., García Coll, C., Erkut, S., Alaracón, O., & Troop, L. (2000). Family values of Latino adolescents. In M. Montero-Sieburth and F. Villarruel (Eds.), *Making invisible Latino adolescents visible: A critical approach to Latino diversity* (pp. 239–264). New York: Falmer Press.

Villarreal, Y. (2009, 4 October). Planet Spanglish; Bilingual and media-savvy, these Latinos host cross-cultural shows that can play in any casa. *Los Angeles Times*, D1.

Viswanath, K. & Arora, P. (2000). Ethnic media in the United States: An essay on their role in integration, assimilation, and social control. *Mass Communication & Society, 3,* 39–56.

Wakefield, W. D. & Hudley, C. (2007). Ethnic and racial idenity and adolescent well-being. *Theory Into Practice, 46*(2), 147–154.

Wentz, L. (2009, 29 October). Ad spend in Spanish-language media falls by 6.3%, Nielsen says. Retrieved on November 11, 2009, from http://adage.com/hispanic/article?article_id=140067.

Wentz, L. (2008). What shaky economy? Hispanic nets bet ad growth will continue. *Advertising Age, 79*, 22.

Wentz, L (2004). SiTV reaches out to young Hispanics. *Advertising Age,* 75, (8), 37.

Wilkin, H., Valente, T., Murphy, S., Cody, M., Huang, G. & Beck, V. (2007). Does entertainment-education work with Latinos in the United States? Identification and the effects of a telenovela breast cancer storyline. *Journal of Health Communication, 12,* 455–469.

Wilmer Valderrama & *Handy Manny* characters to appear at licensing international expo 2009, Las Vegas. (2009, 1 June). Disney Consumer Products Press Release. Retrieved on August 10, 2009, from http://www.smartbrief.com/news/aaaa/industryBW-detail.jsp?id=6B83C120-3B4E-4927-9A55-1EA0E3303C6C.

Wilson, C. & Gutiérrez, F. (1995). *Race, multiculturalism, and the media: From mass to class communication, 2nd edition.* Thousand Oaks, CA: Sage Publications.

Woodard, L. (2010, 21 April). Advertising: Dora the (marketing) explorer: Kid favorite Dora the Explorer takes on a public service marketing role. ABC news. Retrieved on April 24, 2010 from http://abcnews.go.com/Business/ advertising-dora-marketingexplorer/story?id=10431380.

Wyatt, E. (2010, 29 January). After ratings decline, 'Ugly Betty' is canceled. *New York Times.* Retrieved on January 30, 2010, from http://www.nytimes.com/2010/01/29/arts/television/29artsAFTERRATINGS_BRF.html.

York, E. B. (2009, 30 November). Brands prepare for a more diverse 'general market'; with generational shift afoot, ethnic insights are standard in ad efforts. *Advertising Age, 80*(40), 6.

Index

mediated youth

Sharon R. Mazzarella
General Editor

Grounded in cultural studies, books in this series will study the cultures, artifacts, and media of children, tweens, teens, and college-aged youth. Whether studying television, popular music, fashion, sports, toys, the Internet, self-publishing, leisure, clubs, school, cultures/activities, film, dance, language, tie-in merchandising, concerts, subcultures, or other forms of popular culture, books in this series go beyond the dominant paradigm of traditional scholarship on the effects of media/culture on youth. Instead, authors endeavor to understand the complex relationship between youth and popular culture. Relevant studies would include, but are not limited to studies of how youth negotiate their way through the maze of corporately-produced mass culture; how they themselves have become cultural producers; how youth create "safe spaces" for themselves within the broader culture; the political economy of youth culture industries; the representational politics inherent in mediated coverage and portrayals of youth; and so on. Books that provide a forum for the "voices" of the young are particularly encouraged. The source of such voices can range from in-depth interviews and other ethnographic studies to textual analyses of cultural artifacts created by youth.

For further information about the series and submitting manuscripts, please contact:

> SHARON R. MAZZARELLA
> School of Communication Studies
> James Madison University
> Harrisonburg, VA 22807

To order other books in this series, please contact our Customer Service Department at:

> (800) 770-LANG (within the U.S.)
> (212) 647-7706 (outside the U.S.)
> (212) 647-7707 FAX

Or browse online by series at WWW.PETERLANG.COM

www.ingramcontent.com/pod-product-compliance
Lightning Source LLC
Chambersburg PA
CBHW050646280326
41932CB00015B/2795